REASON, REVELATION, AND THE CIVIC ORDER

.

REASON, REVELATION, AND THE CIVIC ORDER

POLITICAL PHILOSOPHY AND THE CLAIMS OF FAITH

Edited by

Paul R. DeHart and

Carson Holloway

NIU Press
DeKalb, IL

This volume was made possible through the financial support of the Agora Institute for Civic Virtue and the Common Good, a research initiative affiliated with Eastern University in Philadelphia. Its purpose is to cultivate open and honest inquiry into the fundamental virtues, truths, values, and habits required for human flourishing within a free and ordered society, while promoting quality interdisciplinary research and programs.

Library of Congress Cataloging-in-Publication Data

Reason, revelation, and the civic order : political philosophy and the claims of faith / edited by Paul R. DeHart and Carson Holloway.
    pages cm
  Includes index.
  ISBN 978-0-87580-484-2 (cloth) — ISBN 978-1-60909-157-6 (e-book)
  1. Religion and politics. 2. Revelation. 3. Political science—Philosophy. I. DeHart, Paul R., 1975– , author, editor of compilation. II. Holloway, Carson, 1969– , author, editor of compilation.
  BL65.P7R38 2014
  201'.72—dc23

                    2013041737

With undying gratitude for their love and support,
the editors dedicate this book to their wives:

ROBYN DEHART AND SHARI HOLLOWAY

And, in hope of a world in which serious inquiry
and the pursuit of transcendent joy
are ever bound together, to their children:

MINA AND ZOE DEHART

MARIA, ANNA, ELIZABETH, CATHERINE,
JANE, AND EMILY HOLLOWAY

CONTENTS

ACKNOWLEDGMENTS

In the course of completing this project, we have accumulated many debts that can never be repaid but can only be acknowledged joyfully and with our unreserved gratitude.

This book was first conceived in conversations that took place in Princeton, New Jersey, during the summer of 2009. The setting for these conversations was that year's Lehrman American Studies Institute, which brought together senior scholars and young academics to discuss statesmanship and the principles of Western political thought. We would like to express our gratitude to the institute and its organizers for this opportunity for intellectual fellowship, from which emerged so many friendships and opportunities to collaborate. Our friend and colleague Joe Fornieri was an integral part of those initial conversations, and without his valuable input this book would not have taken its present form and might not have even gotten underway. We were also helped immensely by the early and continuing support, encouragement, and wise counsel of J. Budziszewski, Rob Koons, and Nick Wolterstorff. Finally, we owe a special word of thanks to Robyn DeHart, Paul's wife, whose unfailing belief in the project encouraged Paul to see it to its conclusion, but who also provided important help in the formatting of the chapters as they were prepared for submission to the Press.

This brings us to Northern Illinois University Press, to which we are grateful for its willingness to publish the present volume. We owe special thanks to our editor, Amy Farranto, for her early support for the project and the sure hand she applied in guiding us through the various stages of bringing it to completion. In addition, we wish to thank Christopher Tollefsen and Phillip Muñoz for their careful attention to the manuscript and their sage suggestions for how it might be improved.

We must also express our thanks to the Agora Institute (www.agorainstitute. org) for its generous financial support for this project, support that was essential to bringing this book to publication. We hope that the volume will contribute to the kind of reasoned dialogue that the Agora Institute seeks to foster, a dialogue that deepens our understanding of the Western tradition of reflection on the good and on the requirements of civic virtue. We are grateful to R. J. Snell, one of the Agora Institute's research directors, and Kelly Hanlon, its executive director, for their encouragement and for their help in arranging the institute's support.

Paul DeHart would like to thank Carson Holloway, Nick Wolterstorff, Justin Dyer, and Micah Watson for helpful comments on his chapter. He would also like to acknowledge the work of Al Plantinga and Nick Wolterstorff in epistemology and philosophy of religion. The quality of their work and their courage has led to a sea change in the discipline of philosophy, and Paul hopes that the present volume may contribute, in some small way, to a similar change in political theory. Paul has also been inspired by the work of Glenn Tinder, Jean Elshtain, and J. Budziszewski within political theory. To him they are shining examples of first-rate scholars for whom the claims of faith play an essential role in theorizing about politics. While an undergraduate at Houghton College, Paul once heard Ron Oakerson, protégé of the late Vincent Ostrom, say that he could not be a rational choice theorist all the way down. Thoroughgoing rational choice theory ruled out free will (at least on any meaningful account of free will). His Christian faith, however, compelled him to affirm human free agency over and against thoroughgoing rational choice theory. Thus, while he thought there were a number of things that such an approach to the study of politics got right, the claims of faith and their attendant anthropology of the human person remained more fundamental for him than his graduate training. These words have remained with Paul as a guide to his own scholarly efforts.

Finally (and most importantly) Paul would like to acknowledge the support, help, and encouragement of his family, and especially of his wife, Robyn. Her love and support breathes life into all of his undertakings. They adopted their children, Mina and Zoe, more than two years ago. They have been the very best of distractions. Together with Robyn, they constantly remind him that life is not for the sake of politics but politics for the sake of life: for the sake of ordinary pleasures, playing tag or catch on a warm summer afternoon.

Carson Holloway would like to thank his teachers Tom Lindsay, Gary Glenn, Larry Arnhart, and the late Morton Frisch. He remains mindful of Aristotle's observation that a man can never repay those who taught him philosophy. Carson also wishes to thank Micah Watson for reading and commenting on an earlier version of his chapter in this volume. In addition, he is grateful for the ongoing intellectual and personal friendship of Brad Wilson and Matt Franck, from whose conversation he derives great pleasure and benefit. Finally, Carson wishes to thank his wife, Shari, and daughters—Maria, Anna, Lizzie, Catherine, Jane, and Emily—for constantly reminding him of the truth that human beings are actually more interesting than books.

REASON, REVELATION, AND THE CIVIC ORDER

INTRODUCTION

Carson Holloway and Paul R. DeHart

This book offers a variety of essays exploring the contribution that revelation, or faith in revelation, can make to the practice of political theory or political philosophy. Its aim is to remedy what we take to be an unjustifiable neglect of the claims of revelation by mainstream secular political theory. Such an undertaking must immediately provoke some questions in the form of a counter-challenge. Is it true that contemporary political theory neglects religion and its claims? If so, might not that neglect be justified? After all, why should secular political theorists pay serious attention to the claims of revelation?

With regard to the first question, we admit that reasoning on the claims of revelation is not entirely excluded from contemporary political theory. Some political theorists are themselves religious believers, and some of them reason from their religious beliefs in their theorizing. Nevertheless, such work is often addressed primarily to their co-religionists and rarely wins attention in the mainstream of the profession.

This is not to say that this mainstream, made up primarily of secular political theorists, entirely disregards religion. But to the extent that it pays attention it treats religious belief as a political or philosophic problem to be addressed rather than as a positive body of thought from which we might derive important insights about the nature of politics and the truth of the human condition. On the academic left, Rawlsians and other liberals, protective of pluralism and individual autonomy, tend to view religion primarily as a threat to freedom. The claims of revelation and, indeed, all comprehensive doctrines, they suggest, are to be kept private and not introduced into the public discourse. On the academic right, Straussians often acknowledge religious belief as necessary to a stable society, but they exclude the claims of revelation from philosophy itself, insisting instead on a strict distinction between political theology and political philosophy, with the latter taking its guidance only from autonomous reason. In other words, secular political theory, to the extent that it takes notice of revelation, does not treat it as a potential fund of wisdom from which something of genuine value might be learned; and this, we contend, is to fail to treat the claims of faith with the seriousness that they deserve.

This last claim, however, moves us to the second question suggested above: why should secular political theorists treat revelation with such seriousness? Why should they agree that such attention is necessary to the soundness of their own theoretical investigations into politics? Ultimately, such questions can be answered satisfactorily only by some attempt at such serious attention followed by reflection on whether anything of value was learned. Or, to frame the point more narrowly, secular political theorists might try reading this book with a view to seeing whether what it contains is fruitful for their own thinking. Nevertheless, it is possible beforehand to sketch some reasons why such an undertaking is likely to prove useful.

There is, in the first place, a practical argument for seriously attending to the claims of revelation: it is probable that one cannot fully understand the world we live in, the civilization we have inherited, without understanding those claims. Political theory, even normative political theory, must concern itself not only with what ought to be but also with what is. To be complete, a normative account of politics must consider not only what is best but also how society might move in the direction of what is best. This latter knowledge, however, presupposes an accurate understanding of the present state of society and how it developed. The fully competent political theorist must be like a fully competent physician: conversant not only with health as such but also with the current state of the patient. Nevertheless, the civilization in which contemporary political theorists find themselves—let us say, the civilization of the West, or of the developed world—was certainly influenced by revelation and by believers in revelation. The exact character of the influence is admittedly elusive. The modern liberal democracies were undoubtedly influenced by an Enlightenment philosophy that was in some measure critical both of the claims of revelation and of the quality of the society to which earnestness about those claims gave rise. On the other hand, the modern liberal democracies, and Enlightenment philosophy itself, first emerged in societies that had been deeply influenced by Christianity. The development of the modern world we inhabit seems inseparable from a certain revolt against the claims of revelation, but on the other hand it seems equally inseparable from the previous acceptance of those claims in the first place. These considerations suggest—and some contributors to this volume make this argument at greater length in what follows—that the democratic, egalitarian, individual-rights-respecting world in which we find ourselves cannot be fully understood apart from the role of revelation. Put another way, modern democracy, with its emphasis on equality and rights, may be intelligible only on the assumption that certain distinctively religious claims are in fact sound.

The role of revelation in making the modern world, moreover, cannot be treated merely as a relic of the past. It is true that the modern world, under the influence of the aforementioned Enlightenment philosophy, has undergone a process of secularization. Nevertheless, that process has not become complete: the total collapse of belief in revelation that was expected by the most confident proponents of secular Enlightenment has not yet come to pass. It is likely, then, that belief in revelation, and believers in revelation, will continue for the foreseeable future to influence our politics. That is to say, revelation will continue to have a valid claim on the attention of the secular political theorist who wants to understand the world as we find it.

Such considerations, however, do not yet get us to our more important claim, or do not fully answer the question that we posed above. After all, to study the claims of revelation as a force that has shaped the world in which we live is not the same thing as to approach them as a potential source of genuine insight into the permanent nature of things. It is to treat such claims as relevant facts rather than as possible truths. Nevertheless, even here we would caution that it might not be possible fully to appreciate revelation's factual role in shaping our society without being open to the possibility of its truthfulness. That is, the claims of revelation—like any claims of truth—are best understood from the inside out, and not from the outside in. They are more likely to be understood, and hence their consequences more likely to be understood, when they are approached with a proper openness and not with dismissiveness or hostility. These reflections would counsel the secular political theorists to attend to revelation's claims sympathetically, although not uncritically.

Again, however, as a preliminary matter, why should the secular political theorist approach the claims of faith in the hope of finding genuine insights that may prove useful or even essential to the enterprise of political theory? Opposition to this possibility often arises from the assumption that the claims of revelation are simply irrational, at least in the sense of not being verifiable by reason. Why pay attention to such claims? In response, it might be noted that even secular political theory relies on claims that are not strictly verifiable by reason, but that are posited as fundamental values, as the beginning point of further reasoning. Much serious and influential work in political theory has taken individual autonomy or the principle of equality as its starting point, even though the absolute validity of such principles cannot be confirmed by reason. It may well be that any normative thinking about politics, even the most rigorous and disciplined, requires as its beginning point some basic principles that cannot be fully vindicated by reason alone. If this is the case, then there is no good cause to exclude the claims of revelation from our political theorizing, since they are no less rational than other claims that commonly animate our academic and public discourse. It may well be, as some of our authors argue, that such cherished values as individual autonomy and equality derived their initial plausibility from—and may finally depend for their continued vitality on—the influence of revelation upon our culture.

Finally, we may offer a more positive response to the concern that the claims of revelation are irrational—beyond, again, suggesting that their degree of rationality can only be known after, and not before, an open and sympathetic inquiry into them. Revelation is either what it claims to be, or it is not. That is, it is either a genuine communication from God, or it is the product of human cultural processes. If it really is from God, then it is unlikely to be irrational. God reveals himself, if he reveals himself, in order to communicate with human beings, who are rational creatures. It is highly unlikely that his attempted communication would be alien and unintelligible to those he is seeking to address—especially when we reflect that on any reasonable supposition the God revealing himself would have to be the same God who created us as rational creatures in the first place. If God is seeking to communicate with us, he would either tailor that communication to the kind of beings we are or make us the kind of beings who could recognize his communication, or both. Anything else would seem strangely pointless for any intelligent being, and especially for the supreme intelligence. But what if revelation is not really from God? In that case, will secular political theorists simply be wasting their time in attending to it? Not at all. If what has claimed to be divine revelation were really just a set of cultural beliefs developed by human beings, it would still be the case that those beliefs had built and sustained various cultures and indeed a whole civilization for millennia. It is unlikely, to say the least, that such a system of thought would be devoid of useful and true insights into the human condition.

On the basis of these considerations, then, and others developed at greater length by the contributors to this volume, we hold that the claims of revelation are worthy of the secular political theorist's attention and that the present neglect of those claims is not justifiable. This book is offered as a partial remedy to this neglect. We contend that efforts to preserve the pristine rationality—or rationalism—of political discourse and philosophy are themselves unreasonable. The claims of faith, we suggest, should be taken even by secular political theorists not only as a problem to be ameliorated, or even as an object of interest, but actually as a possible source of valuable insight. The contributions to this volume seek to defend the role of religious arguments in our most rigorous thinking about politics and to offer examples of some such arguments. Insofar as we are American political theorists addressing our colleagues, and given the movements of thought that have predominantly shaped our civilization up to the present, the revelation on which the following chapters focus is primarily biblical revelation and indeed traditional Christianity.

The volume is divided into three sections. In Part I, "Believing in Order to Understand," we explore the reasonableness of faith, or the part it can play in our efforts to think clearly about politics and the human situation. In Chapter 1, Carson Holloway asks whether revelation possesses even the minimal rationality necessary for it to be attributed any credibility by the individual or the public. That is, can it claim at least to be rational in the sense of being among the plausible alternatives that a reasonable person might choose? Holloway approaches this question by way of a critique of Heinrich Meier's Straussian account of the refutation of revelation by philosophy. Meier, inspired by Leo Strauss's efforts to untangle the theologico-political problem, contends that philosophy can and must refute the very possibility of revelation for the philosopher's choice of philosophy as the best way of life to be rationally evident. This refutation proceeds by way of a philosophic account of the origins of revelation: philosophy can explain, and explain away, revelation as a political invention, a set of beliefs about the origins of divine law necessary to a stable society. In response, Holloway contends that Meier's Straussian explanation-as-refutation does not in fact fully explain or successfully refute revelation. This political account of revelation's origins cannot explain the full content of revelation, at least in the sense of biblical revelation. What political or moral purpose is served, for example, by the claimed revelation of God's inner nature as a trinitarian being? If revelation is rooted in the political and moral needs of society, why is the morality accompanying revelation so much more demanding than is necessary to a functional society? In sum, Holloway contends that Meier's explanation and refutation is more or less plausible, but no more so than the rational defenses of belief in revelation that might be mounted by the believer. Therefore, according to Holloway and contrary to Meier, philosophy cannot succeed in definitively refuting revelation, and belief in revelation can be understood as reasonable, in the sense of being rationally plausible, if not rationally compelling.

In Chapter 2 Paul R. DeHart seeks to refute the view, so common among contemporary political theorists, that political philosophy—in order to remain political philosophy, properly understood, and not political theology—must be practiced without reference to any religious claims. According to DeHart, approaches to political philosophy that directly or by implication debar the invocation of religious reasons—approaches such as the new historicism, the Straussian approach, and Rawlsian political liberalism—are self-defeating, especially when it comes to their claims concerning what can be known and the nature of reality. Moreover, these approaches to political philosophy rest (or depend for their plausibility) upon a specific and untenable epistemology: strong or classical foundationalism, the view that we can rationally hold only such beliefs as are themselves properly basic (i.e., self-evident or incorrigible) or are derived from such beliefs. DeHart notes, however, that the self-referential incoherency of strong (epistemic) foundationalism has been demonstrated by analytic philosophers Alvin Plantinga and Nicholas Wolterstorff. Strong foundationalism's criteria for proper basicality are themselves neither self-evident nor incorrigible nor derived from any beliefs that are (or, at least, no one has shown that they are). Given this fatal flaw, as Plantinga and Wolterstorff suggest, we must either reject (epistemic) foundationalism altogether or embrace a modified version with a less constrictive understanding of proper basicality. Either option, DeHart observes, would acknowledge that at least some religious beliefs are just as rational as nonreligious beliefs and thus would permit the use of such religious reasons in the pursuit of any theorizing that deserves to call itself philosophy.

Can Christian agape be reconciled with classical eudaemonism? That is, can the Christian call to love others selflessly be made compatible with the understanding, first articulated by Greek philosophers like Plato and Aristotle, that virtue is good because it is the road to one's own individual happiness? Philosopher Robert C. Koons contends in Chapter 3 that such a reconciliation is possible, and that it requires a careful exploration of the metaphysics of Thomas Aquinas, which suggests that we are the sort of beings whose nature can be perfected and whose happiness can thereby be attained through habits of deliberation and choice that seek larger ends than our own, including the goods of our neighbors and political communities. Koons maintains that such an inquiry, and the reconciliation it seeks, is proper not only to philosophy but to political philosophy. Such an inquiry is essential to finding a place for Christianity in our politics. For if Christianity were really committed to the view that we are obligated to seek the good of others without any thought of our own good, its moral teachings would have to appear as unintelligible to reason alone, and thus there could be no common ground, no commonly accepted "good," available to believers and unbelievers alike. Koons contends that the way out of this dilemma, and the path to the beginnings of mutual understanding between Christian and non-Christian citizens, is through a proper appropriation of Aquinas's effort to harmonize faith and reason.

In Part II, "Faith and the Foundations of Political Order," we consider the importance of religious belief to what may be termed "regime questions," or faith's implications for the constitutional basis of political society, and especially of the modern liberal society in which we live. According to a widely accepted contemporary view, respect for pluralism requires governmental neutrality as regards religion. Put another way, modern societies have put away the old "confessional state," in which the government was committed to a particular religion, and replaced it with the neutral state, in which the government neither fosters nor discourages religion—or is wholly secular in its character. J. Budziszewski contends in Chapter 4 that this advance, so treasured by modern liberal secularists, is in fact a delusion: there is no such thing as a non-confessional state. Even the modern liberal state is a confessional state, insofar as it, like any other state, is based on some convictional foundations, or a commitment to some foundational truths that are regarded as nonnegotiable. As Budziszewski notes, the mere denial that a state is confessional does not in fact make it non-confessional, since a state may have a convictional foundation that it enforces on citizens even if it does not declare that basis openly. So it is with contemporary liberalism, which uses government power to enforce various ideas about how people should live even when this requires coercing the consciences of traditional religious believers, while using such expressions as "autonomy" to disguise what it is doing. Indeed, Budziszewski contends, the modern liberal confessional state is all the more likely to coerce precisely because it blinds itself to its use of coercion or fails to see that it is enforcing an orthodoxy but thinks it is just enforcing neutral standards. The real question for political theory, therefore, is not whether we will have a confessional state, but what kind. Will the state openly declare the convictions that underpin it? Will it embrace tolerance even for those who dispute its fundamental convictions? Budziszewski defends the possibility of, and advocates the desirability of, a confessional state that includes a religious component to its confession but that is nevertheless tolerant because the content of its religious beliefs require tolerance even of nonbelievers. Such a state will be more likely to resist the temptation of intolerance, he adds, if it makes its confessional foundation broadly ecumenical rather than narrowly sectarian.

Modern politics, Peter Lawler notes in Chapter 5, assumes the reality of free persons and the importance of personal freedom. From left to right, all significant voices are devoted to the flourishing of particular personal lives. We no longer view the individual merely as a part of a larger whole, whether nation or species, but as a person with dignity. This realization of the importance of the person, Lawler contends, has Christian roots and can only continue to flourish if those roots are nourished. For the ancient political philosophers, he contends, nature or eternity was essentially impersonal, and so the individual human personality was understood as a secondary reality or even as ultimately unreal. Only with Christianity's introduction of the personal God did we come to appreciate the genuine significance of each person as unique and unrepeatable. This importance of the person is adopted by, and is fundamental to, our Lockean modernity; but Lockeanism alone, Lawler suggests, cannot sustain our commitment to personal freedom. Locke's teaching is too individualistic, his person too solitary. Solitary persons cannot maintain their freedom against the state. Such freedom instead is sustained by persons bound together by ties of love—that is, by the personal teaching characteristic of Christianity.

Taking as his guide the profound but still underappreciated French political philosopher Pierre Manent, Ralph Hancock asks us in Chapter 6 to ponder the question: can we really know ourselves fully as modern human beings without confronting Christianity? That is, can we accurately understand the nature of modernity without taking into account the role of Christianity in bringing it into being? As

Hancock observes, the idea is commonplace that political and philosophic modernity—with its emphasis on equality and its aspiration to ease the suffering of mankind—represents a "secularization" of Christian ideas and impulses. Nevertheless, the tendency among the partisans of secular modernity is to neglect its Christian roots and thus to evade the question of whether modernity is intelligible or sustainable apart from those roots. And, as Hancock notes, the even more pronounced tendency is absolutely to evade the question whether serious reflection on the nature and origins of modernity requires us to confront not merely the influence but even the truth of Christianity. Hancock also shows, however, that reflection on the Christian roots of modernity is no less important to the self-understanding of Christians themselves. The most ardent and intellectually consistent contemporary Christians, seeing the growth of a secular modernity that is to some extent hostile to traditional Christianity, might be tempted to deny that their own beliefs have anything to do with the emergence of such a modernity. Hancock's exploration reminds us that the origins of modernity were not thinkable without the assistance of certain Christian presuppositions and therefore reminds Christians themselves that full self-understanding requires them to meditate on the connection of their own tradition to modernity.

In Chapter 7, James R. Stoner, Jr., concludes this section of the book by tracing the dynamic and, as he contends, fruitful relationship between Catholicism and American constitutionalism. At first glance, one might be inclined to emphasize instead the gap between the religion of Catholics and the American regime. After all, America was founded primarily by Protestants, and its founding political theory was influenced not only by Protestant thought but also by a secular political philosophy that was often skeptical of both the truth and the political and social wholesomeness of Catholic belief. Nevertheless, Stoner points out, American Catholics in fact played an important part in establishing the American republic. Here he emphasizes in particular the Carrolls of Maryland, whose Catholic orthodoxy nobody could reasonably question and whose support for the revolutionary cause and for the Constitution nobody could reasonably deny. Later events in American history show not only the minimal compatibility of Catholicism and American constitutionalism, Stoner contends, but even the positive contribution of the former to the latter. If we understand the Constitution broadly, as encompassing not only the written document but also the enduring governmental institutions and policies that have grown up around it, we can see that Catholic thought influenced the development of American constitutionalism in the early part of the twentieth century. Our "constitution" in this broader sense now includes various programs, such as Social Security, designed to express and foster a kind of economic solidarity among citizens. While the case for such programs was first popularized by Progressives, Stoner observes, they could not be fully enacted at the national level without the political support of Catholics in the New Deal coalition, a support that was already prepared by the work of American Catholic social thinkers like Father John Ryan. Conversely, Stoner contends, the traditions of American constitutionalism have also influenced the mind of the church. Inspired by the political theory of the Constitution, the American Jesuit John Courney Murray influenced the Second Vatican Council's statement in favor of religious liberty in *Dignitatis Humanae*. In view of this history, Stoner asks, why would either side want this healthy and mutually supportive relationship to end?

Finally, in Part III, "Faith and Contemporary Political Thought," we examine the relationship of religion to various important strands of current scholarship in legal and political theory. In Chapter 8, Micah Watson explores the relationship between the New Natural Law theory and the beliefs of American Evangelicals. Unlike some contemporary theories of politics, the New Natural Law approach is not hostile to traditional religious belief or the traditional morality that often accompanies it. Indeed, as Watson explains, the great pioneers and explicators of the New Natural Law are Catholic thinkers, animated at least in part by a desire to show that traditional moral beliefs could be justified on the basis of reason alone. Watson's account reveals a tension between the New Natural Law's rationalistic aspirations and American Evangelicalism's commitment to faith. According to the proponents of the New Natural Law, human reason is a sufficient moral guide: the basic goods and elementary principles we need to know in order to perform our duties and to establish a decent and just society are evident to reason. Evangelicals, Watson contends, must balk at this affirmation of reason's moral self-sufficiency. For while they can certainly embrace the importance of reason in clarifying moral issues and perhaps even in adequately answering some moral questions, Evangelicals take God's revelation in Scripture to be our most authoritative guide for how to live rightly. Accordingly, they cannot subscribe without qualification to the New Natural Law. This clash would be entirely academic if reason (as understood by New Natural Lawyers) and Scripture (as understood by Evangelicals) were in perfect agreement. Thus Watson highlights the real, practical nature of the conflict by contrasting the New Natural Law's absolute prohibition on lying with certain passages in the Bible that seem to justify the telling of falsehoods in a righteous cause.

Since the ratification of the Constitution, Americans of almost all political persuasions have been united by a belief in the separation of church and state—understood as the prohibition, articulated in the First Amendment, on the establishment of an official religion by the government. In recent decades, however, some Americans have embraced an understanding of the separation of church and state that goes further and is more controversial. They have contended that distinctively religious beliefs and arguments should be excluded from the public square or that they should be forbidden as the grounds of legislation or policy. As Francis Beckwith explains in

Chapter 9, this argument has been pressed by prominent American jurists including members of the Supreme Court as well as legal theorists, on the grounds that religious beliefs are not amenable to reason, that they cannot be characterized as knowledge, and therefore that they are essentially private and cannot be made the matter of public deliberation. Beckwith contends that this is a caricature of religious belief rather than an accurate characterization of it. The irrationality of religious belief is commonly defended on the basis of a secular rationalism, holding that only those beliefs are reasonable that can be demonstrated by science or by reasoning from experience. But as Beckwith observes, that principle of knowledge itself cannot be demonstrated by scientific or empirical reasoning. Moreover, this secular rationalism surely proves far too much, and therefore proves nothing, because many kinds of beliefs that we commonly think we hold reasonably—such as moral, philosophic, or literary opinions—are likewise incapable of the kind of empirical demonstration that secular rationalism demands. In any case, Beckwith continues, the mainstream Christianity that secular rationalism particularly wants to exclude from the public discourse in fact has a long and impressive history of being open to and trying to meet reasonable challenges to its beliefs. Finally, traditional moral beliefs associated with traditional Christianity—for example, regarding abortion, physician-assisted suicide, and the definition of marriage—are ordinarily defensible in rational terms, even if they are also somewhat inspired by or associated with religious beliefs that cannot be confirmed by reason. For these reasons, Beckwith concludes, there is no solid basis on which to exclude religious arguments from our political deliberations.

In Chapter 10, Luigi Bradizza exposes the inconsistencies of Richard Rorty's antireligious philosophy of public life. Rorty elevates individual autonomy, understood as self-creation, and therefore understands traditional Christianity as an enemy to his understanding of human flourishing. Nevertheless, Bradizza contends, Rorty's thought really cannot escape being religious itself. Rorty looks forward to an egalitarian utopia that he describes using religiously charged language. Moreover, since there is no present evidence for the possibility of such a society, Rorty's dedication to it depends on a kind of faith. In addition, Rorty admits that the free self-creativity he admires is really accessible only to a few, to the "strong poets." The majority of human beings depend on these strong poets for their conceptions of value. Thus they remain in a state similar to that of religious believers, dependent on an intellectual authority around which they must organize their lives. Indeed, insofar as Rorty believes that the mind is determined by natural necessity, it turns out that even the freedom of the strong poets is really illusory. In light of these considerations, there is no ground on which anyone could take Rorty's philosophy as more reasonable than the religion he opposes.

Finally, in Chapter 11, R. J. Snell contends that the superficiality of our public discourse—observed and lamented by commentators on the left and the right, secular and religious—can be healed only by a kind of "conversion," not necessarily a spiritual conversion to some particular faith but an intellectual conversion to openness toward religious claims. Such a position runs counter to influential theories of public reason (such as the account put forward by John Rawls), which admonish citizens to respect democratic pluralism by keeping appeals to any controversial comprehensive doctrines out of public debate. Drawing on the philosophic anthropology of Charles Taylor and the work of philosopher and theologian Bernard Lonergan, Snell challenges this conception of public reason. Human beings by their nature construct their identities in relation to their comprehensive beliefs. Thus Rawlsian public reason in effect asks them to check their very selves at the door of our public discourse, which seems to be an extreme and hence unreasonable demand. Moreover, because of our inescapable need for comprehensive doctrines, efforts to exclude these doctrines only foster a tendency to smuggle them into our deliberations surreptitiously, a process hardly conducive to their rational examination. In addition, there may be injustices or corruptions in our common life that cannot be brought to light and corrected on the basis of the pluralist consensus but only by recurrence to the kind of fundamental considerations that comprehensive doctrines, including religious doctrines, address. Finally, it is the nature of reason to ask questions about all things and thus to ponder even the comprehensive questions. In light of these considerations, Snell concludes, those who insist on a Rawlsian public reason are, paradoxically, not reasonable enough and are inadvertently undermining the rationality of our discourse.

The preceding chapters admittedly do not offer a complete defense of the role of revelation in our thinking about politics, much less a comprehensive account of what might be learned about politics from arguments informed by religious faith. We hope, however, that they at least offer a persuasive first step toward opening the study of political philosophy to such arguments or an introduction to religion as more than a political problem to be contained or even a useful political tool to be employed for ends identified by rationalistic political theory but, rather, as a source of genuine insight and a full partner in our dialogue about the aims of politics. We hope, in sum, to have shown that if the claims of faith cannot compel the assent of secular political theorists, those claims at least should win their attention.

PART I

BELIEVING IN ORDER
TO UNDERSTAND

Revelation's Contributions to Philosophy

1

HEINRICH MEIER'S STRAUSSIAN REFUTATION OF REVELATION

Carson Holloway

Is belief in divine revelation reasonable? Such belief surely cannot command simply rational assent, in the sense of a conviction that follows upon rational demonstration: belief in revelation depends in part upon accepting historical claims from the distant past that are no longer subject to independent verification. Indeed, religious believers themselves do not even claim this kind of rationality for their convictions. Hence their emphasis on the need for faith—that is, the need to trust God's revelation and, in addition, to trust the church or community of believers he has constituted to communicate his revelation.[1] But if believers in revelation cannot demonstrate their claims and do not even claim to try to do so, can their position at least be presented as a reasonable one in a less demanding sense? That is, can belief in revelation stake a claim to intellectual respectability equal to that of rival positions, or one at least sufficiently within the bounds of reasonableness that it cannot simply be dismissed as obvious delusion? This question has been pressed with greater than usual vigor and openness in recent years, especially by opponents of revealed religion who have sought to expose it as a mere medley of irrational beliefs, unworthy of continued vitality in an enlightened age.[2]

This question is undoubtedly an important one. It matters for us as individuals. Revealed religion makes claims—about man's ultimate origins, his purpose, and his destiny—that seem impossible for a serious person to ignore. At least, the claims would be hard to ignore, again, if belief in revelation is reasonable in the sense of rationally plausible. The question is also important for the quality of our political life. If belief in revelation is seen as simply irrational, then believers' arguments about how best to organize our common life, their conceptions of justice and the good, will be easily dismissed; while, on the other hand, if that belief is seen as at least plausible, believers' public arguments will be accorded more respect and will probably have more public impact.

As is often the case, however, the most important questions are not always treated with the seriousness they deserve; and the most well-known arguments are not always the ones most worthy of our attention. I propose to investigate a critique of the reasonableness of revelation found not in one of the recent bestsellers but, instead, in the much less widely known work of the German philosopher Heinrich Meier—specifically, that to be found in his book *Leo Strauss and the Theologico-Political Problem*. In Meier's argument we encounter not a polemicist but a philosopher sharing his meditations on this question, which are in turn derived from his long and careful study of one of the foremost figures in political philosophy in the twentieth century. Such a study is also of interest because of Strauss's reputation as a friend of traditional religion. In taking his point of departure from Strauss, Meier is not beginning from a reflexive hostility to religious belief. Such considerations add a certain weight to his ultimate dismissal of revelation as unable to justify itself at the bar of reason.

In this chapter I offer a critique of Meier's treatment of revelation or, rather, I attempt a refutation of his Straussian refutation of revelation. I will first deal with some preliminary matters, which are necessary in order to clarify Meier's argument and hence the nature of the disagreement. Then I will present what I take to be the key argument in Meier's refutation. Finally I will offer my response.

PRELIMINARY OBSERVATIONS: MEIER'S STRAUSS ON REASON AND REVELATION

Meier presents his argument as an interpretation of the thought of Leo Strauss on the theologico-political problem. In doing so he challenges two common conceptions of Strauss. The first is that Strauss was not himself a political philosopher but, instead, only a student of political philosophy, albeit a brilliant one. On this view (which Strauss himself probably encouraged to some extent), he was a scholar or commentator on the ideas of others but did not have any philosophic project of his own. In contrast, Meier contends with great plausibility that Strauss was himself a philosopher and that he spent his life grappling with what he took to be *the* central question: the theologico-political problem or the problem of the relationships among politics, religion, and philosophy and the question as to which alternative offers the true or right way of life. Meier observes: "For anyone who seriously studies [Strauss's] oeuvre, the focal point becomes the intention that the philosopher Strauss pursues when he directs his undivided attention, so it seems, to the history of political philosophy and presents his philosophy in the guise of interpretations of past writings."[3]

Meier contends that many of those who do see Strauss as a philosopher or who believe he did articulate a position on the theologico-political question do not correctly understand his teaching on this question. This is not entirely their own fault because, as Meier holds, Strauss used deliberate misdirection in order to conceal his true teaching with regard to the relationship between revelation and reason or between faith and philosophy. Strauss is famous for, among other things, his emphasis on the use of esotericism among philosophers of the first rank, that is, their tendency to write in such a way as to point to a teaching beneath the surface that is not the same as the exoteric teaching or the surface teaching. Meier holds that Strauss is not only a philosopher but also an esoteric philosopher, who subtly conveyed his teaching using the techniques he exposed in his works on other thinkers.

According to a commonly held view, Strauss believed that philosophy and revelation are in opposition to each other and that this opposition is insuperable. The opposition arises from the different ultimate grounds upon which they stand. The philosopher, although he might find some interesting and useful things in the teachings of revelation, seeks finally to be guided only by rational inquiry into the nature of things. The theologian, although he may use some of the tools of philosophic inquiry in order to refine his beliefs, ultimately rests his deepest convictions on faith or trust in revelation. This opposition is insuperable because neither side can demonstrate that the other is wrong. The theologian cannot offer for revelation the rational evidence demanded by the philosopher, but neither can the philosopher prove to the theologian that the revelation did not in fact occur. The idea of such a standoff, moreover, undermines philosophy's pretensions to a superior rationality to theology. Precisely because of the standoff, or because of philosophy's inability decisively to refute theology, the choice to pursue the life of philosophy is not based on considerations evident to reason but instead on what Meier terms a "decisionistic act" or, in other words, an act of faith—faith, paradoxically, in reason (*Strauss*, 23).

This, again, is the view commonly attributed to Strauss. Meier contends, however, that Strauss's real teaching on this question is different from, or rather opposed to, the one he seemed to make in public. Strauss's public claim that there is an insuperable standoff between philosophy and theology is merely an exoteric teaching concealing a more radical esoteric teaching: that philosophy must and can refute the very possibility of revelation. "Political considerations," according to Meier, led Strauss to impose a certain "restraint on himself" in his "public treatment" of the theologico-political problem. These considerations caused him in fact to "nourish

[the] misleading impression" that he believed the life of philosophy to depend on a "decisionistic" act, because "in the face of revelation, philosophy finds itself in a blind alley," or again, because there is an unresolvable "stalemate between philosophy and faith in revelation." We may suppose that Strauss's public comments to this effect are designed to create a "misleading impression," Meier suggests, because they rest uneasily with other claims that he made no less insistently. Specifically, even as he held that, confronted with revelation, philosophy could justify itself only on the basis of a nonrational decision to opt for the life of reason, Strauss also denied emphatically "that a blind, unproven decision can ever be a sound foundation for the philosophical life." Strauss famously taught that the apparent contradictions in the surface teaching of a philosopher may point to a veiled, but nevertheless discoverable, esoteric teaching, a teaching the philosopher intends to communicate not to all readers but only to dedicated and careful readers. Applying this insight to Strauss himself, Meier contends that Strauss's "insistence on the requirement of a rational justification" for the philosophic life is designed to suggest to his "philosophic readers [that] they may not rest satisfied with a decisionistic position" (23–24). It is an invitation for them to philosophize more deeply, to think for themselves, and to find a way out of the blind alley or stalemate that appears (but only appears) to confront philosophy. Strauss's thought, moreover, points to paths out of this blind alley, paths to a successful philosophic refutation of revelation.

Why, we might ask, did Strauss choose to keep his deepest insights on the theologico-political question veiled in this manner? What are the "political considerations" that led Strauss to create the false impression that he considered philosophy and theology to be locked in a theoretical stalemate? Meier briefly suggests two reasons, both of which relate to the "central concerns of political philosophy" (23n22). In the first place, Strauss was concerned with the "protection and defense of philosophy." In other words, Strauss sought prudently to conceal the extent to which philosophy is wedded to ideas that might provoke public anger. This might at first seem strange. After all, Strauss did not live in a time (America in the 1950s and 1960s) when philosophers were likely to suffer serious persecution by denying revelation in their scholarly writings. Strauss, however, was deeply familiar with the history of philosophy and with the fact that, for most of its history, it did not exist under conditions in which freedom of thought enjoyed legal protection. He might reasonably have feared that a spirit of anti-philosophical persecution could arise again at any time and, accordingly, thought it was better to keep his views hidden.

However that may be, if Meier's interpretation of Strauss's views is correct, Strauss would certainly have had more mundane and practical reasons for concealing his critique of revelation. As Meier observes, Strauss did not merely wish to philosophize himself, he also wished to be the founder of a philosophical school, a possibility that arose when he won a position at the University of Chicago. The founding of this school was essential to Strauss's aspiration to revitalize the study of political philosophy and (even more important) to open up again the possibility of the philosophic life as the best life. Advancing these lofty aims surely would require attention to more pragmatic concerns such as the ability of Strauss's students to win positions in the American academy, which certainly would not be aided if it were known their teacher was an open atheist. Strauss could not have failed to observe that many American colleges and universities had religious foundations and identities, that America in general was a more religious country than the countries of Europe, and that this widespread religiosity influenced—at least at the time—even the faculties of America's secular institutions of higher education. If no one was in real danger of being made to drink the hemlock, it was still necessary for Strauss's students to get jobs, and this would be far easier in America if Strauss was believed to hold views that were, if not religious, at least respectful of religion's claims to intellectual credibility.

Meier suggests a second concern "central to political philosophy" that would have led Strauss to veil his teaching: "the role accorded to religion in a well-ordered commonwealth" (23n32). Meier does not here elaborate on this consideration, but its meaning will be tolerably clear to any student of Strauss's writings. Strauss characteristically emphasized, and Meier appears to follow him in emphasizing, the difference between the philosophic few and the nonphilosophical many. A few can guide their lives by reason alone, but the majority of men cannot. Accordingly, every political society relies on a set of nonrational convictions as its organizing principle—beliefs that are necessary to hold society together but that cannot withstand the careful scrutiny of the philosopher. Moreover, religious beliefs are typically an important part of this element of opinion upon which public order rests. In light of such considerations, Strauss would, out of a certain decent public spiritedness, understandably wish to veil from the society at large his philosophic critique of revelation.[4]

These remarks point to final preliminary reflection, offered before turning to the supposed refutation of revelation itself: the Straussian critique of revelation sketched by Meier is not hostile to religion in the way that is characteristic of the Enlightenment, either as the Enlightenment was presented by the philosophic giants who originated it or by the more recent popularizers of Enlightenment antireligiosity. As Meier develops Strauss's presentation of revelation, although it terminates in rejection, it is nevertheless somewhat respectful both politically and philosophically. Politically, while the proponents of the Enlightenment tend to regard revelation merely as a source of public disorder and sectarian violence, a force that needs to be replaced by the rule of public rationality, Strauss as we have just seen doubts such a rule of reason is possible and so appreciates the role of revelation in providing opinions necessary to hold society together. Strauss's respect for revelation goes beyond a mere recognition of its political utility, however, and acknowledges also a kind of philosophic utility. While Enlightenment thinkers tend merely to dismiss revelation as irrational superstition, Strauss insists that revelation is in fact the truly worthy opponent of philosophy as a way of life, the grand alternative that the philosopher must overcome in order to place his way of life on a solid rational footing. In contrast, the Enlightenment tended not so much to refute revelation as to dismiss it. According to Meier, Strauss believed that the thinkers of early modernity had pursued a "Napoleonic strategy" against revelation. That is, the Enlightenment "strove for victory by marching past the seemingly impregnable fortress of orthodoxy in order to provide proof of its own power through the creation of a new world, trusting that the enemy's position would be historically 'disposed of.'" On Meier's account, whatever its merits or demerits as a political strategy, from a philosophic standpoint this Enlightenment approach is a mere "evasion" (13). It does not attempt a straightforward confrontation with the claims of revelation and so cannot truly claim to have refuted them. The success of the Enlightenment in building modern societies characterized by unprecedented prosperity and power is not so much an answer to revelation as a distraction from its claims. But, again, those claims must be answered if philosophy is to be defended rationally as a way of life. Thus, according to Meier, Strauss presents revelation as the truly worthy opponent of philosophy, the alternative with which philosophy must grapple if it is to justify itself.

To succeed in justifying itself, however, philosophy must not only grapple with revelation but in fact overcome it. Although Strauss's approach to revelation is respectful for the reasons noted above, he does conclude in the end that belief in revelation is irrational; for the philosopher can only move forward with the philosophic life as a rationally grounded and necessarily evident—as opposed to a merely willed—choice if he can claim to have refuted the possibility of revelation. We must now turn to the refutation that Meier draws from Strauss's writings.

THE REFUTATION OF REVELATION

According to Meier, Strauss's thought suggests several paths out of the blind alley, or several ways by which the philosopher might proceed in overcoming the standoff between faith and reason and thereby refuting revelation. Here we will focus on one particular path, however, the one that Meier implies is the most important. This is the path that involves reflection on philosophy's *"explanation of revelation,"* or *"the concentration on politics"* (25; original emphasis). The importance of this particular path is indicated by the amount of space Meier gives to it, as well as the way in which he presents it before undertaking it. This approach, he notes, involves philosophy in developing a "genealogy of revelation" or a historical account of revelation's origins and development (26). Yet Meier presents his unpacking of Strauss's genealogy as an "example that is more than an example" of how philosophy may approach the refutation of revelation and thus suggests that it shows how all the paths of refutation "are to be developed" (xiii, xiv).

Meier's framing of the key path of philosophy's refutation of revelation suggests that it proceeds by way of a "concentration on politics." How, then, does a consideration of politics lead to an "explanation of revelation" that is also a refutation of it? The answer, it would seem, is that philosophy can show that revelation is linked to politics or is part of politics and is therefore not, as it claims, from God. Revelation is a political invention and therefore of merely human origins. Meier's account implies this from the very outset. In the first few pages he notes that Strauss used the term "theologico-political problem" for the "urgent confrontation with the theological and political alternative to philosophy" (4–5). The confrontation, we note, is carefully framed by Meier as being with the singular theological and political alternative—and not plural alternatives—to philosophy. We might at first think that the "theologico-political problem" has to do primarily with the problem of the relationship of theology to politics, but it is, according to Meier, primarily a problem posed, to philosophy as a way of life, by theology/politics as a united alternative to philosophy.

Meier renders the character of this path more clear when he later notes that Strauss discovered it in Plato as a result of his study of certain medieval political philosophers. "The Arabic philosophers and Maimonides," Strauss learned, "followed Plato when they grasped the divine law, providence, and the prophet as objects of politics; they relied on the *Laws* when they treated the teaching of revelation, the doctrine of particular providence, and prophetology as parts of political science (and not at all of metaphysics)." Similarly, they "moved in the politico-philosophical horizon of the *Republic* when they regarded the founding of the 'perfect city' as the *raison d'être* of revelation" (12). According to Meier, "premodern rationalism" begins its confrontation with revelation by focusing on "the law in the original sense, on the comprehensive order of the commonwealth, an order that united religion and politics and that, as religious, political, moral law, lays claim to the individual wholly, existentially." Premodern rationalism "justifies" this "law" in order to "get beyond it." In other words, for the "Platonic political philosophers of the Middle Ages, justifying the law philosophically becomes the grounding of philosophy" (13). By revealing the purely natural basis of belief in revelation, political society's need for a divine law, the philosopher explains and indeed explains away revelation understood as a genuine communication of ultimate truth from God. And with revelation so debunked, the philosopher can proceed with rational confidence that philosophy is the evidently true or right way of life.

Let us now examine this explanation and refutation more closely. Meier traces this account with great care in chapter 2 of *Leo Strauss and the Theologico-Political*

Problem, "On the Genealogy of Faith in Revelation," where he offers his detailed commentary on Strauss's 1948 lecture "Reason and Revelation." The argument proceeds as follows: The seemingly insuperable standoff between theology and philosophy—or revelation's status as a kind of impregnable fortress that, while it cannot overthrow philosophy, also cannot be overthrown by it—arises from the supposed fact, emphasized by the defenders of revelation, that philosophy cannot explain revelation. Revelation claims to be a radically unique communication of God to men in human history. Philosophy proceeds by inquiring reasonably into the regular and intelligible order of nature. To this extent, revelation appears to be simply beyond the ken of philosophy, which perhaps need not accept it but certainly cannot disprove it. In contrast, the Straussian argument sketched by Meier contends that philosophy can, in fact, demonstrate the natural grounding of belief in revelation. It can trace the "transition from nature to historicity" or the "derivation of the asserted singularity" of revelation from "intelligible necessity" (31). The philosopher, in other words, can see through the claim that revelation is from God to the truth of how it was gradually invented by men.

The argument begins from the indisputable fact that humans must live in society and therefore are in need of law. The need is more specifically, of course, for good law, and men at first held that the proper criterion for the good was the ancestral. There is, moreover, a perfectly natural and reasonable basis for making such an equation: the laws of one's ancestors have been tested by time, and they provide a certain necessary stability. If the purpose of the law is the preservation of an orderly society, then the embrace of the ancestral has an obvious natural and rational basis. Nevertheless, to make this law sufficiently binding upon men, it would be further necessary to posit that it has a superhuman source. Thus men conclude that the ancestral law is in fact a divine law, that gods are the authors both of the laws and of the existence of men. It will not, however, escape the notice of even rather primitive societies that there are other communities with their own laws for which they also claim divine status. If the divine law is to fulfill its (natural and political) purpose, then, we must conclude that there is in reality only one divine law and hence only one God who is the author of divine law as well as the creator of all things. From this, it is suggested, arises the demand for full obedience to the law, in several senses. The single creator-lawgiver God is viewed as omnipotent, and his law as the source of all blessings. This God and his law should be valued not merely instrumentally but absolutely, not as means to some other end but as ends in themselves. Thus full obedience requires that one love God with all of one's soul or heart, all of one's power. Moreover, the oneness of God means that he is the father of all men, so that we must love all men as brothers: thus no human relationships escape the gaze of God and his law. In addition, full obedience means that not only one's actions but even one's thoughts and desires must conform perfectly to God's law. Hence the need for an upright intention. Nevertheless, because such integrity is impossible for human beings, the concept of sin arises, and the need to view God as a God of mercy. At the same time, full obedience suggests the notion of humility or self-surrender, the complete rejection of self-assertion on the part of man, and hence a rejection of science and philosophy. At last, this argument suggests, such conceptions of God terminate in the belief that God himself is the source of our ability to live up to the law. God must make us holy; he must communicate himself to us and draw near to us. Hence the belief in an incarnation of God (32–34). Thus, Meier suggests, a set of beliefs about God and man, or a theology, that is recognizable as biblical revelation can be understood to have developed from humanity's natural need for a divine law as the basis of society.

A RESPONSE TO THE REFUTATION

What are we to make of this explanation of and refutation of revelation? Does it succeed in its aims? Does it sufficiently show, for those who have eyes to see, that revelation's claim to be from God is false, and that philosophy alone therefore remains as the way of life that is evidently the true or right one according to reason?

As this framing of the issue makes clear, my concern here is not with whether Meier's interpretation of Strauss is correct. I will not try to solve the question as to whether Strauss really believed and taught, contrary to what he put in writing in certain places, that philosophy can in fact refute revelation. Others will no doubt take issue with Meier's reading insofar as it involves him in the bold—though not necessarily unreasonable—claim that he has understood Strauss's thought on this question more accurately than many of Strauss's own students. Although bold, the claim is not necessarily unreasonable because, as Meier explains, Strauss's undertaking of founding a philosophical school inevitably meant that not all of his students would understand his deepest intentions. Be that as it may, I will leave the question of Strauss's true intention to those better able to inquire into it and concern myself instead with the substantive question presented by Meier's interpretation. Does the argument Meier claims to draw from Strauss succeed in refuting revelation and overcoming the standoff, with the effect that belief in revelation can no longer be viewed as a legitimate alternative for a thinking person? Meier's attempted refutation of revelation falls short, I believe, for the following reasons.

First, the refutation begins from an unreasonable premise, namely, that the philosopher cannot choose the path of philosophy unless that path is "evidently" the right path. On the argument presented by Meier, the philosopher must have rational certainty that philosophy is the right way of life before he can embark on that way of life with integrity and consistency. If such certainty is lacking (if revelation is even possibly true), then philosophy will depend on a choice that is not compelled by reason and will therefore in fact be no more reasonable than the life of faith. It is far from obvious, however, that such certainty is in fact required. The demand for a rationally evident, or irrefutable, starting point for philosophy depends on a prior judgment about what it means to live one's life according to reason. One might understand this to mean that the choice must be a rationally evident one, as the Meier-Strauss position demands. Alternatively, however, one might understand this to mean only that the choice must be the one to which reason on its own directs us. According to this second view, the way of philosophy is a reasonable one not because philosophy can show that revelation is false but simply because philosophy cannot know rationally whether revelation is true. The philosopher who pursues this path will simply say that, as far as anybody can tell on the basis of reason alone, philosophy is the right way of life. The philosopher does not need to know that the claims of revelation are untrue: they cannot compel his assent because he cannot know them to be true. Moreover, it is impossible for reason to determine that the former posture—Meier's posture—is the obligatory one. Meier's philosopher wishes his choice for philosophy to be rationally evident. By insisting on this he is embracing a particular—and rather demanding—standard of deciding what renders a choice reasonable or rationally defensible. Yet there is no way for him to make it rationally evident that this standard is more reasonable than the less demanding standard, which leaves open the possibility that revelation is in fact true. In sum, the demand for a rationally evident starting point for philosophy—in the sense that Meier understands it—cannot itself be made rationally evident or compelling in contrast to the other possible understanding of what constitutes a sufficiently rationally evident starting point—one that does not and need not preclude the possibility of revelation.

Indeed, of the two possible standards of rationality in play here, the latter, less demanding one, the one open to the possibility of revelation, would seem to be the more reasonable. Given the vastness and complexity of the universe and the weakness of our own powers of reason, it is doubtful that any of our important choices could achieve the kind of rationality demanded by Meier's philosopher, a rationality that excludes all possibility of error. Philosophy is, as Strauss himself never tired of repeating, a rational *quest for* the truth, not the *possession of* the truth. It presupposes that the truth has not yet been fully grasped, which is a very plausible supposition. Such an understanding necessarily, however, includes the possibility that the full truth does not disclose itself to rational inquiry alone.

According to Meier, Strauss resists this view, contending instead that philosophy must refute the very possibility of revelation. "If there is revelation," Strauss says, then "philosophy becomes something infinitely unimportant—the possibility of revelation implies the possible meaninglessness of philosophy. If the possibility of revelation remains an open question, the significance of philosophy remains an open question." Yet, according to Strauss, "philosophy stands and falls by the contention that philosophy is the One Thing Needful, or the highest possibility of man. Philosophy cannot claim less: it cannot afford being modest" (quoted in *Strauss*, 22–23). Let us leave aside the point that the truth of revelation would not in fact bring about the absolute meaninglessness or infinite unimportance of philosophy—any more than it would necessitate the meaninglessness of any other noble use of our noble faculties—but would only render philosophy less than self-sufficient. Things incomplete in themselves are not for that reason meaningless or unimportant. In any case, the possible meaninglessness of philosophy is something the philosopher would have to live with even if no one had ever heard of divine revelation. That possible meaninglessness would arise from the possibility—which the philosopher cannot definitively rule out—that the ultimate truth about the whole cannot be known by reason, or that this truth, once discovered, will require some other activity than philosophic activity. Meier correctly suggests that the philosopher needs courage to question his own most dearly held convictions. In view of the insistence that the beginning point of philosophy be absolutely rationally evident, however, it begins to look as if Meier means that the philosopher needs the courage to question other people's most dearly held convictions—that is, nonphilosophers' most dearly held convictions, in other words, moral and political convictions—but not his own convictions. Needless to say, stated in this way, the philosopher's courage looks less impressive. In fact the human situation, the necessary incompleteness of our knowledge, requires of the philosopher the courage to philosophize even while knowing that philosophy is conceivably not the best way of life.

The second reason I believe Meier's attempted refutation of revelation falls short is because it must be considered imperfect to the extent that his explanation of revelation is imperfect. Meier contends that philosophy can refute revelation by explaining it, by bringing to light its roots in man's natural needs, or showing how it arises from natural and political necessity. The argument Meier presents, however, does not in fact explain revelation completely or adequately, that is, it leaves some important things unexplained, and it explains other things in ways that lack persuasion. By "revelation" Meier and Strauss would appear to have in mind the teaching of the Bible, the most obvious source of belief in an omnipotent God who creates man and gives him a law, who asks total obedience, and who forgives sin and draws near to man. The explanation in fact appears to end in the claim to explain Christianity as a result of the logical development of an idea that originates with the need for a divine lawgiver. This explanation, we recall, concludes with the idea of the "incarnation." Even if we were to concede the power of the explanation so far as it is traced by Meier, relying on Strauss, it would still leave unexplained important beliefs that are held to be part of this revelation, such as the Trinity, which Christians hold to be central to their belief, as well as Christ's suffering and death. Why would revelation—which, again, is finally a set of conventional beliefs developed for political reasons—feel the need to reveal the inner life of God as a Trinitarian being? Perhaps Meier would contend that this is part of the drawing near of God that is required by the anxiety created by the sense of sin: God draws near by showing us what he is in himself and not only in relation to us. Like a friend he opens himself up to us. This is perhaps plausible, but it does not explain why men would come to conceive the idea that God's inner being is specifically three persons in one nature. Moreover, it is not even obvious that such a self-revelation would be necessary to alleviate the problem of sin. Put another way, the revelation turns out to be more "theological" than the Meier-Strauss account can explain. Similar considerations apply to the belief that God became incarnate not only to draw near to man but also to suffer and die in expiation of sin. The philosophic explanation and refutation suggests that God is posited as a God of mercy in order to remedy the sense of sin. Because we cannot live up to God's demands, we come to believe that he will himself communicate holiness to us. Again, whatever merits such an explanation might have, it cannot explain definitively why the belief in revelation took the form it did. A God of mercy could simply forgive the sins of those who make an honest effort to be good, and he could communicate his grace to those who ask for it earnestly, without having to suffer the punishments himself.

Furthermore, the Straussian explanation developed by Meier lacks full persuasiveness even in relation to the aspects of revelation that it does address. The account of the development of belief in revelation has the character of a Rube Goldberg machine: it is more complicated than it needs to be for the purposes it is supposed to perform. Put simply, the morality of revelation is more demanding than it needs to be in order to fulfill its original political purpose. According to the Meier-Strauss account, men posit the existence of a single omnipotent and all-good God as the source of the law required by men in order to live in an orderly and peaceable way in society. This God then turns out to demand absolute obedience to his law, including the obedience even of one's desires and thoughts. Since men are incapable of such righteousness, they develop the belief that this God is forgiving and will communicate his righteousness to us. The kind of purity demanded by this revelation is far beyond what is required by a functional society. Social order may well need—or at least can be understood to be supported by—a belief in a God who demands just conduct and who will punish the unjust and reward the just. We can well understand how men might invent a belief in such a God. What is not clear is why they would embark on the invention of a socially useful religion and then go so far as to impute to their God demands that even the best human beings cannot fulfill and then try to ameliorate the unsettling consequences of that strange step by further imputing a spirit of mercy and condescension to such a God. It seems more likely that men would evolve religious beliefs that satisfy the requirements of society without going further. Of course, men might also develop beliefs along the lines of the revelation Meier describes because they have a natural sense that there really is some absolute transcendent goodness to which they must try to conform. But this explanation would suggest that man is by nature a religious being, which would in turn call into question whether philosophy is the best way of life (at least, philosophy as Meier understands it, as an autonomous and rationalistic quest for knowledge), which is obviously not the kind of explanation in which Meier is very interested.

In fact, Meier's argument does touch upon the possibility that man is somehow by nature a religious being. We can bring this part of his argument to light by stating another objection to the political explanation and refutation of revelation and then noting the materials from which Meier could fashion a plausible rejoinder. In addition to the difficulties noted above, we might object further to the critique of revelation on the grounds that it does not fully acknowledge why men are so apt to embrace belief in God. The need for divine law in the service of social order might explain why founders and rulers would invent a civic religion, but it does not explain any inner desire that would lead ordinary men so readily to embrace such a creed. Men, we might say, are led to embrace belief at least as much because they are aware of and fear death as for any moral needs of the community. Yet this aspect of the problem is ignored by the genealogy of belief in revelation, which therefore fails to give a full explanation of revelation and, therefore, cannot fully succeed in refuting it according to the terms set by Meier.

Meier does touch on this aspect of the problem, however, elsewhere in his book—specifically in his account of some of Strauss's reflections on Heidegger. Those reflections suggest that man experiences a certain call. Defenders of revelation present this call as the call of God, God's revelation of himself to man, but it is in fact the call of death. Man is uniquely aware of death. He knows that he is drawn irresistibly to union with this nothingness, and he reacts by transforming it into a positive being. Belief in revelation, then, is based on the soul's effort to solve the problem of death by personifying death. Some of the most powerful parts of the human soul, Strauss suggests, support this tendency toward personification. *Thumos*—or spiritedness, the power by why which we desire honor, and thereby assert our individual self-importance—personifies. Here we might think of Melville's Captain Ahab, lashing out at a whale in order to exact revenge on an apparently hostile cosmos. *Eros*—our desire for the beautiful—also personifies. On this view, man's openness to revelation results from the soul's projection of its desires onto the cosmos. It wants to believe in the eternity of the things it loves (45–51).

Like the genealogy derived from man's need for divine law, this is certainly a plausible account of the origins of revelation. This account is not, however, more plausible than the alternative explanation—or at least not compellingly more plausible. To note that *thumos* and *eros* personify begs the question as to why they are constituted such as to personify? The soul might have evolved the capacity to personify—to project personality on the universe—in order to heal, or at least treat, the wounds left by the intolerable truth of man's personal insignificance. On the other hand, the soul might tend to personify precisely because it owes its origin and nature to God. The soul may be created to personify precisely because God made man with the intention of revealing himself to man. Or, to state the issue differently, the critics of belief in revelation could with reason contend that it is strange that a God who intended to reveal himself to man would leave himself almost entirely cloaked in silence and invisibility, that he should directly reveal himself only to the smallest number of men and only at certain times, leaving the rest of humankind to rely on secondhand reports and leaving even the direct recipients of his revelation to carry on most of the time by faith that the revelation was in fact from God. We might well wonder whether such a God is really even there. The proponents of revelation have answers to these objections but would have to admit their force. On the other hand, however, the proponents of revelation could contend that it is no less strange that a cosmos that is fundamentally indifferent to particular beings would give rise to a being who so insistently desires to believe in his own personal significance. And, the proponents of revelation might further ask, if nature is so indifferent to our desires, why should we even think that the philosophic life is, as the philosopher insists, really good for us? Both interpretations have a certain plausibility and involve certain problems. In view of this rough parity between them Meier's plausible but not rationally compelling explanation cannot succeed in being a refutation.

Indeed, the fundamental problem with Meier's account is that a plausible—but necessarily somewhat speculative—explanation of something cannot succeed in being a refutation of an alternative explanation, or at least, not to the extent that Meier seems to demand, which is to the extent of rendering the preferred explanation simply "evident," so that the philosopher has a rationally rock-solid starting point for his choice of the philosophic way of life. If we find a man dead in the street, struck in the head by a piece of metal that has fallen from the building above, we might well conclude that he was murdered. After all, there are doors that allow access to the roof of the building. On the other hand, someone might object that the wind was blowing hard on the day the man was killed, so it is also possible that a gust blew the piece of metal off the building, resulting in a death by accident. Both explanations are plausible. Both fit with the known facts, but in the absence of additional verifiable facts we cannot say that one explanation can evidently exclude the other. This is precisely the situation that confronts us in evaluating the competing explanations of revelation. We might ask, for example, did Abraham experience something truly extraordinary, something he might reasonably have understood as a call from God? Or was he a prudent founder of a people who understood the natural need for a divine foundation for the law that would bind that people together? This is not a question philosophy can answer so definitively that the answer can be presented as simply evident and a satisfactory refutation of the competing possible explanations.

Those skeptical of revelation might point to the remarkable coincidence that its teaching conforms so closely to the moral, political, and emotional needs of human beings. May we not suspect on that basis that what purports to be revelation was in fact invented by humans to satisfy those needs? While it is certainly not unreasonable to entertain such suspicions, it is unreasonable to pretend they constitute a refutation of belief, especially when the believers in revelation can respond to those suspicions in a way that is consistent within their own assumptions. What the skeptic regards as suspicious coincidences the believer in revelation regards as perfectly natural and predictable. After all, for the believer, the God who reveals himself to men is also the same God who created men in the first place. Revelation is an effort at communication. It is to be expected—or it is at least plausible—that God would create men in such a way that they would be ready to receive his revelation. Indeed, it would be strange if it were otherwise, if revelation appeared as something wholly alien or useless to men.

These reflections on Meier's argument return us, I believe, to the standoff on which Strauss publicly insisted: the life of philosophy and the life of faith in revelation are equally plausible contenders for the right way of life. There is no purely rational path by which this impasse can be resolved in favor of philosophy. This is not to say, however, that there is no path at all by which it could be so resolved. While we need not agree with Nietzsche that *all* thought is merely will to power, we may concede that, given our human limitations, much thought, and even some of the most impressive thought, is tainted by the will to power. Meier's Straussian refutation of revelation is not so powerful that it can refute revelation for the wholly impartial person considering the two alternatives. It may well succeed, however, in appearing to refute revelation for the person who, for whatever nonphilosophical reasons, is already disposed not to believe in revelation.

NOTES

1. Of course, this is not to deny that believers in revelation can and do claim that their faith is held reasonably in a certain sense.

2. Here we might mention, as prominent examples, Richard Dawkins's *The God Delusion* (New York: Mariner Books, 2008), Christopher Hitchens's *God Is Not Great: How Religion Poisons Everything* (New York: Twelve, 2009), and Sam Harris's *The End of Faith: Religion, Terror, and the Future of Reason* (New York: W. W. Norton, 2005).

3. Heinrich Meier, *Leo Strauss and the Theologico-Political Problem* (New York: Cambridge University Press, 2006), xiv. Page references will henceforth be given parenthetically in the text.

4. These considerations point to a further possible inquiry. Why does Meier choose to rip away the veil concealing Strauss's supposed refutation of revelation, a concealment that Strauss himself thought necessary and just? Does Meier disagree with Strauss's view that religion is necessary for decent order among ordinary human beings and that therefore the philosopher should try not to disturb it? Or does Meier agree it is necessary, but he does not agree with Strauss that it is the responsible philosopher's duty not to disturb it? Or perhaps Meier agrees that religion is necessary but thinks that, at this point in our history, unveiling Strauss's real thoughts on the rational status of belief in revelation can do no harm? These and other possibilities might fruitfully be explored, but they are not the concern of this chapter.

2

POLITICAL PHILOSOPHY AFTER THE COLLAPSE OF CLASSICAL, EPISTEMIC FOUNDATIONALISM

Paul R. DeHart

Standard approaches to the practice of political philosophy debar (directly or by implication) the invocation of theological propositions or narratives or what might be called religious reasons. Insofar as one is a political philosopher, one is to set religious convictions aside (supposing for the moment one entertains any such convictions) and proceed on the basis of rationality or public reasonableness or some such thing. Any such requirement presupposes, as a matter of course, that the relation between faith and reason or faith and rationality is oppositional. But political philosophy has not always been committed to strident secularism. How has this come about? Is such a commitment tenable anymore? I shall answer this latter question in the negative. Political philosophy came to debar the invocation of religious reasons or the claims of faith because, with the Enlightenment, political philosophy came to be premised upon a particular epistemology. The name for that epistemic point of view is classical foundationalism. But, due in large measure to the work of analytic philosophers such as Alvin Plantinga and Nicholas Wolterstorff, classical foundationalism has collapsed and is now irretrievably lost. And with the collapse of classical foundationalism, the very ground of the ban on religious reasons in the practice of political philosophy has fallen away. Consequently, I will argue that it is permissible, as an exercise of philosophy in general and of political philosophy in particular, to begin with the claims of faith and to reason to conclusions that are generally the purview of political philosophy (e.g., conclusions concerning the relation of church and state, the relation of consent to legitimate government, the nature of the just regime, the necessity of constitutional limitations on the exercise of political authority, etc.). First, however, I would like to construct the approaches to political philosophy that directly or by implication debar the claims of faith; and I would like to show how these various approaches fail on their own terms.

THE PRACTICE OF POLITICAL PHILOSOPHY IN VIEW OF THE COLLAPSE OF CLASSICAL FOUNDATIONALISM

The Place of Religious Faith in the Practice of Political Philosophy at Present

There are various approaches to the practice of political philosophy. What these approaches (or most of them, at any rate) hold in common is the impropriety of invoking religious reasons when doing work in political philosophy. That is the contemporary situation. The contemporary situation follows the modern situation and follows an approach to political philosophy that became ascendant during the so-called Enlightenment. Early modern political thought (such as Locke's) did not debar the invocation of religious reasons as such in the practice of political philosophy. But early modern thought (or method) did require that religious reasons only be invoked insofar as they were underwritten by rationality.[1] Eventually, we arrived at a state of affairs in which religious claims are no longer considered rational and so no longer allowed. But the Enlightenment has now gone out.[2]

One approach to political thought that, by virtue of its very method, debars the invocation of the claims of faith, is historicism. By *historicism* I refer to what is now sometimes called the new historicism. And the new historicism must be distinguished from nineteenth-century historicism. The old historicism was epitomized by Leopold von Rank, for whom historical inquiry constituted uncovering the facts and allowing the facts to speak for themselves. In contrast, what is sometimes called the *new historicism* is more akin to the historical relativism of Charles Beard, Carl Becker, and F. R. Ankersmit.[3] The new historicism must be characterized as, in some sense, reactionary. It more or less (especially in Ankersmit) rejected the old approach to history (seeking to uncover the past or the facts about the past or things said in the past that have abiding importance for us)—an approach new historicists take to be wedded to philosophical objectivism. In contrast, the new historicism begins with skepticism of eternal verities or timeless truths or, at least, skepticism that the study of the past can bring us to any such thing. This is especially true when it comes to the study of political thought. Thus, Richard Ashcraft laments the old approach to political theory, an approach that conflated political theory with philosophy by converting political theory into a search for objective or eternal truths: "What is sought, through the medium of political theory, is a knowledge of principles that are 'universally applicable to all men at all times.'" As a result, political theory "becomes identified with 'timeless truths' or the 'perennial problems' of human existence." This confusion of political theory with philosophy, according to Ashcraft, produces two negative consequences: "First, it reflects and enforces a divorcement of an understanding of political theory in terms of the specific historical-social context within which it arose. Secondly, it severs political theory from precisely those political objectives which, to its author, or to the audience, made the theory a recognizable force in society." To be sure, Ashcraft does not expressly reject the "philosophical approach" to political theory. He laments, rather, the dominance of the philosophical approach over a more historical approach.[4]

In an older essay, Quentin Skinner affirms his skepticism that study of the history of thought or of political philosophy can bring us to eternal truths, while maintaining that this skepticism is in no way a denial that such truths exist:

> Insistence on the claim that there are no perennial problems in philosophy, from which we can hope to learn directly through studying the classic texts, is not of course intended as a denial of the possibility that there are propositions (perhaps in mathematics) the truth of which is wholly tenseless. (This does not yet amount to showing their truth is any the less contingent for that.) It is not even a denial of the possibility that there may be apparently perennial *questions*, if these are sufficiently abstractly framed. All I wish to insist is that whenever it is claimed that the point of the historical study of such questions is that we may learn directly from the *answers*, it will be found that what *counts* as an answer will usually look, in a different culture or period, so different in itself that it can hardly be in the least useful even to go on thinking of the relevant question as being "the same" in the required sense after all. More crudely: we must learn to do our own thinking for ourselves.

But having advanced so qualified a position, he proceeds to make the breathless claim that study of the history of thought results in recognition of the variety of moral convictions and the recognition that truths one has taken as timeless are really just the product of one's own time and place. The one who studies political thought will come to realize that there are no "timeless concepts":

> The classic texts, especially in social, ethical, and political thought, help to reveal—if we let them—not the essential sameness, but rather the

essential variety of viable moral assumptions and political commitments. . . . A knowledge of the history of ideas can then serve to show
the extent to which those features of our own arrangements which we
may be disposed to accept as traditional or even "timeless" truths may
in fact be the merest of contingencies of our peculiar history and social
structure. *To discover from the history of thought that there are in fact no*
such timeless concepts, but only the various different concepts which have
gone with various different societies, is to discover a general truth not merely
about the past but about ourselves as well.[5]

Now it is less than clear that Skinner's account of the revelation of the history of
thought—namely, the radical variation in moral and political convictions—is the
sober truth of the matter. In fact, I think Skinner is wrong here. Rather than addressing Skinner's eminently contestable claim just now, however, I would like to note
how these two claims could support two variants of the new historicism. The first
variant appears in the lines from Ashcraft and in the first quote from the Skinner essay. Let's call that view *humble new historicism* (HNH for short). What we see in the
second Skinner quote can be called *grandiose new historicism* (GNH for short). As I
see it, both are flawed. Let's take them in reverse order.

Drawing on the second quotation from Skinner, we might say that GNH moves
beyond skepticism that timeless truths can be apprehended through the study of
the history of thought and beyond the expression of epistemic doubt (or agnos-
ticism) that such truths exist to the outright denial of their existence. The GNH
defender claims (1) that there are no eternal verities, no timeless truths at all,[6] and
(2) that the study of the history of ideas demonstrates the truth of (1) by revealing
the contingency of truth claims in matters social, ethical, and political. The study of
the history of ideas seems to accomplish this demonstration by revealing just how
varied moral and political views really are. "Different strokes for different folks" is
the revelation of the history of thought. But in that case, (3) the study of "canoni-
cal texts" in the history of political thought can be nothing other than the study of
the goals of the author in writing the text and the use to which the text was put by
those who read it. It is the context in which the text was written, the rhetorical or
persuasive goals of the author, and the use to which the text has been put or the
way in which it has been received by its readers that determines the meaning of the
text and what can be learned from the study of it. There are no objective or aeon-
transcendent truths to be gained in the study of Plato's *Republic*, Aristotle's *Politics*, Augustine of Hippo's *City of God*, Hobbes's *Leviathan*, or Locke's *Two Treatises*.
Likewise, there are no timeless or aeon-transcendent truths of moral and political
import to be gleaned from the study of Hebrew or Christian sacred texts. What are
we to make of GNH?

I submit that our first reaction should be to find the seeming widespread acceptance of GNH a bit surprising. For GNH is self-referentially incoherent. Consider, premise (1). The very denial of timeless truths is the expression of one such truth: that there are no timeless truths. Consequently, it is impossible to deny the existence of timeless truths without affirming that at least one exists. As a result, GNH is self-defeating. Anyone who subscribes to GNH has a defeater for GNH—a defeater that removes all warrant for affirming GNH. Put another way, to affirm GNH is to affirm the denial of GNH, for to deny the existence of any and all timeless truths is to utter one. Thus, given (1), we have (4)—namely, the self-referential incoherency of GNH.

What about (2)? Well, (2) may well be unsound. Honest study of moral beliefs across cultures fails to reveal radical or complete variance. There is variance. But there is also convergence. Indeed, something like cultural norms or universals has been discovered to be necessary for cultural anthropology even to proceed. And if we find agreement in moral convictions across culture (even if we also find difference), then we might expect to find some agreement in the political and moral texts across cultures as well.[7] But even if we did not, we would have to note that (2) utterly fails to support (1)—Quentin Skinner notwithstanding. For suppose all the texts in political theory say (whatever they appear to say) fundamentally different things. Suppose those texts contradict each other left and right as to their most fundamental teachings. Nevertheless, it remains possible that at least one text (even if only one) instantiated or gave expression to a timeless and universal truth—a truth that might even help us today, if only we could apprehend it. If such a truth were given expression in a historical text, there is an a priori possibility that we might uncover the truth through a careful study of the text. My point is this: The mining of texts written in preceding generations for the wisdom of the ages is not built on the presupposition that all or most or even any of the great texts in political theory teach the same thing. Perhaps Aristotle and Hobbes teach fundamentally different things. Perhaps also Aristotle is right and Hobbes is wrong (or vice versa). In sum, the very different moral and political teachings of texts in moral, political, and religious teaching says nothing one way or the other about our ability to apprehend universal or objective truths from the study of political thought.

The third component of GNH is problematic as well. All the arguments that suggest we cannot discover timeless or objective truths in the study of the past mitigate against our being able to study the past at all. The study of history—whether of ideas or anything else—becomes nothing other than the construction of our own narratives about what we call the past. Put another way, the denial of timeless truths—or of the connection of any such truths to the study of history—entails the rejection of an objective past that we can accurately capture in the present.[8] The rug has been yanked out from under the new historicist project by nothing other than new historicism itself.

What about HNH? I submit that HNH fails as well. Suppose HNH maintains only that we cannot know whether or not there are timeless truths. Well, that proposition is itself still one such truth. Consequently, the expression of epistemic doubt concerning the existence of timeless truths is self-referentially incoherent. What if we modify the claim to say only that the study of the history of ideas—of past political theory—cannot lead to the discovery of such truths? But how could the study of past political theory (or of the past more generally) lead to such a conclusion (that study of the past cannot lead to timeless truths)? If the claim is true, then the study of past political theory cannot lead to it—otherwise the study of past political theory would have led us to a timeless truth about the study of political theory. But, according to the claim, the study of past political theory can lead to no such truths. Where then did the claim come from? There is no argument in contemporary political theory that is divorced from the study of past political thought *and* that demonstrates the truth of the claim. Nor is there any purely abstract, deductive argument that demonstrates it. Indeed, there presently exists no demonstration of it at all. The claim seems to be nothing other than sheer assertion. But sheer assertion is no reason to accept it.

So there is no reason to accept either GNH or HNH. But, in that case, there is no reason to reject the invocation of religious claims in the practice of political theory just because those claims derive from historical texts or because those claims make or include timeless truths.

A second approach to the practice of political philosophy that debars the invocation of religious reasons is the Straussian approach. Strauss famously endeavored to partition theological claims from political philosophy by distinguishing political thought, political theology, and political philosophy. Strauss frames the relation of political philosophy to political thought as that of species to genus, where political philosophy is a species of the larger genus of political thought: "Hence all political philosophy is political thought but not all political thought is political philosophy." What's the difference? Well, political thought is "reflection on, or the exposition of political ideas." But political thought as such is "indifferent to the distinction between opinion and knowledge." In contrast, "political philosophy is the conscious, coherent and relentless effort to replace opinions about political fundamentals by knowledge regarding them" (not that Strauss thinks such knowledge can ever be attained in practice—he denies that it can).[9] Strauss also holds that "we are compelled to distinguish political philosophy from political theology." Political theology encompasses "political teachings which are based on divine revelation." But "political philosophy is limited to what is accessible to the unassisted human mind."[10] Given the foregoing, invocations of religious reasons or of the claims of faith in the practice of political philosophy are debarred as a matter of definition. Political theology trades in special revelation. Political philosophy does not. In an earlier lecture entitled "Reason and Revelation," Strauss frames the relation between the two (or between philosophy and revelation, as he puts it in the body of the talk) as oppositional.[11] Philosophy and revelation are said to be inherently opposed. It follows that philosophical reason (or rationality) and revelation are also opposed. Faith is one thing, the exercise of reason another (though in "Reason and Revelation" Strauss concedes that theologians do in fact reason—it's philosophy or philosophical reason, he says, which is opposed to revelation).

I think Strauss's position is premised on an untenable view of rationality. I think Strauss's sharp distinction between faith and rationality or faith and philosophy is premised on a view that analytic philosophers call classical or strong (epistemic) foundationalism.[12] And classical (epistemic) foundationalism is irredeemably incoherent. So I find his attempt to exclude political theology or religious reasons from the practice of political philosophy to be incoherent as well. Without going into the details of that portion of the argument just yet, we can raise some other objections to the Straussian view. First, why understand faith and reason or faith and philosophy as inherently oppositional? If the definitions employed by Strauss lead to inherent opposition, then instead of saying, "It's either revelation or philosophy," we might rather say, "So much the worse for those definitions of reason and philosophy." Revelation may be opposed to *Straussian* philosophy. But so what? More importantly, why should the religious believer care? Why shouldn't she define political philosophy differently and proceed from there? Given the opposition of her faith to Straussian philosophy, why shouldn't she opt instead for Augustinian philosophy or for Christian philosophy or for a conception of philosophy in which philosophy refers to the tools of investigation instead of stipulating a priori conclusions that philosophy is not allowed to reach (as Straussian philosophy avowedly does)?

Moreover, Strauss claims, "Philosophy is essentially not the possession of the truth, but the quest for the truth. The distinctive trait of the philosopher is that 'he knows that he knows nothing,' and that his insight into our ignorance concerning the most important things induces him to strive with all his power for knowledge."[13] But doesn't just this understanding of political philosophy give up the game? First, it is impossible for anyone, the political philosopher included, to know that he knows nothing. To know that one knows nothing is to *know* it; in which case the political philosopher really does know something; in which case, it is *not* the case that the political philosopher knows nothing. So the political philosopher cannot know that he knows nothing. He may believe that he knows nothing. But if he knows nothing, then he cannot know it (and cannot *know* that he believes that he knows nothing; for, in that case, the political philosopher would still know something—namely that he believes that he knows nothing). Consequently, if Strauss wants to claim this degree of epistemic humility for political philosophy, then wouldn't it be best to admit that he doesn't know whether or not political philosophy and political theology intersect? Shouldn't Strauss refrain from claiming to *know* that political philosophy cannot accept, cannot begin with, or cannot reason to (perhaps by confirming) the claims of faith? As I see it, Strauss's own account of the nature of political philosophy precludes him from knowing that political philosophy as such must eschew the claims of theology.

Finally, we come to *political liberalism* and its chief proponent, John Rawls. As I see it, political liberalism has two components: (1) a recommendation to citizens and officials concerning how they should conduct themselves in the public sphere when debating and voting on constitutional essentials and matters of basic justice and (2) a conception of political philosophy and the work of political theorists in modern constitutional democracies. While I need to say something about both of these components, I'm mainly interested in this question: Does the practice of political philosophy as understood by Rawls debar the invocation of religious claims or propositions?

Let's begin with the first component of Rawls's political liberalism. Can citizens and officials invoke religious reasons when publicly debating or discussing constitutional essentials and matters of basic justice? In a handful of essays written after *A Theory of Justice* and in the first edition of his *Political Liberalism*, Rawls develops a more or less negative answer to this question.[14] In these works Rawls famously maintained that citizens and officials, when publicly debating (or even voting on) constitutional essentials and matters of basic justice, (ideally) should not invoke reasons unique to their comprehensive doctrines about the nature of the world and our place within it.[15] In particular, citizens or officials should not advocate or repudiate positions on the basis of metaphysical conceptions of justice (i.e., based upon conceptions of justice with metaphysical presuppositions). By implication, the Rawlsian position also prevents citizens from invoking religious reasons when engaged in public discussions of justice or of constitutional essentials (to be sure, reasons grounded in comprehensive liberal theories such as those proffered by Mill, Kant, or Rawls, in *A Theory of Justice*, are ruled out too)—at least, in *normal* circumstances. Thus, the usual rule for citizens and officials goes as follows: "in discussing constitutional essentials and matters of basic justice we are not to appeal to comprehensive religious and philosophical doctrines—to what we as individuals or members of associations see as the whole truth—nor to elaborate economic theories of general equilibrium, say, if these are in dispute."[16]

What justifies this Rawlsian prescription? So far as I can tell, the Rawlsian prohibition is grounded in two claims: a descriptive claim about modern, constitutional democracies and a normative claim concerning what might make such a regime legitimate. The descriptive claim is that modern, constitutional democracies encompass an *ineliminable pluralism* of conflicting but reasonable conceptions of the good (or, perhaps more aptly, an ineliminable pluralism of competing but reasonable conceptions of the good inevitably obtains within such regimes). Thus, Rawls: "political liberalism supposes that there are many conflicting reasonable conceptions of the good, each compatible with the full rationality of human persons." Moreover, this ineliminable pluralism of "conflicting and incommensurable" yet reasonable conceptions of the good is the normal result of practical reason operating under "enduring free institutions." Consequently, "no comprehensive doctrine is appropriate as a political conception for a constitutional regime" (*Political Liberalism*, 135). This brings us to the normative claim or to what Rawls calls the "liberal principle of legitimacy": "[O]ur exercise of political power is fully proper only when it is exercised in accordance with a constitution the essentials of which all citizens as free and equal may reasonably be expected to endorse in light of the principles and ideals acceptable to their common human reason." And so, "only a political conception of justice that all citizens might be reasonably expected to endorse can serve as a basis of public reason and justification" (137). We might put the point this way: political power is only rightly exercised by some free and equal persons over other free and equal persons when the exercise of that power is justified in terms that may be viewed as reasonable by all.

But if political liberalism concedes that fully rational persons may (reasonably) differ as to conceptions of the good, what resources remain for the development of a liberal conception of justice? Put another way, if the differences concerning the good and the good life are ineliminable in a liberal democracy, then on what basis can citizens discuss or even debate the most appropriate way to order their common life? One answer Rawls rejects, because he takes it to be unstable, is a modus vivendi.[17] For Rawls, a modus vivendi is a purely pragmatic compromise between parties or groups who view the world in fundamentally different ways. These groups agree to live together by shared principles just because circumstances require them to live together and no group at present has the upper hand. Should some group gain the upper hand, however, then the purely pragmatic justification for the compromise is gone. In which case Rawls thinks that the terms of the compromise will no longer be observed. The instability of the modus vivendi leads Rawls to reject, as a basis of shared rules for living together, a compromise grounded in nothing but the self-interest of the parties to the agreement.[18] Where then to turn?

Rawls proposes, as an alternative to a modus vivendi, the idea of an overlapping consensus or, more aptly, the idea of an overlapping consensus in conjunction with the idea of public reason. The notion is that in a liberal democracy (constituted in part by the fact of ineliminable pluralism) each group, insofar as it is reasonable, may, as part of its comprehensive view, subscribe to some tenets to which each of the other groups in the society also subscribes. Each group would subscribe to such principles for its own reasons. In order for the overlapping consensus to be stable, these reasons must be *essential* to each group's comprehensive doctrine. If the principles or ideas that comprise the overlapping consensus are merely contingent for each group (or for some groups) in the society, then, according to Rawls, the overlapping consensus will be no more stable than a mere modus vivendi.[19]

The overlapping consensus, should one exist, provides more than stability. It also lays the foundation for conditions under which citizens and officials can satisfy the *liberal principle of legitimacy*. For, given the existence of such a consensus, it becomes possible for citizens and officials to deliberate and justify their votes by appealing to reasons on which all can agree (i.e., public reasons). And, in fact, the liberal principle of legitimacy would seem to require citizens and officials (when deliberating or voting upon constitutional essentials or matters of basic justice) to refrain from invoking reasons distinctive to their comprehensive views (which is to say, nonpublic reasons) and so to advance their cause in terms of public reason alone. This seems to be what Rawls means by "the ideal of public reason": "The point of the ideal of public reason is that citizens are to conduct their fundamental discussions within the framework of what each regards as a political conception of justice based on values that the others can reasonably be expected to endorse and each is, in good faith, prepared to defend that conception so understood" (226–27).[20]

Now the upshot of the foregoing *seems* to be that citizens and officials run afoul of the Rawlsian prescription (that they recur to public reason when discussing or justifying votes concerning constitutional essentials and matters of basic justice) when they invoke reasons peculiar to their philosophic or religious view—that is, when they employ nonpublic reasons in such debates. And the articles written between *A Theory of Justice* and *Political Liberalism* seem to point in that direction. But in a "puzzling" passage in *Political Liberalism* Rawls distinguishes between the *exclusive* and *inclusive* view of public reason.[21] On the exclusive view, it is never appropriate for citizens and officials to invoke nonpublic reasons (including religious reasons) when discussing or justifying votes concerning constitutional essentials or matters of basic justice. On the inclusive view, however, there are states of affairs in which the invocation of nonpublic (indeed, of religious) reasons is appropriate. And just here is the rub; for Rawls affirms the inclusive view (*Political Liberalism*, 248).

Rawls distinguishes three states of affairs: (1) a well-ordered society wherein the members affirm a stable overlapping consensus and in which there are no "deep disputes"; (2) a "nearly well-ordered society," in which "there is a serious dispute" concerning the application of "one of its principles of justice"; and (3) a society that "is not well-ordered" and in which "there is a profound division about constitutional essentials" (248–49). He then suggests that, while it would be inappropriate to invoke nonpublic (and so religious or metaphysical) reasons in the first state of affairs, nonpublic (and, indeed, religious) reasons may be invoked in the second and third state of affairs. Reflecting on the second state of affairs, Rawls considers a disagreement among religious groups concerning public support for religious schools. Perhaps one group thinks such support not only good policy but also constitutional. Meanwhile, another group believes such support violates the separation of church and state. In this situation, according to Rawls, "those of different faiths may come to doubt the sincerity of one another's allegiance to fundamental political values" (248). One way to address this doubt "is for leaders of the opposing groups to present in the public forum how their comprehensive doctrines do indeed affirm those values" (249). But the far more interesting case is the third state of affairs. In a disordered or significantly unjust society, citizens and officials may invoke reasons grounded in their comprehensive doctrine in public discussion and debate concerning constitutional essentials and matters of basic justice. But there is an important qualification. Citizens and officials may do so only to the extent that their actions and the policies they promote foster (or would bring about, should the policies be adopted) a well-ordered or just society in which the ideal of public reason can be followed (249–51). Reflecting on religiously grounded abolitionism in the United States, Rawls says, "The nonpublic reason of certain Christian churches supported the clear conclusions of public reason" (249–50).

The Rawlsian ban on nonpublic, and so also on religious, reasons in a well-ordered society but allowance of nonpublic, and so also religious, reasons in a disordered society is sufficiently strange (and arguably inconsistent)[22] that it is perhaps unsurprising that Rawls eventually discarded the inclusive view in favor of the *wide* view of public reason and what he called the *proviso*.[23] According to Rawls's revised view, in public discussion of constitutional essentials and matters of basic justice, citizens and officials may justify their positions and votes in terms of nonpublic reasons (i.e., in terms of reasons distinctive to their comprehensive view) *so long as* they stand ready to justify their position and votes (say to fellow citizens who are not members of their group) in terms of public reason *as well*. By implication, religious reasons are admissible so long as the position being advanced admits of justification in terms of public reason as well. Thus, public reasonableness stands as the rule and measure for when nonpublic reasons can be admitted into public discussion of constitutional essentials and matters of basic justice.

When it comes to the openness of the public realm to religious and metaphysical views, the position of the later Rawls seems more generous than that of the early Rawls or even the Rawls of the first edition of *Political Liberalism*. Even so, the proviso might be a less generous concession than it first appears. But instead of exploring that matter further, I want to ask whether the more capacious view of the later Rawls also applies to the practice of political philosophy. I submit that it does not.

Rawls distinguishes two approaches to political philosophy. He refers to the first approach as the "dominant tradition" (we can also call it the standard approach), which he distinguishes from political philosophy as conceived by political liberalism. On the standard approach, there is but one reasonable and comprehensive conception of the good. There are, of course, various accounts of the one "reasonable and rational" good. For instance, there are the classical, antique views advanced by Plato and Aristotle and the traditional, Christian conceptions of Augustine and Aquinas. Rawls suggests that classical utilitarianism "belongs to this dominant tradition" of political philosophy as well. Despite their evident differences, such views hold in common the notion that "institutions are justifiable to the extent that they effectively promote" the one "reasonable and rational" good. On this view, "the aim of political philosophy" is "to determine" the "nature and content" of the one rational good. Political liberalism rejects this approach to political philosophy. Rather, as noted above, political liberalism posits an ineliminable pluralism of conflicting and incommensurable but also *reasonable* conceptions of good. As a result, "the question the dominant tradition has tried to answer [i.e., What is the nature and content of the one rational good that our institutions, if they are to be justifiable, ought to promote?] has no answer: no comprehensive doctrine is appropriate as a political conception for a constitutional regime" (*Political Liberalism*, 134–35).

The upshot of rejecting the method of "the dominant tradition" is a shift in the purpose of political philosophy. Thus, in "The Idea of an Overlapping Consensus," Rawls characterizes what he deems the proper work of political philosophy as follows:

> The aims of political philosophy depend on the society it addresses. In a constitutional democracy one of its most important aims is presenting a political conception of justice that can not only provide a shared public basis for the justification of political and social institutions but also helps ensure stability from one generation to the next. . . . [T]his political conception needs to be such that there is some hope of its gaining the support of an overlapping consensus, that is, a consensus in which it is affirmed by the opposing religious, philosophical and moral doctrines likely to thrive over generations in a more or less just constitutional democracy, where the criterion of justice is that political conception itself.[24]

But a few pages later he says this: "[S]uccess in achieving consensus requires that political philosophy try to be, so far as possible, independent and autonomous from other parts of philosophy, especially from philosophy's long-standing problems and controversies. For given the aim of consensus, to proceed otherwise would be self-defeating."[25] Similarly, in "Justice as Fairness: Political not Metaphysical," Rawls describes what he considers "the task of political philosophy at the present time": "Briefly, the idea is that in a constitutional democracy the public conception of justice should be, so far as possible, independent of controversial philosophical and religious doctrines. Thus, to formulate such a conception, *we apply the principle of toleration to philosophy itself:* the public conception of justice is to be political, not metaphysical."[26] So the work of "political philosophy at the present time" is to apply the principle of toleration to philosophy. The principle is so applied for the sake of developing a political conception of justice that has no *metaphysical* foundation (or one for which no particular metaphysical ground is essential). Put another way, the work of political philosophy is to produce a public conception of justice that does not depend upon ideas, principles, or reasons unique to any comprehensive view—including religious and philosophical ones. Thus, according to Rawls:

> The aim of justice as fairness as a political conception is practical, and not metaphysical or epistemological. That is, it presents itself not as a conception of justice that is true, but one that can serve as a basis of informed and willing political agreement between citizens viewed as free and equal persons. . . . To secure this agreement we try, so far as we can, to avoid disputed philosophical, as well as disputed moral and religious, questions. . . . Thus, justice as fairness deliberately stays on the surface, philosophically speaking. Given the profound differences in belief and conceptions of the good at least since the Reformation, we must recognize that, just as on questions of religious and moral doctrine, public agreement on the basic questions of philosophy cannot be obtained without the state's infringement of basic liberties. Philosophy as the search for truth about an independent metaphysical and moral order cannot, I believe, provide a workable and shared basis for a political conception of justice in a democratic society.[27]

Based on this passage and others like it, Jean Hampton proffers this depiction of "the justificatory methodology Rawls is urging political philosophers to follow":

> A political philosopher should justify any principle or doctrine to a pluralist community by finding or seeking to develop an "overlapping consensus," and she should do so while relying on the prevailing conception of free public reason and any shared virtues that encourage political cooperation, either by articulating the values or principles that are instrumentally necessary for the achievement of certain universally held objectives, or by looking for or else seeking to develop a theoretical overlap among the disparate groups in the society, so as to define a fund of implicitly shared ideas and principles.[28]

According to Hampton, "Rawls calls this the 'method of avoidance' (JFPM, p. 231); by using it one avoids argument on the basis of any contested premise and any controversial claim about what is true."[29]

Given the foregoing, it's exceptionally difficult to see how the greater openness of the later Rawls to the invocation of religious and metaphysical reasons in the public realm—by citizens and officials—can be extended to political philosophers in modern, constitutional democracies. To be sure, political philosophers, following the Rawlsian procedure, might endeavor to show adherents to some view of the good just how their comprehensive view also supports the tenets of an overlapping consensus and the political conception of justice most appropriate for that society. But political philosophers working in modern, constitutional democracies must make sure the conception of justice they develop in no way depends on particular philosophical or religious views. Consequently, it would seem that political philosophy (like the original position) has *no* room for the claims of faith. It excludes them from playing any foundational role in the practice of political philosophy just as such. Indeed, the kind of political philosophy that invokes metaphysically or religiously grounded claims stands on the side of the dominant tradition. And it is over and against that tradition that Rawls frames his *political* liberalism.

The foregoing impels us to ask why Rawls frames liberal political philosophy in such a way as to debar metaphysical or religious claims from playing any sort of meaningful role in the practice of political philosophy just as such. More aptly, why would Rawls hold that reasons, principles, or ideas distinctive to some comprehensive view or other cannot supply premises in the construction of a public conception of justice? One possible argument that Rawls might proffer (though he doesn't provide any clear and direct argument for his position) derives from what has been called *chastened epistemology*.[30] The argument—call it *Argument I*—might be rendered as follows: It is unreasonable for citizens or officials who subscribe to a particular, comprehensive view (whether religious or philosophical)—call it *V*—to make arguments about constitutional essentials or matters of basic justice (or to cast votes concerning these) on the basis of *V* just because, in modern, constitutional democracies, there obtains an *ineliminable* pluralism of *reasonable* conceptions of the good. On this argument, the unreasonability of invoking *V* flows from the fact of (reasonable) pluralism. Of course, *Argument I*, as it stands, is a non sequitur. We have a minor premise and a conclusion. But the major premise is missing. And it's unclear as to what might fit the bill. Why does an ineliminable and reasonable pluralism of conceptions of the good entail the wrongness of invoking reasons distinctive to *V*?

To make *Argument I* go, Rawls might proffer *Argument II*: In view of an ineliminable and reasonable pluralism of conceptions of the good, no one can impose their views on others just because no one can rightly claim to know their view is true. And invoking reasons from *V* (whatever the contents of *V*) in discussions about constitutional essentials and matters of basic justice is to impose *V* on others. Several problems with *Argument II* present themselves immediately.

First, on what basis can Rawls distinguish reasonable from unreasonable pluralisms (or reasonable from unreasonable views)? Suppose there is such a basis. How can it be that such a basis is not itself part and parcel of some comprehensive view? After all, distinguishing some set of views as reasonable over and against others that are not implicates a particular account of reason and, in all likelihood, a particular epistemic ethic. Isn't it therefore likely that adherents to some views of the good, reasonable from the Rawlsian vantage, would reject the ground for distinguishing reasonable from unreasonable views while others would not? Wouldn't that make use of the ground for distinguishing reasonable from unreasonable pluralisms objectionable from the standpoint of public reason? To state my point more directly: The Rawlsian notion of a *reasonable* pluralism of conceptions of the good trades on a putative consensus about the nature of reason and the appropriate epistemic ethic (perhaps included as part of the conception of reason on which we allegedly concur). But there is no such consensus.[31] The nature of reason (or rationality) and the appropriate epistemic ethic by which we ought to regulate our noetic structure are in dispute. Thus, there is no uncontested ground from which we could distinguish reasonable from unreasonable pluralisms.

Second, inferring that no one knows the truth of their view just because there is (if indeed there is) a plurality of irreducible and conflicting conceptions of the good is a non sequitur. So *Argument II* is insufficient to make *Argument I* work. There is still a missing premise. After all, we can ask this question: Why should a pluralism of conceptions of the good entail that no one can rightly claim to know that their conception is true? One candidate for that missing premise (one that many in the modern academy would advance) is *epistemic skepticism* or *radical epistemic humility*: Given a pluralism of views (whether of the good or of anything else), no one can know the truth of their view—in consequence of which no one can intelligibly *claim* to know the truth of their view. So we can imagine an *Argument III* that adds this premise to *Argument II*. But this position (radical epistemic humility) is self-referentially incoherent. For our skeptic is *claiming to know* that no one knows (or can rightly claim to know) the truth of their view. That is, the skeptic (at least implicitly) is claiming to know the truth of his skepticism. But such a claim entails the rejection of the skeptical claim itself. Consequently, no one can claim, as an article of knowledge, the impossibility of knowing something, whether *V* or anything else. In short, if radical epistemic humility is true then no one can know or intelligibly claim to know that it's true. But in that case, the plurality of conceptions of the good does not entail that no view is true; nor does it entail that we are unable to know the truth of some view. In which case the plurality of conceptions of the good appears *not* to rule out political philosophy as traditionally practiced (the so-called "dominant tradition")—something Rawls clearly means to do.

Third, liberal political philosophy, as conceived by Rawls, refrains (or tries to refrain) from taking any stand as to truth or knowledge. Thus, if liberal political philosophy is to remain neutral on questions of metaphysics *and epistemology* (if it is to embody Rawls's "method of avoidance"), then it must reject *Argument III's epistemological* claim that no one can know the truth of their comprehensive view just because (in view of an ineliminable pluralism of incommensurable conceptions of the good) no view is true. *Radical epistemic humility*, precisely because it is an *epistemic* position, is incompatible with avoidance of taking a stand on metaphysical and epistemological questions.

Nevertheless, I submit that radical epistemic humility or some substantially similar premise is necessary to make *Argument II* valid. Consequently, the self-referential incoherency of *Argument III* suggests rejecting *Argument II*. Moreover, *Argument II's* epistemic claim—that (in view of an ineliminable pluralism of rational comprehensive views) no one can rightly claim to know the truth of their view—also seems incompatible with the metaphysical *and epistemic* neutrality to which Rawls aspires.

Is there any other way to make *Argument I* go? Well, suppose Rawls rejects radical epistemic humility. Suppose instead that he thinks some comprehensive view or other is the correct one—that it's true and maybe even rationally known.[32] Or, instead, suppose that he simply thinks some view or other *might* be true or known. In that case, his claim must be something like this: "Even if some comprehensive doctrine is not only true but also rationally known to me, this does not imply that I can rightly impose it upon others." Why not? Well, perhaps for the reason underlying the liberal principle of legitimacy and the prescription that we use only public reasons or (per the later Rawls) stand ready to justify our positions in terms of public reason—namely, the duties of civility and reciprocity.[33] These, after all, are the *moral* duties upon which Rawls grounds his prescription of public reason (on both the inclusive and wide views). And these duties would seem to provide the ground for the liberal principle of legitimacy as well. But, quite obviously, civility and reciprocity are moral duties that belong to some comprehensive views and not to others. Note what follows: The answer to the question "Why ought I, when discussing constitutional essentials and matters of basic justice in public, use only public reason or stand ready to justify my position in terms of public reason?" derives from particular metaphysical or religious views that insist I have a duty to be civil and to reciprocate. In other words, the ultimate justification for using public reason is grounded in what can only, reasonably, be considered nonpublic reasons. So when it comes to defending the theory of public reason, Rawls more or less has to reject public reason.

It seems to me, however, that the logic of Rawls's position compels him to reject the idea that civility and reciprocity are metaphysically or religiously grounded duties. In that case, so far as I can tell, one route remains open to him. He must insist that civility and reciprocity are not part of some view or other but, rather, are deep norms or conventions of our culture—and so, perhaps, shared by all groups (or at least by all reasonable groups, whatever that might mean). Given its commitment to Kantian constructivism, after all, political liberalism refrains from judging whether civility or reciprocity are real moral norms or objective duties, on the one hand, or merely subjective convictions (though perhaps shared by each person), on the other.[34] Thus, *from the standpoint of political liberalism*, the only thing that can matter is that these norms are *ours*.[35] The ground of public reason, of the liberal principle of legitimacy, and of the political conception of justice would, in that case, be nothing other than convention. But, as I've demonstrated elsewhere, conventionalism is self-referentially incoherent.[36]

The short version of the argument, applied to political liberalism runs as follows: (1) it is logically impossible to distinguish among exercises of will on the basis of will alone; (2) consequently, it is impossible to distinguish obligatory from non-obligatory exercises of will on the basis of will alone; (3) consequently, any intelligible designation of some exercises of will as normative or obligatory for other exercises requires positing some standard external to or transcendent of mere will; (4) the conventions of any given community (however intentional or reflective, on the one hand, or subconscious or latent, on the other) can be construed as instances of communal will; (5) it is therefore impossible to distinguish some instances of the will of the community from others on the basis of nothing other than community will such that a given instance of community will becomes normative for others; (6) but if, per Rawls, the moral duties of civility and reciprocity are, at least for the purposes of political liberalism, nothing other than the conventions of the community, then these "moral duties" cannot obligate other instances of willing. Put another way, if civility and reciprocity are merely conventions, then they are in no sense normative. Thus we have (7): given (3), treating civility and reciprocity as normative for other instances of human willing—for instance, by treating them as duties to which we must conform when publicly discussing constitutional essentials and matters of basic justice or as moral constraints upon a society's choice of its public conception of justice—entails positing a standard external to (indeed, transcendent of) the community's will. Any conventional account of justice or of moral duties more broadly is therefore self-referentially incoherent. But Rawls ultimately seems to ground political liberalism in nothing else. Consequently, Rawlsian political liberalism is self-referentially incoherent.

So I think Rawlsian political liberalism is deeply problematic. It can either treat civility and reciprocity as real moral duties, thereby making political liberalism depend upon metaphysics, or it can treat such duties as conventional, in which case the position collapses into self-referential incoherence (I have only sketched that argument here, but I take it the reader can see how it goes from what's been said). But I have also hinted at another problem. The Rawlsian view seems to depend on an account of reason or rationality. How else can we tell what propositions may be viewed as reasonable by all rational persons or which comprehensive doctrines are compatible with the full rationality of human persons? How else can we distinguish between reasonable and unreasonable pluralisms? But, as Wolterstorff notes, Rawls nowhere supplies the requisite epistemology.[37] As to the nature of reason, he says nothing at all. Moreover, Rawls says political liberalism endeavors to remain neutral not only on metaphysical questions but on epistemic ones as well. Thus, while the coherence of his project seems clearly to require an epistemology, the strictures of his theory seem clearly to prevent him from providing one. Even so, I think it is likely that political liberalism's strictures on the claims of faith both in public debate and in the practice of political philosophy get what plausibility they have from the assumption that religious beliefs are legitimate only insofar as they are validated by reason or evidence (and perhaps from the widespread assumption among academics that they cannot be so validated). But even if this is *not* the case, I submit that political liberalism's insistence that political philosophy remain neutral as to comprehensive doctrines is rendered implausible as a result of the collapse of strong, epistemic foundationalism.

Before proceeding to the collapse of classical, epistemic foundationalism and its implications for the practice of political philosophy, a word of clarification is in order. For Rawls (or Rawlsian political liberalism) is often taken to be anti-foundationalist. How then can the fall of classical or strong foundationalism have negative implications for political philosophy as conceived by political liberalism? I have two replies, both already present in the preceding argument. *First*, Rawls attempts to construct a political conception of justice and an account of public reason that presume the truth of no particular metaphysic. Consequently, Rawlsian political liberalism (if he succeeds) is without *metaphysical* foundations. But we must distinguish metaphysical or ontological foundationalism (and essentialism) from *epistemic* foundationalism. Moreover, we must distinguish strong (or classical) epistemic foundationalism from epistemic foundationalism more generally (both described below), the former being a species or instance of the latter. My argument is that the fall of strong, epistemic foundationalism has dire implications for Rawlsian political philosophy. I am not mounting an argument concerning essentialism or metaphysical foundationalism (which seem perfectly coherent to me). Nor am I entering an argument concerning the coherence of epistemic foundationalism just as such.[38] *Second*, to underscore the point at the end of the previous paragraph, I believe the incoherence of strong, epistemic foundationalism has dire consequences for Rawlsian political liberalism and its attendant method for practicing political philosophy *whether or not* Rawls is aptly described as a strong, epistemic foundationalist or even as an epistemic foundationalist of any sort.[39] For the collapse of classical or strong, epistemic foundationalism has implications as to the sorts of beliefs that are plausibly epistemically basic and so as to the sorts of beliefs that can rightly be invoked in philosophical or political-philosophic argumentation. The collapse of classical or strong, epistemic foundationalism means that (at least some) religious beliefs are plausibly properly basic. But it seems to me that epistemically basic propositions are eligible for use in philosophic (and in political-philosophic) argumentation—indeed, that they are eligible to be the starting points for such arguments.

The Fall of Classical (Epistemic) Foundationalism

I have suggested that the fall of classical, epistemic foundationalism poses a significant problem for attempts to banish religious reasons or claims of faith from the practice of political philosophy.[40] I should note that I take classical foundationalism to be a necessary—though not sufficient—condition for that claim. There have been, after all, classical foundationalists who endorsed the use of religious reasons in the practice of moral and political theorizing, so long as those reasons were also endorsed by reason, construed in the classical foundationalist way (Locke and Leibniz come to mind). But I have been putting off, until now, giving an account of classical, epistemic foundationalism. It is time to present that account and to show how analytic philosophers such as Alvin Plantinga and Nicholas Wolterstorff demonstrated that account of rationality to be hopelessly flawed. The reader should bear in mind that classical foundationalism is what Plantinga and Wolterstorff call an epistemic ethic, which we are to follow in governing our beliefs (at least when it comes to what Locke called matters of maximal concernment—such as morality, politics, and religion). This epistemic ethic assumes something about the noetic structure of knowing and believing, and discussion of this ethic came most to the fore perhaps in discussions about belief in God.

Though we could produce passages from John Locke, Rene Descartes, W. K. Clifford, or Bertrand Russell in order to illustrate classical (epistemic) foundationalism, I think Thomas Jefferson's famous letter of August 10, 1787, to his nephew Peter Carr instantiates the idea quite nicely.[41] In that letter, Jefferson tells Carr that he should "fix reason firmly in her seat, and call to her tribunal every fact, every opinion." And fixing reason firmly in her seat requires, according to Jefferson, following a particular program:

> Question with boldness even the existence of a god; because, if there be one, he *must* more approve of the homage of reason, than that of blindfolded fear. You will naturally examine first the religion of your own country. Read the Bible then, as you would read Livy or Tacitus.

The facts which are within the ordinary course of nature you will believe on the authority of the writer, as you do those of the same kind in Livy & Tacitus. The testimony of the writer weighs in their favor in one scale, and their not being against the laws of nature does not weigh against them. But those facts in the Bible which contradict the laws of nature, must be examined with more care, and under a variety of faces. Here you must recur to the pretensions of the writer to inspiration from god. Examine upon what evidence his pretensions are founded, and whether that evidence is so strong as that its falsehood would be more improbable than a change in the laws of nature in the case he relates. For example in the book of Joshua we are told the sun stood still several hours. Were we to read that fact in Livy or Tacitus we should class it with their showers of blood, speaking of statues, beasts, &c. But it is said that the writer of that book was inspired. Examine therefore candidly what evidence there is of his having been inspired. The pretension is entitled to your inquiry, because millions believe it. On the other hand you are astronomer enough to know how contrary it is to the law of nature that a body revolving on its axis as the earth does, should have stopped, should not by that sudden stoppage have prostrated animals, trees, buildings, and should after a certain time have resumed its revolution, & that with out a second of general prostration. Is this arrest of the earth's motion, or the evidence which affirms it, most within the law of probabilities?

Jefferson goes on to commend this program for analyzing the New Testament accounts of the life of Jesus—warning against two, quite opposite, pretensions:

Keep in your eye the opposite pretensions 1. Of those who say he was begotten by god, born of a virgin, suspended & reversed the laws of nature at will, & ascended bodily into heaven: and 2. Of those who say he was a man of illegitimate birth, of a benevolent heart, enthusiastic in mind, who set out without pretensions to divinity, ended up believing them, & was punished capitally by the Roman law which punished the first commission of that offense by whipping, & the second by exile or death *in furca*.[42]

Jefferson then tells Carr that these questions are examined in books whose titles occur under the heading of "religion" on a list he has enclosed. Included therein are works by Hume and Voltaire.

Now this letter, as I say, is an instantiation of a particular account of rationality. I dare say that it is not the only account of rationality, even as bears on theistic belief. Nor do I take the account proffered by Jefferson (following Locke and perhaps Hume at this point) to be the sober truth of the matter. But before showing why, following Plantinga and Wolterstorff, we ought to reject this account of rationality, I must first say something about the account itself. The sort of rationality to which Jefferson urges Carr is a species of what epistemologists call *evidentialism*. Consider Jefferson's advice to Carr concerning belief in the existence of God. Carr is to question the existence of God because, if God exists, he *must* more approve the homage of reason than of fear. So Jefferson presents Carr with unreflective belief grounded in fear, on the one hand, and rational belief arrived at as a conclusion from rational inquiry, on the other. Jefferson says, to Carr, "Your own reason is the only oracle given you by heaven." It seems quite clear that Jefferson is suggesting something like this proposition: Belief in the existence of God is rational *only if* such belief is a conclusion arrived at as a result of rational inquiry. This rather presupposes that belief in God is rational only to the degree that it is established by rational argumentation. Locke and Descartes both held this position (both also held that theistic belief could be so justified). In one of the most important essays of the last century on rationality and religious beliefs, analytic philosopher Nicholas Wolterstorff characterizes what he and Plantinga refer to as the evidentialist challenge to theistic belief as follows: "It was insisted [by the evidentialist], in the first place, that it would be *wrong* for a person to accept Christianity, or any other form of theism, unless it was *rational* for him to do so. And it was insisted, secondly, that it was not rational for a person to do so unless he holds his religious convictions on the basis of other beliefs of his which give those convictions adequate evidential support. No religion is acceptable unless rational, and no religion is rational unless supported by evidence. That is the evidentialist challenge."[43] That, I submit, is the position of Jefferson. And while it is possible, of course, to be a theist and an evidentialist at the same time (Descartes, Locke, and Leibniz all were), it is also possible (as W. K. Clifford and Bertrand Russell did) to advance religious skepticism under the garb of evidentialism.

To get at the evidentialist objection to belief in the existence of God or religious belief more generally, it is helpful, as Plantinga notes in a similarly important essay, to consider foundationalism.[44] For, as Michael Peterson, William Hasker, Bruce Reichenbach, and David Basinger note, "Modern philosophers who are evidentialists have for the most part been committed to . . . *strong foundationalism*."[45] And to understand strong foundationalism we must first understand foundationalism more generally. Foundationalism, as described by epistemologists such as Plantinga and Wolterstorff, distinguishes between two sorts of beliefs (indeed, between two sorts of rational beliefs). On the one hand, there are beliefs that we hold on the basis of other beliefs. Such beliefs are *derived* beliefs. And, on the other hand, there are beliefs that we hold but that are *not* held on the basis of anything else we believe. Such beliefs are *basic*. The question for the foundationalist is this: What constitutes a *properly basic* belief? That is, when is it that any given person *rightly* or *rationally* holds a belief *not* on the basis of anything else he or she believes? Put another way, when can one be said rationally to hold an *underived* belief? Foundationalists such as Descartes, Locke, and Clifford—theorists from across a wide spectrum—have a strikingly similar answer to this question. These otherwise very different theorists all subscribe to what has come to be called *strong foundationalism*.[46]

Now, foundationalism is not equivalent to strong (or classical) foundationalism (though strong foundationalism is an instance of foundationalism). Moreover, evidentialism is not equivalent with foundationalism, strong or otherwise. One could be an evidentialist without being either a foundationalist or a strong foundationalist.[47] Nevertheless, the correlation between evidentalism and strong foundationalism is sufficiently strong that (as noted by Peterson et al.) "evidentialists have usually . . . been strong foundationalists" and such that "there do not seem to be well-developed examples of the evidentialist position that are *not* instances of strong foundationalism."[48] So, while strong foundationalism and evidentialism are not conceptually identical, no theorist worthy of note seems to have operationalized their evidentialist commitments in any other way. Descartes, Locke, most likely Jefferson, Clifford, and Russell are both evidentialists and strong foundationalists. Indeed, it's plausible that these theorists (and others) simply equate strong foundationalism with evidentialism. But if the only evidentialists of note are strong foundationalists, then this poses a problem for early and late modern evidentialists.[49] For strong foundationalism, as Plantinga and Wolterstorff have demonstrated, is hopelessly, logically flawed.[50]

In order to get at the logical incoherence of strong foundationalism (and here I am following Plantinga's now well-known argument), we must consider the strong foundationalists' criteria as to the sorts of belief to which we can attribute proper basicality.[51] According to the strong foundationalist, only those beliefs that are self-evident (such as $2 + 2 = 4$) or incorrigible (such as I am feeling pain now) are properly basic. Sometimes undeniable propositions, such as the law of noncontradiction, are said to be properly basic as well. This seems to be because undeniable propositions are self-evident. Recall that, for the foundationalist, beliefs are only rationally held if they are properly basic *or* if they are *derived* from beliefs that are properly basic. Consequently, for the strong foundationalist, a person is rational in holding some belief x only if x is self-evident or incorrigible *or* is deduced from a belief that is either self-evident or incorrigible. But just here the problem emerges.

For the requirement that, to be rational, one must believe only that which is self-evident or incorrigible *or* that which derives from self-evident and incorrigible beliefs (or propositions) *and* nothing else—that requirement is neither self-evident nor incorrigible, nor is it deducible from anything that is.[52] Strong foundationalism is therefore self-referentially incoherent. For, as Peterson et al. put it, if strong foundationalism is true and given that strong foundationalism is neither self-evident nor incorrigible nor deducible from anything that is, then *no one* is rational in believing strong foundationlism to be true.[53]

Following arguments originally developed by Plantinga and Wolterstorff, we have seen that strong foundationalism (the only way in which modern theorists like Locke operationalized evidentialism concerning perceptual and religious beliefs) is self-referentially incoherent. The position's self-referential incoherency suggests that we ought to reject it. But if we must reject strong foundationalism, on account of its self-destructiveness, then we must either reject foundationalism (as a correct account of human rationality) altogether or we must embrace what might be called *weak foundationalism*. It seems to be the case that most of us hold some beliefs on the basis of other beliefs that we hold and other beliefs that can only be described as underived. This suggests that most of us are foundationalists to some degree. The incoherence of strong foundationalism does *not* require rejecting foundationalism as such. Nor does it require letting go of the notion of proper basicality. Rather, the incoherence of strong foundationalism means rejecting strong foundationalism's *criteria for proper basicality*. But then a very interesting implication emerges. If we reject strong foundationalism's criteria for proper basicality, then a belief need not be self-evident (or undeniable) or incorrigible in order to be properly basic. Moreover, a properly regulated noetic structure can be such that derived beliefs are held on the basis of underived briefs that are neither self-evident nor undeniable nor incorrigible. That is, there may be many properly basic beliefs that do not meet the criteria of strong foundationalism but that are properly basic nevertheless. Indeed, it is possible that many or even most of the beliefs that we in fact hold, and hold rationally, are such that they are properly basic. In particular, it is at least an a priori possibility that belief in other minds or in one's own existence or in the existence of God are all instances of beliefs that are properly basic. Plantinga has argued rigorously that, if God exists, then belief in his existence is probably properly basic. (Note: I think it's clear that a belief can *both* be properly basic and held as such *and* simultaneously be derived or deduced—that is, we can hold a proposition as properly basic and argue for it at the same time; no logical contradiction is involved.) But in that case, whether or not belief in God, without evidence, is rational depends upon whether God exists. Or, put another way, denials that belief in the existence of God is properly basic seem premised on an a priori rejection of the existence of the divine.

Given the fall of classical foundationalism, it is plausible to argue that at least certain theistic beliefs, such as the existence of God, are warranted even in the absence of foundations. Put another way, certain theistic beliefs are arguably rational even if rational evidence is not adduced for them. Such beliefs are, arguably, properly basic. But then one might rationally move from such beliefs to the implications of such beliefs for moral and political theory. Certain theistic beliefs (including, for instance, the existence of God) may serve as a set of underived beliefs from which other beliefs are derived. But if some theistic beliefs are or may be properly basic, then on what grounds can the exclusion of such beliefs from the practice of political philosophy be justified? I submit that there are no such grounds, *save perhaps* some comprehensive doctrine that includes as its entailment the rejection of such beliefs as the existence of God (or, perchance, the resurrection of the dead)—perhaps secularism, materialism, physicalism, Protagorean antirealism, etc. But then the debarment of theistic belief from the practice of political philosophy requires the view in question to be such that we have greater warrant for believing that view than for believing theism. And as things presently stand, there are no available arguments that establish the greater probability of or greater warrant for such a view vis-à-vis theism. Until such arguments are forthcoming, banishing religious claims from the practice of political philosophy seems premature.

Consider, as an alternative to classical foundationalism, the sort of epistemology developed by Plantinga over a series of seminal works.[54] According to Plantinga's epistemology, any person x can be said to know something y just in that instance where y is a true belief that x holds precisely as a result of the proper functioning of his (or her) cognitive faculties. And x's cognitive faculties are functioning properly if they are functioning in accordance with their design plan and in their proper environment. If Plantinga is right (and no one has demonstrated that he is wrong), then it is possible to have not only rational belief but even knowledge *without* certainty. We may know all sorts of things without knowing that we know them. We may know that y is the case even if we don't know whether our cognitive faculties are functioning properly or functioning in the right environment—all that matters is that they are. Moreover, it's plausible that our cognitive faculties are designed to produce true beliefs in accordance with the testimony of others—so long as that testimony is truthful and *even if* we don't know whether it is. Thus, it is plausible that one knows the claims of faith (or some of them) to be true even without any evidence. Such claims could be properly basic. It is possible that I hear such claims from a trustworthy source, that I believe them, and that they are true. In such a case, if my cognitive faculties were designed to produce true beliefs as a result of testimony from some trustworthy source, it is plausible that I have knowledge of such claims. But given all this, it is plausible that a person of religious faith knows that the claims of her particular faith are true (or at least that certain of those claims are true)—and knows that these claims are true whether or not she can prove (or establish) the truth of such claims by rational demonstration (and whether or not she is certain of them). Suppose the person in question subscribes to the tenets of Christian faith. Then, given the incoherence of strong foundationalism, she might rationally know the truth of Christian faith (or the truth of at least some of the central claims of the faith) without any rational demonstration. Now the tenets of Christian faith rather clearly have implications for moral and political theorizing. One cannot read the New Testament canon in context and reach any other conclusion.[55] But given this, why shouldn't our Christian political theorist take into account the claims of her faith in the practice of political philosophy? Why shouldn't her theorizing be informed by all that she knows?

And now the problem for those who would banish political theology, putative revelation, or religious reasons from the practice of political philosophy should be apparent. For such ones, instead of taking the last question above as rhetorical, must insist upon a negative answer to it. But what ground can be proffered for a negative answer? The only ground I can imagine is that our would-be banisher denies that our religious political theorist *knows* what she claims to know. But what ground is there for such a denial? The reply for many such political theorists is that she cannot know the truth value of claims of revelation. She can believe such claims, but she cannot know them. But if that's the case, then what is the basis for saying that she cannot know the truth of revelatory claims? The only conceivable answer seems to be that what she *claims* to know is neither properly basic nor derivable from anything that is. To be sure, Descartes, Locke, and Leibniz thought that what she claims to know *is* derivable from things that are properly basic. But for the sake of argument, let's suppose that Clifford and Russell are right and these others are wrong. For the sake of argument, let's suppose that our theorist's claim cannot be demonstrated from that which is properly basic. The question then becomes whether our theorist's claim to know certain things from revelation can be considered properly basic. Our would-be banisher must insist that it cannot be. But if the revelatory claims that our political theorist claims to know are not properly basic, then it can only be either because what she claims to know fails to meet the criteria for proper basicality or because the revelatory claims in question are not true. And the only criteria for proper basicality that prevent special revelation or religious claims from being properly basic are the criteria for strong foundationalism—or perhaps somewhat different criteria for strong foundationalism (whatever those might be, given that no one has proposed other criteria) that look so much like it as to be subject to the same criticism that the new position is also self-referentially incoherent. But given the self-referential incoherence of strong foundationalism, then our would-be banisher has failed to show that our religious theorist stands on irrational ground. Given the incoherence of strong foundationalism, the rationality of debarring religious reasons from the practice of political philosophy seems to turn entirely on the truth of the beliefs in question. If certain religious beliefs are true, then banning their invocation in the practice of political philosophy arguably makes no sense. But in that case, it only makes sense to proscribe moral and political theorizing derived from any given religious perspective if we are warranted in taking that perspective to be false. And there are, at present, no knock-down arguments showing that theism in general or Christianity in particular are incoherent or simply false.

CONCLUSION

The upshot of the foregoing seems rather clearly to be that the Christian political philosopher qua political philosopher is well within her epistemic rights to invoke claims distinctive to her faith in the practice of political philosophy—indeed, to invoke such claims as starting points for arguments in political philosophy. Thus, for instance, the Christian political philosopher might reject the lodestar of Hobbesian political theory—the preeminence of the fear of death—on account of the Christian doctrine of the resurrection of the dead. Or, the Christian political theorist might reject versions of consent theory that make consent both necessary and sufficient for authority just as such, and so for the authority of the state, in view of the Christian proclamation that Jesus of Nazareth is King of kings and Lord of lords (i.e., that he is king over all kings and lord over all lords). This would not entail the rejection of consent as necessary for the authority of some persons over others. Rather, the Christian political philosopher qua political philosopher might maintain that consent is necessary for the exercise of authority by some merely human persons over other merely human persons on account of the equality of such persons. And the Christian political philosopher might hold that human persons are equal in terms of ontological value and on account of being made and in the image of God and on account of being loved by him. My point is that arguments of this sort, given the collapse of classical epistemic foundationalism ought to be considered instances of political philosophy that take the claims of faith as starting points and proceed from there. I am not suggesting that this is the only way to do political philosophy but only that this is a legitimate way to do it. Those who disagree, rather than asserting their disagreement, must demonstrate that this is not a legitimate way to proceed. At present no such demonstration exists.

NOTES

Note: I am grateful for very helpful comments on earlier drafts of this essay from Justin Dyer, Carson Holloway, Micah Watson, and Nick Wolterstorff.

1. Which is to say, insofar as they (i.e., religious reasons) were underwritten by nonreligious reasons deemed more fundamental (or basic) in the order of knowing.

2. Not, as Garry Wills wrongly surmises, with the 2004 reelection of George W. Bush to

the presidency but long before that. See Garry Wills, "The Day the Enlightenment Went Out," *New York Times,* November 4, 2004. The Enlightenment (a dubious label in view of the fact that there were many "enlightenments," not all of them reconcilable with each other) went out long before Wills's op ed.

3. F. R. Ankersmit, "The Dilemma of Contemporary Anglo-Saxon Philosophy of History," in "Knowing and Telling History: The Anglo-Saxon Debate," *History and Theory* Beiheft 25 (1986): 1–27; Carl Becker, "What Are Historical Facts?" in *The Philosophy of History in Our Time,* ed. H. Meyerhoff (Garden City, NY: Doubleday, 1959), esp. 130–31. For a depiction and critique of the new historicism (or historical relativism), see William Lane Craig, *Reasonable Faith,* 3rd ed. (Wheaton, IL: Crossway Books, 2008), 215–40.

4. Richard Ashcraft, "Political Theory and the Problem of Ideology," *Journal of Politics* 42, no. 3 (August 1980): 687–88, 688, 690.

5. Quentin Skinner, "Meaning and Understanding in the History of Ideas," *History and Theory* 8, no. 1 (1969): 52–53 (emphasis added).

6. I once heard a well-regarded historian claim that there are no timeless truths or eternal verities and that historical inquiry of any sort should have nothing to do with the search for such truths. He went on to express his fervent hope that this was the unifying thread of the social sciences—the denial of such truths and so the rejection of any search for them. He seemed blissfully unaware of the self-contradictory nature of his claim.

7. As to the empirical failure of cultural relativism, see Paul R. DeHart, "The Dangerous Life: Natural Justice and the Rightful Subversion of the State," *Polity* 38, no. 3 (July 2006): 369–93; C. S. Lewis, "The Poison of Subjectivism," in *Christian Reflections,* ed. Walter Hooper (Grand Rapids, MI: Eerdmans, 1994); John M. Cooper, "The Relations between Religion and Morality in Primitive Culture," *Primitive Man* 4, no. 3 (July 1931): 33–48.

8. See Craig, *Reasonable Faith,* 221.

9. Leo Strauss, "What Is Political Philosophy?" in *What Is Political Philosophy? And Other Essays* (Chicago: University of Chicago Press, 1988), 12. As to Strauss's claim that we can never attain knowledge of "political fundamentals," we are compelled to ask how he knows that. His very claim seems to undermine itself. Is the claim therefore *not* a matter of knowledge but rather merely an opinion? But the claim itself is a claim to *know* that we cannot attain such knowledge in practice rather than a claim about what Strauss *believes* to be the case—namely, that he believes we cannot attain such knowledge in practice.

10. Ibid., 13.

11. See Leo Strauss, "Reason and Revelation," which is published as an appendix in Heinrich Meier, *Leo Strauss and the Theologico-Political Problem* (Cambridge: Cambridge University Press, 2006).

12. Given that classical (epistemic) foundationalism is most prominent in certain modern theorists, such as Locke, my claim that Straussian political philosophy presupposes classical foundationalism in epistemology may seem odd. But the oddness should dissipate in light of two considerations. First, while prominent modern theorists such as Descartes, Locke, Leibniz, and

Hobbes are aptly described as classical (epistemic) foundationalists, classical foundationalism is not a uniquely modern view. Other Western theorists, ancient and medieval (Plato, for instance) have also been described as classical, epistemic foundationalists. Second, in "Philosophy and Revelation" (also in Meier), Strauss equates Spinoza with philosophy (see Meier, p. 178). Spinoza, for Strauss, is philosophy as such. And Spinoza is as much a classical, epistemic foundationalist as one could hope to find.

13. Strauss, "What Is Political Philosophy?" 11.

14. John Rawls, "Justice as Fairness: Political not Metaphysical," *Philosophy and Public Affairs* 14 (1985): 223–51; "The Idea of an Overlapping Consensus," *Oxford Journal of Legal Studies* 7 (1987): 1–25; *Political Liberalism* (New York: Columbia University Press, 1993).

15. These works, as I see it, have been subjected to decisive criticism. See Jean Hampton, "Should Political Philosophy Be Done without Metaphysics?" *Ethics* 99 (July 1989): 791–814; Nicholas Wolterstorff, "The Role of Religion in Decision and Discussion of Political Issues," in Robert Audi and Nicholas Wolterstorff, *Religion in the Public Square: The Place of Religious Convictions in Political Debate* (Lanham: Rowman and Littlefield, 1997); Nicholas Wolterstorff, *Understanding Liberal Democracy: Essays in Political Philosophy*, ed. Terence Cuneo (Oxford: Oxford University Press, 2012), chapters 1–4; Justin Buckley Dyer, "Public Reason and the Wrong of Slavery," in *Natural Law and the Anti-Slavery Constitutional Tradition* (Cambridge: Cambridge University Press, 2012), chapter 6. For a similarly devastating critique of Rawls's earlier work, see T. K. Seung, *Intuition and Construction: The Foundation of Normative Theory* (New Haven: Yale University Press, 1993), chapters 1–3; Michael Sandel, *Liberalism and the Limits of Justice*, 2nd ed. (Cambridge: Cambridge University Press, 1998).

16. John Rawls, *Political Liberalism*, with a new introduction and the "Reply to Habermas" (New York: Columbia University Press, 1996), 224–25; all quotations and citations are to this edition and will be given parenthetically in the text.

17. Rawls, "Overlapping Consensus," 10–12.

18. Jean Hampton believes that Rawls is wrong about this. And I'm inclined to concur. The modus vivendi is stable, given that the pluralism in question is, per Rawls's assertion, ineliminable. Rawls says it's unstable because the social consensus will collapse *when one group gets the upper hand*. But, as Hampton notes, pluralism's ineliminability means that *no group will get the upper hand*. See Hampton, "Should Political Philosophy be Done without Metaphysics?" 805–6.

19. Wolterstorff notes, rightly I think, that Rawls here more or less endorses the notion of a *consensus populi*, though without using that terminology. See "The Role of Religion," 91–92.

20. In the "Introduction to the Paperback Edition," Rawls puts it this way: "[The idea of public reason] is that citizens are to conduct their public political discussions of constitutional essentials and matters of basic justice within the framework of what each sincerely regards as a reasonable political conception of justice, a conception that expresses political values that others as free and equal also might reasonably be expected reasonably to endorse" (1).

21. Sandel, *Liberalism*, 213–14.

22. On this, see ibid., 214.

23. See the "Introduction to the Paperback Edition" of *Political Liberalism*, li–lii. See also

John Rawls, "The Idea of Public Reason Revisited," *University of Chicago Law Review* 64, no. 3 (Summer 1997): 765–807 (esp. 783–87); and see the *Commonweal* interview with John Rawls (1998), republished as chapter 27 of *John Rawls: Collected Papers*, ed. Samuel Freeman (Cambridge: Harvard University Press, 1999).

24. Rawls, "Overlapping Consensus," 1.

25. Ibid., 8.

26. Rawls, "Justice as Fairness," 223 (emphasis added).

27. Ibid., 230–31.

28. Hampton, "Should Political Philosophy be Done without Metaphysics?" 798–99.

29. Ibid., 799.

30. Wolterstorff, "The Role of Religion," 91.

31. Thus Alasdair MacIntyre's *Whose Justice? Which Rationality?* (Notre Dame, IN: University of Notre Dame Press, 1988).

32. See for instance, John Rawls, "On My Religion," in *A Brief Inquiry into the Meaning of Sin and Faith*, ed. Thomas Nagel, with commentaries by Joshua Cohen and Thomas Nagel, and by Robert Merrihew Adams (Cambridge: Harvard University Press, 2009). "On My Religion" advances or depends upon the truth of what Rawls calls a comprehensive doctrine or view. Moreover, I suspect Rawls never rejected the comprehensive Kantian liberalism he elaborates in *A Theory of Justice*.

33. *Political Liberalism*, 217, 248, 253; see also the Preface to the Paperback Edition, xliv, xlvi, l–li, liv.

34. See Rawls, "Justice as Fairness," where he says, "Kantian constructivism" avoids "the problem of truth and the controversy between realism and subjectivism about the status of moral and political values. This form of constructivism neither asserts nor denies these doctrines" (231).

35. "We look, then, to our political culture itself, including its main institutions and the historical traditions of their interpretation, as the shared fund of implicitly recognized basic ideas and principles. The hope is that these ideas and principles can be formulated clearly enough to be combined into a conception of political justice congenial to our most firmly held convictions. We express this by saying that a political conception of justice, to be acceptable, must be in accordance with our considered convictions" (ibid., 228).

36. Paul R. DeHart, "Covenantal Realism: The Self-Referential Incoherency of Conventional Social Contract Theory and the Necessity of Consent," *Perspectives on Political Science* 41, no. 3 (July 2012): 165–77.

37. Wolterstorff, "The Role of Religion," 98.

38. In fact, the conclusion I will advance—that political-philosophic arguments can begin with the claims of faith and reason to conclusions premised, at least in part, upon such claims—presupposes the validity of some account of epistemic foundationalism (even as it is premised on the rejection of the classical, epistemic foundationalism of Locke and others).

39. Though there is a sense in which even the wide view of the later Rawls parallels the classical, epistemic foundationalism of Locke and others described below. On Rawls's wide view of public reason, in order to be eligible for use in debate about constitutional essentials or matters

of basic justice, a proposition or belief must either be a public reason or be defensible in terms of public reason. Of course, the doctrine of public reason is controversial and so lacks the sort of consensus necessary for it to meet the liberal criterion of legitimacy. Thus, I submit, the doctrine of public reason is self-defeating: the justification for the requirement of public reason (that positions advanced in public debate be advanced in terms of public reason or at least be defensible in terms of public reason), given that this requirement is controversial, can only be made in terms the reasonableness of which is rejected by some; thus, to defend the doctrine of public reason, one must step outside its bounds.

40. Herein *classical foundationalism* refers only to epistemic foundationalism. Nothing in what follows should be construed as an argument against ontological foundationalism.

41. The term *classical* may be misleading. *Classical*, here, does not refer to theorists in the classical *moral* and *metaphysical* tradition. In epistemology, *classical* does not denominate theorists such as Plato, Aristotle, Cicero, Augustine, or Aquinas. Rather, it refers primarily to modern theorists of knowledge and their followers. Plantinga places Locke at the fountainhead of classical (epistemic) foundationalism; see Alvin Plantinga, *Warranted Christian Belief* (Oxford: Oxford University Press, 2000), 88.

42. *Thomas Jefferson: Writings* (New York: The Library of America, 1984), 900–906.

43. Nicholas Wolterstorff, "Can Belief in God Be Rational If It Has No Foundations?" in *Faith and Rationality: Reason and Belief in God*, ed. Alvin Plantinga and Nicholas Wolterstorff (Notre Dame, IN: University of Notre Dame Press, 1983), 136.

44. Alvin Plantinga, "Reason and Belief in God," in ibid., 48.

45. Michael Peterson, William Hasker, Bruce Reichenbach, and David Basinger, *Reason and Religious Belief* (Oxford: Oxford University Press, 1991), 119 (original emphasis). The ensuing discussion of classical foundationalism and its self-referential incoherence follows closely the summary of the arguments of Plantinga and Wolterstorff in ibid., 119–21. See also Plantinga, "Reason and Belief in God"; Wolterstorff, "Can Belief in God Be Rational If It Has No Foundations?"

46. Plantinga, "Reason and Belief in God," 48; Peterson et al., *Reason and Religious Belief*, 119–21.

47. See Plantinga, "Reason and Belief in God," 62–63. I don't think the reverse is true. That is, I don't think one could plausibly be a foundationalist with regard to religious or perceptual beliefs without also being an evidentialist. Perhaps being an epistemic foundationalist is one way of being an evidentialist, just as being a strong foundationalist is one way of being a foundationalist.

48. Peterson et al., *Reason and Religious Belief*, 121.

49. Though I think my conclusion holds even if we discover instances of evidentialism that are not also instances of strong foundationalism.

50. Perhaps the problem posed for evidentialism by the collapse of strong foundationalism is even more pronounced. For it is on the basis of this collapse that Plantinga and Wolterstorff posit the possibility that belief in the existence of God and perhaps other beliefs of the religious variety are properly basic. But if such beliefs are properly basic, then it is quite obviously wrong to insist on evidentialism with respect to such beliefs.

51. Plantinga, "Reason and Belief in God," 55–59.

52. Or no one has demonstrated the strong foundationalist criteria, which, given strong foundationalism, is necessary for affirming the position.

53. Peterson et al., *Reason and Religious Belief*, 121.

54. In addition to "Reason and Belief in God," see Alvin Plantinga, *Warrant the Current Debate* (Oxford: Oxford University Press, 1993), *Warrant and Proper Function* (Oxford: Oxford University Press, 1993), and *Warranted Christian Belief* (Oxford: Oxford University Press, 2000).

55. See, for instance, Oliver O'Donovan, *The Desire of Nations: Rediscovering the Roots of Political Theology* (Cambridge: Cambridge University Press, 1993); N. T. Wright, *Paul in Fresh Perspective* (Minneapolis: Fortress Press, 2005), chapter 4; N. T. Wright, *How God Became King* (New York: HarperOne, 2011). Nicholas Wolterstorff, *The Mighty and the Almighty* (Cambridge: Cambridge University Press, 2012) is also of relevance.

EROS AND AGAPE REVISITED

RECONCILING CLASSICAL EUDAEMONISM WITH CHRISTIAN LOVE?

Robert C. Koons

Anders Nygren (1890–1978), the professor of theology and bishop of Lund, Sweden, was the author of one of the most influential books in twentieth-century theology: *Agape and Eros*, published in 1930–38 in Swedish and eventually in English and seven other languages.[1] Nygren's work contains a trenchant statement of the fundamental incompatibility of the classical eudaemonism of Socrates, Plato, and Aristotle (the object of Eros) with the new Christian ethic of selfless and "unmotivated" Agape. According to Nygren, the Eros of the Greek philosophers is primarily selfish (the pursuit of some good for oneself) and dependent on the prior value of its object (one loves the good because it is good). In contrast, Christian Agape is selfless (one loves another for the sake of the good of the other) and utterly unmotivated by any worthiness of its object (God loves the sinner despite the sinner's absolute unworthiness).[2] For the Christian, the unconditional love of God and of the neighbor is fundamental and independent of any love of self, while for the erotic philosophical tradition, any love for one's friend is grounded in one's love for oneself.

Unsuprisingly, Nygren sees these stark contrasts as forming absolute barriers to any harmonization of the two traditions. In particular, Nygren asserts emphatically that Thomas Aquinas's synthesis of the two was "doomed to failure."[3]

These questions carry grave political implications. If Nygren's absolute dualism were correct it would, by separating Christian political theology from political philosophy, undermine any possibility of a rationally graspable natural law as the foundation for civic life. Nygrenian theology would entail the nonexistence of any rational common ground or via media between believers (motivated by God's Agape) and nonbelievers (still in the grip of Eros).

Nygren's challenge can also be approached from a second angle: interpreting it as a challenge to the coherency and adequacy of the eudaemonistic theory of friendship and politics in the works of Plato and Aristotle. The eudaemonists insist both (1) that it is possible to love one's friend for his own sake and not merely as a means to one's own fulfillment, and (2) that it is rational to sacrifice oneself for the good of one's community, through courageous action in war, for example.[4] However, these actions seem possible only on the alternative theory of selfless, Agape love. How can an egoist, however rational and high-minded, avoid treating the good of his friends as merely instrumental to his own happiness? And how can such an egoist justify the sacrifice of his own life, together with all possible future happiness, for the sake of others, however many and however dear? If these challenges to classical eudaemonism are sound, then it cannot provide a rational basis for the effective social bonds needed for civic life.

THE THOMISTIC SYNTHESIS AND ITS APPARENT DIFFICULTIES

Although, as Nygren pointed out, Augustine attempted a synthesis of Platonic Eros and Christian Agape, the most careful and systematic harmonization of the two traditions is to be found in the work of Thomas Aquinas. It is by examining the Thomistic synthesis that we can best judge whether any such attempt is "doomed to failure," as Nygren put it. Here are eight relevant Thomistic theses, drawn from David M. Gallagher's "Thomas Aquinas on Self-Love as the Basis for Love of Others":[5]

(1) Each complete substance has only one ultimate end, and two distinct substances must have numerically distinct ultimate ends (ST I-II 1.5).[6]

(2) Each complete substance aims at or seeks its own perfection (the full realization of its natural potentialities) as its sole and unique ultimate end (ST I 60.3, ST I-II 1.6, 7).

(3) The ultimate end of any human being is the beatific vision—that is, the enjoyment of the beatific vision by that very human being (ST I-II 3.8).

(4) Self-love is the foundation and principle of all other loves, including one's love for God (ST II-II 25.4c, SCG 3.153, In III Sent. 29.3 ad 3; Aristotle's *Nicomachean Ethics* book 9, 1166a1–2).

(5) The *ordo amoris* (order of charity) requires that one love one's self more than one's friends, and one's friends and families more than the strangers making up the rest of the polis (ST II-II 25.4c, ST II-II 26.4–12).

(6) One loves one's friend for his own sake, and not merely as a means to one's own fulfillment. This is true especially of our love for God (ST II-II 26.3, In III Sent. 29.3). "But St. Thomas's theory provides for an extension of the self to include the others, such that a person can be willing his own good in willing that good for the other and willing it precisely as being in the other."[7]

(7) The whole is prior to and therefore superior in importance to its parts; consequently, the member of the community rationally loves the community more than himself, and the creature rationally loves God more than himself (ST II-II 47.10ad2, ST I 60.5).

(8) The perfected saint loves God above all else and loves himself only for the sake of God (ST II-II 19.10a). "According to Thomas, as one grows in charity, one adverts less and less to these things [one's own individual good], being more and more consumed by the goodness of God."[8]

There are at least six ways of drawing out what appear to be contradictions from these eight theses:

(i) There is tension between thesis 7 and thesis 5: the priority of the whole versus the *ordo amoris*. If the whole were always superior to its parts, then one's love for the many who make up the city would take priority over one's love for one's immediate family. However, if there were a strict priority corresponding to the *ordo amoris*, then it would follow that one's love for a single family member ought to outweigh one's love for any number of strangers, even if those strangers make up the majority of one's community.

(ii) Can thesis 7 be justified even to the point of complete self-sacrifice, given the priority of self-love, as expressed in theses 2 and 4? Thomas Aquinas, along with Aristotle, presumes that it is always rational for a member of the community to sacrifice himself for the whole, even apart from any hope for the individual's survival of death. However, such sacrifice cuts off all possibility of future happiness. Even if the shamefulness of cowardice significantly reduces one's prospects for flourishing, it cannot reduce those prospects to zero, much less to a level somehow below zero. It may be rational in some cases to sacrifice the prospects for a long but ignoble life for a short but glorious one, but this would depend on many factors in each particular case, including one's life expectancy and the likelihood that one's cowardice might be forgotten or forgiven. This would not seem to justify a universal preference for the good of the whole community over one's individual survival, as required by Thomas's theory.

The apostle Paul provides a vivid version of this tension. Paul was willing to be "accursed and cut off from Christ for the sake of his kinsmen according to the flesh, that they might be saved" (Romans 9:3). Paul was willing to exchange the realization of his own ultimate end for the salvation of others. How could such an exchange have been rationally choosable for Paul, given that his unique ultimate end was his own salvation?

(iii) Don't friends become instrumentalized, given theses 2–4, in outright contradiction to thesis 6? If my own perfection is my sole ultimate end, then mustn't I somehow treat the good of my friends as merely a means to my own happiness?

(iv) Given the connection between ontological diversity and the diversity of ends from principle thesis 1, don't theses 6–8 threaten the ontological distinctness of human persons? If we share a numerically identical ultimate end (the common good of friends or of the polis or the greater glory of God), don't we become merely dependent parts of a single substance?

(v) If we resolve the apparent conflict between theses 2–4 and theses 6–8, by supposing that each human being has more than one ultimate end, doesn't this fragment the individual human being into distinct substances, given thesis 1?

(vi) How can one's love for self be the basis of one's love for God (thesis 4) and yet how can one love oneself only for the sake of God (thesis 8)?

METAPHYSICAL CONSTRAINTS ON THE SOLUTION

The simplest path to resolving the conflicts would be simply to abandon thesis 1: the one-to-one correspondence between ultimate ends and complete substances. In the absence of thesis 1, we could weaken thesis 2, asserting only that the perfection of one's nature is *one* of one's ultimate ends. This immediately resolves tensions (ii) through (iv). The remaining tensions, (i) and (vi), could then be resolved by simply giving priority either to the community as a whole or to the *ordo amoris* and by denying that one's love for oneself is the basis for other loves.

This simple resolution comes at too high a metaphysical cost, however. The Aristotelian tradition provides compelling grounds for maintaining thesis 1, with its perfect correspondence between complete substances and their ends. Thesis 1 consists of two sub-claims: (1a) that every complete substance has a single ultimate end and (1b) that numerically distinct complete substances have numerically distinct ultimate ends.

The combination of the two sub-claims means that we can count complete substances simply by counting the ultimate ends being pursued. Each ultimate end corresponds to a distinct, complete substance, and no substance has more than one end. Why believe in such a correspondence? There are three reasons.

The first is epistemological. The correspondence thesis 1 provides us with criteria for distinguishing cases in which several things constitute a single complete substance from cases in which they constitute more than one. If thesis 1 were false, we would have no way of distinguishing mere parts from complete wholes, or real unities from mere "heaps."

The second is theological. Unified substantial being is (as Aristotle argued in *The Metaphysics*) the paradigm case of "being."[9] All creatures exist by participating in the being of God. God's being is absolutely simple. The only way for a composite, material substance to participate in God's simplicity is by having a single ultimate end. Therefore, every substance must have (by its very essence) a single ultimate end. Since creaturely being consists in having a single end, two creatures can be distinct from one another only by having distinct ends.

The third is metaphysical. This argument depends on the assumption that reality is ultimately intelligible: that an adequate reason can be given for each fact. In order for reality to be ultimately intelligible, it must be partitioned into a number of minimal units of complete intelligibility (MUCIs). Every finite thing must be either a MUCI or part of exactly one MUCI, since anything outside of all MUCIs would be ultimately unintelligible, and anything simultaneously belonging to more than one would have a nature that is overdetermined in an inexplicable way.[10] We can then identify substances with MUCIs. No substance can be a part of another substance, since either the first would be unintelligible in itself or the second would not be a *minimal* unit of complete intelligibility.

No substance can have two or more metaphysically ultimate ends, since such a binary substance could provide no explanation in and of itself for the conjunction of the two ends. No two substances could share numerically the same ultimate end, since neither substance would be able to supply the grounds for its own distinctness from the other.

As Aquinas puts it, the final cause is the cause (or explanation) of all the other causes.[11] Every process (including the persisting existence of a substance) is intelligible only in terms of its ultimate terminus: each process either is a moving toward some definite end or is a stable self-sustaining activity, in which case the activity is its own end. In either case, the ultimate end of a substance's existence provides the grounds for understanding why it has the internal constitution it has and for discerning the boundaries (both spatial and temporal) that distinguish it from all other substances.

THE PATH TO RESOLUTION: TWO CRUCIAL DISTINCTIONS

The fundamental problem to resolve is this: on ontological grounds, we must posit a single ultimate end for each human being (his own perfection), but on ethical grounds, we must posit a plurality of ultimate ends, including the glory of God and the good of one's friends and neighbors. An "ultimate" end is one than which no other end is strictly "more final." To resolve the contradictions, we must distinguish between two ways in which an end is "more final" than another: (a) those cases in which the first end is chosen *for the sake of* another, and (b) those cases in which the first end is choiceworthy *in virtue of* another. Let's call the first relation that of "practically rational" or simply "rational" priority, and the second "metaphysical" priority.

The idea of metaphysical priority or ontological grounding has been the subject of intensified interest among metaphysicians in recent years: see Kit Fine (2001), Jonathan Schaffer (2009), and Gideon Rosen (2010), for example.[12] One fact p is ontologically grounded in another, more metaphysically fundamental fact q if p is true by virtue of the truth of q, if the fact that p is constituted by the fact that q. For example, the lateral movement of an ocean wave is ontologically grounded in the successive up and down movements of various volumes of water near the surface. The existence of a crowd is ontologically grounded in the presence of various individuals in the same place. The fragility of a vase is ontologically grounded in its molecular structure. The incurring of a debt is ontologically grounded in the intentional signing of a loan agreement. These grounding relations are all noncausal in nature. Similarly, the value or *choiceworthiness* of some end for some agent can be ontologically grounded in the value of some other, more fundamental end for that same agent.

By way of illustration of this distinction, consider the case of a nonrational animal. A nonrational animal engages in an "estimative" process that is an analogue of practical rationality. Consider the following "desire-perception" syllogism:

1. E is good (because desired sensually).
2. Doing A now would (or might well) result in E (given by immediate perception).

Therefore, do A now.

The notion of "result" employed in premise 2 is not supposed to be understood as necessarily causal in nature. It could be that doing A would simply constitute the realization of E. For example, an animal might desire to engage in an act of sexual congress with a potential mate. A particular act of congress would not cause but would by itself be the thing desired.

There is also a corresponding "aversion-perception" syllogism:

1. E is bad (because feared).
2. Doing A now would or might result in the avoidance of E (given by immediate perception).

Therefore, do A now.

These are analogous to the practical syllogism of rational animals:

1. E is good. (A rational judgment of value.)
2. Doing A now would result in E. (A rational judgment of ground and consequence.)

Therefore, do A now.

We might take the practical syllogism in this form to be composed of two more fundamental inferences:

1. E is good.
2. Doing A now would (might) result in E.
3. Therefore, A is good to do (now). (From 1, 2)
4. Therefore, do A now. (From 3)

That which moves both nonrational animals and us into action is the perception or judgment that some action is now good to do. This can come about through judging that the action would *cause* some good effect (and that it has no disqualifying defect), or that it would more directly *constitute* some good state of affairs.

The connection between sensual or nonrational desire and the nonrational animal's *ontologically ultimate end* is a complex one. It is not the case that each animal sensitively desires its own fulfillment *as such*. Instead, its desires (like the "particular affections" described by Bishop Joseph Butler in his Sermon XI) have specific and narrow objects, such as food, water, warmth, and sexual congress.[13] What we can expect is this: the animal's desires and aversions, taken as a whole and given the animal's perceptual capacities, lead with some reliability to the fulfillment of the animal's nature. The desires and aversions must at least tend collectively in the right direction and do so better than any other configuration of affections would.

In a similar way, we should expect a human being's rational judgments about what it is good for him to do in each situation to work together collectively in guiding the person toward his own individual fulfillment (eudaemonia). Each action judged to be good must be judged to be good either as an end in itself or as a means to some further end (or both). Simplifying somewhat, we can assume that there will be a reliable connection between the realization of the *rationally ultimate natural ends* of a human being (that is, those ends that figure in an ultimate way in the practical syllogisms a human being is naturally disposed to employ) and that human being's attaining of *eudaemonia*. As in the case of the desires of nonrational animals, however, we cannot assume that the sole rationally ultimate natural end (in this sense) of a human being must be that human being's eudaemonia *as such*.

Of course, there is a critical difference between rational and nonrational animals: the rational animal can (and the nonrational animal cannot) understand itself, including its nature and that nature's perfection. Reflecting on these facts can enable a human person to evaluate his conception of his ultimate ends, to see if that conception is properly calibrated to the successful fulfillment of his nature. This reflection on human nature is to be found in Plato's *Republic*, Aristotle's *Nicomachean Ethics*, Boethius's *The Consolation of Philosophy*, and the "Treatise on Happiness" in Thomas's *Summa Theologica* (I-II, Questions 1–48).[14] Such philosophical reflection can reveal the erroneousness of certain conceptions of happiness, including happiness as wealth, power, pleasure, or honor, and it can point to the correct conception of happiness, ultimately in terms of the beatific vision.

Such philosophical reflection does provide human persons with a kind of Archimedean point or God's-eye perspective, from which they can evaluate the appropriateness of their conception of their own ultimate natural ends. This reflection does not require that all ultimate natural ends be consolidated into a single end (that of one's own happiness), however. The right conception of happiness can play a regulative role over one's deliberative practices, but it doesn't play this role by supplanting all ultimate ends with itself. If I can see that my current understanding of what it is good for me to do would not in fact tend toward my own eudaemonia, then I have a compelling reason for believing that my current understanding is in error. However, it does not follow that the way to correct this error is to suppose that every action can be good only by being a means to my own happiness.

We must distinguish carefully between a regulative use of metaphysical insight about eudaemonia and the having of a second-order desire for desires that promote eudaemonia. I can, from a metaphysical point of view, evaluate the appropriateness of my first-order desires and intentions in relation to the perfection of my nature (my eudaemonia). However, this is not the same thing as desiring to have those desires *for the sake of* my happiness. I might desire to have appropriate desires as the means to achieving the greater glory of God or the betterment of my community: my own happiness need not figure as my rationally ultimate end, even when I am deciding which of my desires to promote or suppress.

As I mentioned earlier, we must carefully distinguish between the two ways in which one end can be "ultimate": rationally ultimate (ultimate in terms of practical rationality) and metaphysically ultimate. Scientific and philosophical reflection on human nature reveals that I (and all other human beings) have only one natural end that is metaphysically ultimate: the perfection of my own nature by the beatific vision. However, this reflection does not indicate that I have only one rationally ultimate end. That is, it does not indicate that I ought to alter my deliberational practices in order to engage in only those practical syllogisms in which my own perfection figures as the ultimate end. In fact, a fully accurate understanding of human nature reveals quite the opposite: that my nature can be fulfilled only by means of habits of deliberation that include other ultimate ends: especially the good of God, of my community, and of my neighbor (as modified by the *ordo amoris*).

What, then, does it mean to claim that I have only one metaphysically ultimate end? It does not mean that all other ends are chosen *for the sake of* my own perfection, in the sense that they are perceived to be good by virtue of causing my own perfection as their effect. What it does mean is this: the good of my neighbor is a good for me *by virtue of* the fact that pursuing it as a rationally ultimate end fulfills and perfects my nature and does so constitutively or intrinsically, not causally. It is not that I realize that pursuing my neighbor's good is a reliable way of producing (as a separate effect) the condition of my perfection. If this were the connection, then I should pursue my neighbor's good only for the sake of my own—only when the corresponding practical syllogism is available for employment. Instead, what I should understand is this: my pursuing of my neighbor's good as such is partly constitutive of the perfection of my nature as a rational creature. It is precisely by being an altruist of a certain kind that my own happiness is realized. Hence, reflection on the self-centeredness of my sole metaphysically ultimate end does not in any way undermine the altruism of many of my rationally ultimate ends; in fact, far from undermining this altruism, the metaphysical insight reinforces it.

Thus, a human end can be final in either of two senses: those natural ends that are final in the order of practical reason, and that one end that is final in the order of nature. Some ends are final in the order of practical reason but not in the order of nature. The good of God, the good of one's community, and the good of one's neighbor fall into this category. The good of one's community, for example, is a natural end in virtue of one's eudaemonia but not for the sake of it.

In order to secure the unique metaphysical priority of that end that is final in the order of nature, there must be a nomological, reliable correlation between *realizing* the end that is final in the order of nature and *pursuing* those ends that are final in the order of practical reasoning.

There are two sorts of realization-pursuit correlation of this kind: success-dependent (indirect) and success-independent (direct). In the case of success-dependent correlation, we have a nearly perfect correlation between the pursuit of an end final in the order of practical reasoning and the successful attainment of that end, and also a nearly perfect correlation between the successful attainment of the end and the greater realization of one's own perfection or happiness. In addition, the correlation between the pursuit of the end final in the order of practical reasoning and one's own happiness is grounded in this pair of nearly perfect correlations. That is, the correlation between pursuit of the end and one's happiness depends on the correlation between success in that pursuit and one's happiness.

In the case of success-independent correlation, the correlation between the *pursuit* of the end final in the order of practical reasoning and the realization of one's own happiness is more direct: there is a direct, nearly perfect correlation between *pursuing* the end final in the order of practical reasoning alone and one's own happiness, and either only an imperfect correlation between pursuit of the end and success, or between success in pursuing that end and one's own happiness. It must be the case, however, that there are still positive if imperfect correlations between pursuit and success, and between success and happiness.

For example, a case of success-dependent or indirect correlation to happiness would be the pursuit of friendship or marriage. One's own happiness is seriously impaired by the absence of friendship, and success in developing friendship is nearly perfectly correlated with some increase in one's own happiness.

A case of success-independent or direct correlation to happiness is the pursuit of excellence in one's profession or craft. Not everyone is capable of actually achieving such excellence, so the correlation is imperfect. However, the mere pursuit of excellence is an important component of one's individual happiness. Pursuing excellence in one's craft contributes greatly to one's happiness even when one doesn't succeed. Of course, there is *some* positive correlation between *attaining* excellence and attaining one's own happiness and the happiness of others: otherwise, it couldn't be rational to pursue professional excellence in the first place.

Since human beings are rational animals, every natural end that is final in the order of practical reasoning must be in itself good in some way or to someone. A rational being could not pursue an end not understood as good in some way. However, the realization of an end final in the order of practical reasoning need not be sought *as good for oneself*, as contributing to one's own natural perfection or eudaemonia. It is enough for the realization of the end to be good for someone or in itself, so long as one's having and *pursuing* the end for its own sake contributes *in fact* to one's own happiness.

CONCLUSION: RESOLVING THE SIX TENSIONS

A. Tension (vi), the conflicting priorities of loving God and loving oneself:

Love for oneself is *metaphysically* prior to one's love for God: it is because one's love for God perfects one's own nature that loving God is good. However, love for God is fundamental *in the order of practical reasoning*. For the perfected saint, one's own happiness is only instrumentally good in the order of practical reasoning: to be sought only as a means to God's greater glory. Nonetheless, it remains true that the good for me of seeking God's greater glory is grounded in my nature: it is good insofar as it perfects my nature to love God for his own sake.

B. Tensions (iv) and (v), the threats to the unity and diversity of human beings:

The disparate ends final in the order of practical reasoning are *naturally* unified with the single end final in the order of nature. If it were metaphysically possible to engage in the exchange that St. Paul said he would be willing to make, then Agape and Eros would divide St. Paul into two substances, but the exchange is impossible.

Similarly, there is a metaphysical, in-principle correlation between the common good and the eudaemonia of each citizen. There is, however, a pattern of metaphysical dependencies that singles out the eudaemonia of each citizen as that citizen's unique metaphysically final end. The common good is good for each citizen in virtue of the fact that the pursuit of the common good perfects that citizen's nature, and not vice versa: the fact that the perfection of the citizen's nature (eudaemonia) is good for the citizen is *not* grounded in the fact that the citizen's eudaemonia contributes to the common good.

C. Tension (iii), the instrumentalization of friendship:

True friendship involves, as Aristotle recognized, valuing the happiness of the friend for its own sake and not merely as a means to one's own end.[15] It is true that one's own happiness serves as a kind of regulative ideal: the life of friendship, in order to be affirmable in rational reflection, must reliably maximize one's own eudaemonia. However, this does not mean that the good of one's friends ceases to be an ultimate end in the order of practical reasoning. To the contrary: a rational reflection on the value of friendship reinforces the importance of seeking the good of the friend for his own sake.

D. Tension (ii), the possibility of radical self-sacrifice:

The virtuous man loves his own country for its own sake and is certainly willing to sacrifice his own life and future happiness for its welfare, even in the absence of any hope for life after death. Loving one's country in this way is directly connected (in a success-independent way) with one's own happiness or eudaemonia. Most patriots of this sort live long and happy lives: it is only the exceptional patriot who is actually called upon to give up his life. Moreover, as Aristotle argued, most patriots who sacrifice their lives in this way do increase their happiness (or at least, avoid a catastrophic decrease), since they gain the opportunity to perform extremely noble acts and avoid the shame of cowardice. Thus, it is only in the exception of the exception that love for one's own country results in any loss of individual happiness. Therefore, such love is nearly perfectly correlated with an increase in individual happiness, and any rational reflection on the fitness of such love to the needs of human nature must end in validating it. Since the patriot loves the good of his country for its own sake and not merely as a means to his own happiness, his act of self-sacrifice is perfectly rational.

In the case of the apostle Paul's extraordinary willingness to sacrifice his own eternal good for others in Romans 9, it is of critical importance that the exchange Paul considers is a metaphysical impossibility. There is absolutely nothing that Paul or anyone else could do that would simultaneously increase the prospects of salvation for others while decreasing it for himself. Paul's willingness was a mere wish or velleity, not a potential intention. Such extreme love for one's neighbors' good for its own sake is perfectly correlated with one's own continuation in a state of grace. If it really were possible to sacrifice one's eternal good in this way for the sake of others, such a disposition would have to be counted as a vice and not a virtue, since it would increase the probability that one's nature be destroyed. However, the de facto impossibility of such a sacrifice makes all the difference.

E. Tension (i), the conflict between the priority of the polis and the *ordo amoris*:

As we have seen, the virtuous human being is moved by a plurality of distinct loves, each corresponding to some end final in the order of practical reasoning. Human nature demands that these loves be themselves ordered, with love of God given first priority, followed by love of self, of spouse and children, family and friends, compatriots, and other unrelated human beings. This *ordo amoris* corresponds to an allocation of time and resources among a number of inner homunculi of practical reason, collaborating harmoniously in a regime of internal justice.

Insofar as I am motivated by a love of my polis, I must treat the good of myself or my family as outweighed by the greater good of the whole. However, this love of the polis is only one of many coexisting spheres of love in the well-ordered soul. Rational reflection on the needs of human nature provides grounds for regulating the priorities of the different loves without depriving them of their respective spheres of sovereignty. When called upon to act in one's capacity as a public servant, one must act without favoritism or bias, but in one's role as spouse, parent, or friend one rightly puts the needs of one's loved ones above those of others.

F. Added bonus, resolving the tension between perfect and imperfect happiness: There's one more tension within the Thomistic synthesis that I haven't mentioned yet, which is that between the ends of perfect or eternal happiness (beatitude) and imperfect or earthly happiness (felicity). Both are clearly treated as rational ends of action (ends final in the order of practical reasoning), but only beatitude is the *metaphysically* final cause of human nature. Once again, the coexistence of multiple final ends in the order of practical reason is perfectly consistent with the existence of a uniquely final end for human beings in the order of nature. Rational reflection reveals that my pursuit of my metaphysically ultimate end is *enhanced* and not obstructed by my genuinely loving other goods, including my own felicity and that of my neighbors, for their own sake. Consequently, it is possible for the Christian to be a fully committed and loyal participant in institutions, like the state, that have only felicity as their intrinsic end. Christians must recognize an order here, giving absolute priority of the church within its appointed sphere, without depriving the state of its own rights and dignity.

NOTES

1. Anders Nygren, *Agape and Eros*, trans. Philip S. Watson (1938; Philadelphia: Westminster Press, 1953).

2. Ibid., 75–99.

3. Ibid., 645.

4. Aristotle, *Nicomachean Ethics*, trans. J. A. K. Thomson, with revisions by Hugh Tredennick, introduction by Jonathan Barnes (London: Penguin, 2004). For (1), see ibid., books 8–9 (1155b32); for (2), see book 1 (1094b8–10) and especially book 9 (1169a20).

5. Daniel M. Gallagher, "Thomas Aquinas on Self-Love as the Basis for Love of Others," *Acta Philosophica* 8 (1999): 23–44.

6. References to the *Summa Theologiae* are from the *Summa of St. Thomas Aquinas*, trans. Fathers of the English Dominican Province (New York: Benziger Bros., 1947–1948).

7. Gallagher, "Thomas Aquinas on Self-Love," 35.

8. Ibid., 43.

9. See Aristotle's *Metaphysics* in *The Complete Works of Aristotle: The Revised Oxford Translation*, vol. 2, ed. Jonathan Barnes (Princeton, NJ: Princeton University Press, 1984).

10. Of course, no creature is completely intelligible apart from God. We must take "complete intelligibility" of a finite substance to mean that it is, together with God and apart from any other creature, fully intelligible.

11. St. Thomas Aquinas, *De Principii Naturae*, ed. John J. Paulson (Fribourg: Société Philosophique, 1950), 29.22

12. Kit Fine, "The Question of Realism," *Philosophers' Imprint* 1, no. 2 (June 2001): 1–30; Jonathan Schaffer, "On What Grounds What," in *Metametaphysics: New Essays on the Foundations of Ontology*, ed. David Manley, David J. Chalmers, and Ryan Wasserman (Oxford: Oxford University Press, 2009), 347–83; Gideon Rosen, "Metaphysical Dependence: Grounding and Reduction," in *Modality: Metaphysics, Logic, and Epistemology*, ed. Bob Hale and Aviv Hoffman (New York: Oxford University Press, 2010), 109–36.

13. Joseph Butler, *Five Sermons, preached at the Rolls Chapel and A dissertation upon the nature of virtue*, ed. Stephen L. Darwall (1736; Indianapolis, IN: Hackett, 1983).

14. Plato, *Republic*, 3rd ed., trans. C. D. C. Reeves (Indianapolis, IN: Hackett, 2004); Boethius, *The Consolation of Philosophy*, trans. Joel Relihan (Indanapolis, IN: Hackett, 2001).

15. *Nicomachean Ethics*, book 8, chapters 4 and 7, and book 9, chapter 4.

PART II

FAITH AND THE FOUNDATIONS OF POLITICAL ORDER

THE STRANGE SECOND LIFE OF CONFESSIONAL STATES

J. Budziszewski

I

Liberal political thinkers who wish to push faith out of the public square conjure up the frightening apparition of a confessional state. In reality, a certain sort of confessional state is just what Liberal political theory proposes and has very nearly achieved: A Liberal confessional state, which, being Liberal, must describe itself as something else. Officially, Liberalism is "neutral" about things like religion, not only among different religions but even between having and not having a religion. As the majority held in *McCreary County v. ACLU*, a Ten Commandments case:

> Given the variety of interpretative problems, the principle of neutrality
> has provided a good sense of direction: the government may not favor
> one religion over another, or religion over irreligion, religious choice
> being the prerogative of individuals under the Free Exercise Clause.[1]

I have argued the inauthenticity of "neutrality" at length in other places, so here I present only the gist, before trying to press further.[2] A religion is a system of life and thought based on commitments taken to be supreme and unconditional. We may loosely speak of a religion's supreme and unconditional commitment as its god, with a lower case "g." One need not be a theological relativist to recognize that

different religions propose different such commitments, and that they follow different gods. The god of Christianity and Judaism, for example, is the Creator: The First
Being, God with a capital "G." By contrast, Theravada Buddhism, which is also a religion, denies the reality of all supernatural beings. A Theravada Buddhist's supreme
and unconditional commitment, in this sense his god, is escape from suffering. Now
if the distinguishing mark of religion is a supreme and unconditional commitment,
and the supreme and unconditional commitment need not be a supernatural being,
then it follows that so-called secular creeds too are religions. To say that Theravada
Buddhism with its flight from suffering is a religion, but that Utilitarianism with
its pursuit of aggregate pleasure is not a religion, is arbitrary. Rather we should say
that Utilitarianism is one of those religions that do not call themselves religions and
get away with it. True, when people speak of religions, they often mean only particular sorts of religions, and there may be a great many helpful distinctions among
systems of life and belief—theistic versus nontheistic, fideistic versus non-fideistic,
particularistic versus non-particularistic, organized versus unorganized versus dis-
organized, and so on. Taking the terms generally, though, "religions versus nonreli-
gions" is not one of these helpful distinctions; it clouds the issues.[3]

Concerning the question "What might actually deserve supreme and unconditional commitment?" there is no such thing as neutrality. I do not mean that everyone has a complete and conscious answer but only that everyone lives as though
certain answers might be true and as though others are surely not. As Aristotle
pointed out, every human action is performed for the sake of a particular good, and
at the apex of aspiration is a good taken to be worthwhile for its own sake rather
than just for the sake of something else.[4] Whenever anyone, whether a private individual or a legislator, makes a choice to do X, for the sake of P, rather than Y, for the
sake of Q, he is at least partly specifying what he thinks important. He is eliminat-
ing certain candidates for commitment from consideration and allowing others to
remain in the race.

One may anticipate protests. "You are assuming that everyone is consistent," someone says. "Don't some people choose inconsistently?" But no one is completely inconsistent; there is always a drift toward pursuing some things in preference to others.

Another objector responds, "So you say, but what if someone deliberately sets
out to be inconsistent?" Well, someone might. But wouldn't that too be a commitment? Anyone who undertook such a resolution would have a reason for doing so.
He might say, for example, "I refuse to be chained to any god. If the price of my
freedom from supreme and unconditional commitments is utter inconsistency, I
gladly pay it." This would merely demonstrate that his supreme commitment was to
freedom, conceived in this perverse way.

Yet another objector protests, in a Kantian spirit, "We should never choose acts
as mere means to other goods such as happiness; acts are moral only if they are right

in themselves." But to choose as Kant recommends is not to choose apart from a supreme commitment; it is only to identify the supreme commitment as moral duty.

Someone might even protest, "But what if my supreme and unconditional commitment *is* to neutrality?" Such a commitment is no commitment at all, because choice, by its nature, is never neutral. One may as well swear loyalty to square circles. A so-called commitment to neutrality is always a cloak for some other commitment that refuses to let itself be seen.

Since genuine neutrality is impossible, the way neutralist doctrine actually functions in law and policy is inevitably to generate a bias. It gives the advantage to religions that do not call themselves religions, at the expense of religions that do. To put it another way, it discriminates against transparency. My second-grade public-school teacher, who probably read the Bible, led us at lunch in giving thanks for our food. My fifth-grade public-school teacher, who probably read Jeremy Bentham, taught us in civics class to believe in the Greatest Happiness of the Greatest Number, which to me at that age, God forgive me, sounded plausible. These two pieties, biblical and Benthamite, were equally reflective of supreme commitments; they merely reflected different ones, and each one excluded the other. To mention but a single point of difference, Benthamite morality denies that there is such a thing as an intrinsically evil act, holding that the end justifies the means, but biblical morality insists that there is such a thing as an intrinsically evil act, proclaiming that we must not do evil so that good will result.[5] Yet what do neutralists say? That the second-grade teacher's piety is "religious" and has no place in the classroom, while the fifth-grade teacher's piety is "nonreligious" or "secular" and may stay.

This bias is enshrined in judge-made law. According to the U.S. Supreme Court, to survive judicial scrutiny a governmental action must satisfy a three-pronged test: (1) It must have a "secular" legislative purpose. (2) It must not have the principal or primary effect of either advancing or inhibiting "religion." (3) It must not foster an excessive government entanglement with "religion."[6] Yet because the Court denies that so-called secular systems of life and belief are religions, the way the three-pronged test actually plays out is like this: (1) A statute may not be motivated by concerns originating in the Jewish or Christian systems of life and belief, but it may be motivated by concerns arising in, say, the "Queer Nation" system of life and belief. (2) It must not have the principal or primary effect of advancing things that Jews or Christians believe, but it may have the principal and primary effect of advancing things that, say, Marxists believe. (3) It must not foster an excessive involvement with the institutions of Church or Synagogue, but it may foster any degree of involvement whatsoever with the institutions of, say, Planned Parenthood.

Some of the results of neutralism are almost comical. The first so-called Humanist Manifesto (in 1933) insisted that secular humanism is a religion; the second (in 1973) was silent on the point; the third (in 2000) not only denied that secular humanism is a religion but slammed people who said that it was.[7] For the rules of state patronage have changed. Once upon a time, a religion that wanted to hold the levers of power had to call itself religious. Now it must say it is not. I would agree with secular humanists that, strictly speaking, secular humanism is not "a" religion, but I would do so only because it is a coalition of religions, of various anti-theistic creeds.

Then what do I suppose? That laws and policies be *free* from bias? That would be logically impossible. Rules are necessarily biased; bias is in the nature of a rule. The rules of baseball are biased toward skill, because skillful competition is what baseball is about; the rules of education toward knowledge, because the extension of knowledge is what education is about. Rules can and should be fair, but the notion that fairness means lack of bias is merely neutralism in different words. But surely *laws* should be unbiased, shouldn't they? Certainly not. They should be biased toward the common good, along with its corollaries, justice and the greatest possible protection of conscience. Lady Justice is blindfolded not because she has no criterion but because she is blind toward all other criteria; she uses her scales, not her eyes.

Could we admit that the common good, justice, and protection of conscience are biases, but deny that they are *religious* biases? If only this were true, but it is not. Some religions accept the trifecta, others reject it. In certain religions, like Santerra and Voodoo, the supreme concern is to gain individual power; they would not accept it. The fact that many world religions propose loftier moralities is a tribute to the power of natural law, but of course some religions deny natural law. Insofar as natural law appeals to human reason, it is common ground, but this does not make it neutral ground, for some people refuse to stand on it. One can, after all, reject universal reason, as fundamentalists and postmodernists do. There is such a thing as motivated irrationality.

What about the Liberal creeds? Do they accept the trifecta? Even today they still say they do, yet today the agreement is nominal, for they have refashioned all the words. "Justice" has been redefined in terms of achieving desired ends by any means; "common good" in terms that deny the reality of intrinsic evils; "protection of conscience" in terms of allowing people to do what they desire, rather than in terms of not forcing them to do what they think wrong. The greatest redefinition concerns truth, now commonly viewed as a "social construction," for whatever one can get away with enforcing counts as true.

If we admit that rules cannot be neutral, then aren't we authorizing the tyranny of some religion, or coalition of religions, over others? We are certainly conceding the inevitability of religious influence, even of unequal religious influence, on public policy. Shall we protest this inequality? Why? What sane person would suppose that Satanism or Thuggee should have the same influence as Christianity or Judaism? But whether the influence of a religion will be irenic or tyrannical depends on the nature of that religion—on just what supreme and unconditional commitment it proposes, and how it understands it. Take the early Christian writers, who gave *Christian* reasons for respecting *non*-Christian conscience. "God does not want unwilling worship, nor does He require a forced repentance," says Hilary; "human salvation is procured not by force but by persuasion and gentleness," says Isidore; "no one is detained by us against his will," says Lactantius, "for he is unserviceable to God who is destitute of faith and devotedness . . . Nothing is so much a matter of free-will as [the virtue of true] religion, in which, if the mind of the worshipper is disinclined to it, [the virtue of true] religion is at once taken away, and ceases to exist."[8] According to Hilary, Isidore, and Lactantius, the foundation for toleration lies not in an impossible suspension of judgment about the good and the true but precisely in following the good and the true. God really does desire only willing worship. Faith really cannot be coerced. True religion really is destroyed by compulsion. According to the document *Dignitatis Humanae*, considered authoritative doctrine by the Catholic Church, just to the extent that some generations of Christians have departed from such principles, they have violated the spirit of their faith.[9]

In Islam, the matter stands differently. In his venerable commentary to al-Misri's classic work of Shafi'i jurisprudence, *Reliance of the Traveller*,[10] 'Umar Barakat writes that "*Jihad* means to war against non-Muslims, and is etymologically derived from the word *mujahada*, signifying warfare to establish the religion." To be sure, he adds, "As for the greater jihad, it is spiritual warfare against the lower self (*nafs*), which is why the Prophet (Allah bless him and give him peace) said as he was returning from jihad, 'We have returned from the lesser jihad to the greater jihad.'" On the other hand, according to 'Umar Barakat the scriptural basis for jihad lies in verses like "Fighting is prescribed for you" and "Slay them wherever you find them,"[11] as well as haditha[12] such as the following: "I have been commanded to fight people until they testify that there is no god but Allah and that Muhammad is the Messenger of Allah, and perform the prayer, and pay zakat. If they say it, they have saved their blood and possessions from me, except for the rights of Islam over them. And their final reckoning is with Allah."[13] Plainly, Islamic scriptures like the latter refer not to war against the lower self but to war to compel religious belief. If they supply the very basis for jihad, as 'Umar Barakat asserts, then it would appear that the "lesser" jihad is the *central* meaning of jihad even if it is in some sense lesser—and that it cannot be set aside.

What about that puissant religious alliance, that mighty coalition of systems of life and belief, that travels under the common name of Liberalism? In the name of not being biased, its bias is becoming more and more belligerent and its resort to coercion more frequent. Religious adoption agencies are under pressure to place children with homosexual couples; religious hospitals, to perform abortions; religious medical students, to be trained in them; religious doctors and nurses, to participate in them; religious pharmacists, to dispense the lethal drugs; religious charities, to include abortifacient drugs, sterilization, and artificial contraception in their employee "health" plans. If such assaults on conscience go much further, it may become difficult for traditional Catholics, Protestants, and Jews to share in public life at all. Could this be the idea?

Like John Calvin's Geneva, the Liberal state is a confessional state. It only pretends that it isn't. This pretense is the basis of its power.

II

We are not used to speaking of Liberal states in such terms, not only because of the neutralist pretense but also because expressions such as "confessional state" were coined in the days before camouflage. The term, however, fits. Consider the late John Rawls, who has proposed what is called "public reason" as a binding norm for all public discussion.[14] One would expect such a term to mean freedom to reason in public; actually it means limits on the reasoning allowed there. In the state that Rawls desires, no one would be permitted to make arguments that depend on a "comprehensive" theory, or at any rate, no one would be permitted to base policies on them. A "comprehensive" theory turns out to mean any considered view of reality that admits the impossibility of neutrality and therefore tries to supply more adequate reasons for doing things than Liberalism can supply. Prohibited from offering more adequate reasons, the citizens of the Liberal state would be limited to incomplete and inadequate reasons. But this is a dodge, for they would be allowed to base their policy proposals on any views of reality that they might wish—so long as these views were not recognized *by Liberalism* as views of reality. In other words, citizens would be allowed to appeal only to those views that Liberalism—by virtue of refusing to admit that they were views—deemed acceptable.

But a state can be "confessional" in more than one sense. Just now we have been using the term "confessional" for a state that seeks to circumscribe public reasoning within the limits of the official coalition of religions, Liberalism. Rather than allowing citizens to reason for their views of reality as both true and consequential for policy, it limits the views of reality from which they may draw such consequences. Insofar as it regulates confessions, this is plainly one kind of confessional state, but let us consider others.

Classification might begin with the observation that, like the decisions of every life, the constitution and laws of every state are based on certain fundamental commitments. At the moment we are not considering what a given state's commitments happen to be (whether they are high, like the well-being of the commons, or low, like the well-being of the high), but what it does about them. We might call a state that acknowledges and solemnizes its fundamental commitments a *declaratory* confessional state. Because it makes laws, and because laws direct behavior, a state that is *merely* declaratory certainly coerces citizens to act in certain ways, but it does not coerce them to believe in the commitments on which this coercion is based. Such a state's confession may be more or less ecumenical; it may include only general beliefs shared by a number of religions, or it may privilege the beliefs of a particular religion.

A *coercive* confessional state is a different sort of fish. It does coerce the citizens to believe in a certain way—or at least to act as though they did. For example, it might punish belief in nonapproved religions, or prohibit proselytizing for them. If this state in question is Liberal, it will probably be somewhat more subtle (at first). As we saw earlier, for example, the U.S. Supreme Court declares that laws motivated by religious purposes are invalid,[15] but it does not consider secularist ideologies as religious.[16] Imagine, then, two different mandatory public-school sex-education programs. One teaches children that they are more than mere animals and can therefore control their impulses by reason. The other teaches them that they *are* mere animals, *cannot* resist their impulses, and must therefore seek outlets in "safe" sex, meaning non-procreative sex. If challenged, the former policy would almost certainly be deemed religious and disallowed, but the latter would almost certainly be deemed nonreligious and allowed. Or imagine two mandatory public-school ethics programs. One teaches students that there are universally valid moral laws, discoverable by reason, quite apart from revelation. The other teaches the students "values clarification," the premise of which is that there is no such thing as a universally valid moral law—that any "value" is as good as any other so long as a person is clear about what it is. Such is the influence of the Supreme Court that a program of the former kind would be much less likely to be developed in the first place, just because of the near certainty of successful legal challenge.

This is a good time to remember another point about coercion: That willingness to coerce people to accept one's beliefs is not a measure of how fervently one believes, but of *what* one believes. A religion fervently convinced, with Hilary of Poitiers, that God does not want unwilling worship, cannot coerce belief, at least not without betraying its commitments. A religion fervently convinced, with the late Osama bin Laden, that Allah urges death to all infidels, certainly will. A religion fervently convinced, with John Rawls, of an absolute right to impose its will, which is "political, not metaphysical," will act more and more like bin Laden.

Now it is tempting to think of the different kinds of states as forming some kind of ladder, beginning with non-confessional states and ending with states that not only have confessions but enforce them. For several reasons, I think this picture is misleading. For the fact that a state does not solemnly avow its convictional foundations does not mean that it has none; in this sense, although there is such a thing as an *officially* non-confessional state, there is no such thing as a non-confessional state.

Moreover, even if the state does not declare its convictional basis, it may still enforce it. For example, it may require citizens to change or violate their consciences on pain of exclusion from degree programs, the professions, charitable activities, and other spheres of public life. Such, in fact, is the Liberal state, for under the auspices of neutralism, it insists that it has nothing to profess; more and more, what it does not profess in words it professes in acts of force. Perhaps, then, rather than a ladder, what we have is a two-by-two table (see table 4.1).

TABLE 4.1

Type I confessional regimes: The convictional basis of the state is neither declared nor coerced.	**Type II confessional regimes:** The convictional basis of the state is declared but not coerced.
Type III confessional regimes: The convictional basis of the state is not declared but coerced.	**Type IV confessional regimes:** The convictional basis of the state is both declared and coerced.

Not even a Type I regime, if there could be such a thing, would be religiously neutral. To say that the state should neither declare nor enforce its convictions is to imply that those religions that want it to do so are—at least to this extent—simply wrong. That is not a suspension of judgment; it is a judgment. Besides, just as there would have to be reasons for declaring or enforcing the convictional basis of the state, so there would have to be reasons for not doing so, and although some systems of life and belief would find these reasons acceptable, others surely would not. Of course we need not suppose that all who were committed to the Type I arrangement would have the *same* reasons for it. But even if they had differing reasons, they would have to concur that the reasons for another kind of arrangement were mistaken or had insufficient weight—and no doubt they would "confess" or declare to each other their shared conviction that such was the case. So even though the state does not officially acknowledge and solemnize the confessions that drive it, the culture of governing will.

England under Henry VIII and China under Mao Zedong were Type IV confessional regimes. The fundamental convictions underlying state policy were explicitly acknowledged and solemnly avowed—in the former case, the Protestantism of the Church of England, in the latter case, the eschatology of the Communist Man forming under the Dictatorship of the Proletariat. Moreover, these confessions were enforced. Both in England and in China, those who followed different systems of life and belief suffered persecution, even if they did not upset public order in any way other than by following different systems of life and belief. I certainly do not say that the two regimes were equally rigorous. Henry's was no picnic but Mao's was infinitely harsher.

Though claiming to seek a non-confessional state, Liberalism seeks a Type III confessional state. Under its influence, the state increasingly attempts to coerce the consciences of those who follow non-Liberal systems of life and belief, even while pretending to be neutral. To be sure, such a state is not transparently or coherently confessional, in the sense of solemnly avowing its true commitments. Yet it is not without solemn avowals. It is an opaque and incoherent confessional state, solemnly avowing that its discriminatory acts are required by its determination not to discriminate.

At the time of its founding, the American republic was a Type II confessional state, for although it frankly declared its commitments, it declined to compel belief in them. The convictional basis of the state is most clearly expressed not in our founding legal document, the Constitution, but in our founding political document, the Declaration of Independence. Not only did it identify commitments to natural law and natural rights, but it went on to identify their source, for it said that "the laws of Nature" were the laws of "Nature's God." This confession was fairly ecumenical. Though most of the Founders were Protestants, the Declaration did not go so far as to identify Nature's God with God as Protestants understood Him. It went only so far as to privilege systems of life and belief that shared a view of God that was creational, monotheistic, moral in a Decalogical sense, and providential, with a high view of the inviolable worth of every human being.[17]

Of course the Founders knew that not all systems of life and belief impute these four qualities to the First Being, or believe in the First Being, or for that matter, take such a high view of man. Hinduism is not creational. Animism is not monotheistic. Voodoo is not moral in the Decalogical sense. Buddhism is not providential. Few systems of thought and belief have consistently acknowledged the inviolable worth of every human being. However, the Founders, having a higher view of the possibilities of human reason than fideists or Rawlsians, considered the truth of these principles to be accessible to all men of goodwill, even apart from the biblical revelation from which they drew them. Concerning what Rawls calls "reasonable pluralism," they would have made a distinction. It may be reasonable *to expect* some people to reject the laws of Nature and Nature's God. But it is not reasonable *to reject them.*

Let us coin an expression, "Classically Theist religions," or "CT religions," for all systems of life and belief, whether biblical or not, that are creational, monotheistic, moral, providential, and impressed by inviolable human worth. Within the bounds of public order, the Founders seem to have intended that both CT and non-CT religions would enjoy free exercise. Obviously this principle has not always been followed consistently—but what would consistently following it require? No one would be forced to believe; no one would be forced to do what the certain judgment of his conscience forbade; and within the bounds of public order, no one would be prevented from doing what his conscience demanded. There might arise cases in which CT and non-CT religions disagreed about which acts lay "within the bounds of public order" and which acts fell outside it. No doubt, in such a case, the Founders would have hoped that the views of CT religions would prevail, but even so, the non-CT religions would be free to press their case, not only privately but even in a legislative context. Precisely this liberty to press their case would be denied to *all* religions under Liberal strictures such as "public reason"—*unless* they happened to be among the lucky ones that Liberal theory does not call religions. The CT policy is "Suffer a hundred flowers to bloom." The Liberal policy is "Nothing that blooms shall be suffered."

For the foreseeable future, the chief danger to religious liberty arises not from our avowed religions but from the unavowed and illiberal religions of Liberalism itself. To defend against this danger, four intellectual goals must be achieved, quite apart from whatever political actions must be taken. Perhaps enough has already been said to explode the fallacy of neutralist toleration, which is goal 1; to explain the classical theory of toleration, which is goal 2; and to expose the real nature of the Type III confessional state, which is goal 3. Certainly not enough has been said to explore the nature and limits of the Type II confessional state, which is goal 4.[18]

III

I commented earlier that a regime's confession may be more or less ecumenical, less or more particular. This raises a question: just how ecumenical, or in the other direction, how particular, may such a confession be? One extreme—a *completely ecumenical* confession—is impossible. One cannot be open to everything, whether assassination cults, pederastic cults, what have you. Belief in the possibility of an absolutely ecumenical confession is just neutralism again. Even if one were to refuse to avow any convictional basis for the regime, it would have a convictional basis. Some systems of life and thought would mesh with it, others would not. To govern is to make distinctions. On the other hand, it is certainly possible to associate a nation with a confession that is *somewhat* ecumenical and *somewhat* particular. As we have seen, the Declaration of Independence associated the nation with Classically Theist religions in general, or at least dissociated itself from non-CT religions. Finally, a confession can be *completely particular*. The Founders might have gone further than they did; they might have associated the nation not with CT religions in general, not with Judeo-Christian heritage in general, not with Christianity in general, not even with Protestantism in general, but with, say, Lutheranism.

But let us ask our question not about confessional regimes in general, but about Type II confessional regimes, in which the confession is declared but not coerced— "declared" in the sense that the regime openly admits its convictional basis, "not coerced" in the sense that no one is forced to do or believe what his conscience forbids. Of course, there will be other forms of coercion. Those who drive recklessly, for example, will still be punished, and such a punishment certainly reflects a belief that reckless driving is wrong. But there is a difference between coercively preventing people from doing things they like to do and coercively requiring them to change their beliefs or to do things they consider wrong. The latter is a violation of conscience; the former is not.

From the fact that confessions in general may be more or less ecumenical, more or less particular, it does not follow that the same is true of Type II regimes. With the exception of the most well-indoctrinated Liberals, Americans in general do not mind that the convictional basis of their nation's Founding was Classically Theist. On the other hand, the idea that it might have been more particular makes them nervous. Why? I think because they suspect that if the state becomes associated with a particular religion, it will inevitably become coercive—that beyond a certain threshold of particularism, a Type II state turns into a Type III state.

Is this suspicion true? If it is, the reasons for it might be either purely logical (P entails Q), or psychological (people who are P are likely to do Q). Let us first consider whether there is any logical reason for such fear. Does associating the political community with a single religion entail that belief in it be enforced?

The answer is, "It depends": If the religion in question *requires* civic enforcement of belief, yes; if it *allows* civic enforcement of belief, probably; but if it *forbids* civic enforcement of belief, no. This is the same thing we saw much earlier when we were considering toleration as a virtue; the only difference is that now we are considering it as a policy. To illustrate, consider Ireland and Iran.

Article 44, Section 1, of the 1937 Constitution of the Republic of Ireland begins, "The State acknowledges that the homage of public worship is due to Almighty God. It shall hold His Name in reverence, and shall respect and honor religion." So far, it resembles the American founding documents, but then it goes on to say, "The State recognizes the special position of the Holy Catholic Apostolic and Roman Church as the guardian of the Faith professed by the great majority of the citizens." This confessional language, removed by amendment in 1973, is completely particular; Americans would fear that such language would lead to religious oppression. Yet the rest of the section expresses friendly respect to the other empirically extant CT religions, saying that "the State also recognizes the Church of Ireland, the Presbyterian Church in Ireland, the Methodist Church in Ireland, the Religious Society of Friends in Ireland, as well as the Jewish Congregations and the other religious denominations existing in Ireland at the date of the coming into operation of this Constitution." By itself this language may not be important—if these extant religions are not guides to faith, what does it mean to "recognize" them? But the language does not stand by itself, for the next section specifies in detail the protections guaranteed to believers of other religions:

1. Freedom of conscience and the free profession and practice of religion are, subject to public order and morality, guaranteed to every citizen.

2. The State guarantees not to endow any religion.

3. The State shall not impose any disabilities or make any discrimination on the ground of religious profession, belief or status.

4. Legislation providing State aid for schools shall not discriminate between schools under the management of different religious denominations, nor be such as to affect prejudicially the right of any child to attend a school receiving public money without attending religious instruction at that school.

5. Every religious denomination shall have the right to manage its own affairs, own, acquire and administer property, movable and immovable, and maintain institutions for religious or charitable purposes.

6. The property of any religious denomination or any educational institution shall not be diverted save for necessary works of public utility and on payment of compensation.[19>]

So even though a single religion was singled out as the guardian of faith, the state did not lose its Type II character: A Catholic convictional basis for the state was declared but not coerced. If one bears in mind the teaching of the Catholic Church, this was only to be expected, for as the Second Vatican Council clarified (albeit some three decades later), "the right to religious freedom has its foundation not in the subjective disposition of the person, but in his very nature. In consequence, the right to this immunity continues to exist even in those who do not live up to their obligation of seeking the truth and adhering to it and the exercise of this right is not to be impeded, provided that just public order be observed."[20]

Contrast the constitution of the Republic of Ireland with the constitution of the Islamic Republic of Iran as adopted in 1979 and amended in 1989. Like the former, the latter associates the nation with a particular religion, for as Article 12 states, "The official religion of Iran is Islam and the Twelver Ja'fari school, and this principle will remain eternally immutable."[21] From this point on the resemblance disappears. Although the document contains some language suggestive of religious liberty, this language is far more restrictive. Article 13 recognizes Zoroastrians, Jews, and Christians as religious minorities but emphasizes that they are "the only" such recognized minorities. It goes on to state that "within the limits of the law, [they] are free to perform their religious rites and ceremonies, and to act according to their own canon in matters of personal affairs and religious education," but the meaning of the expression "within the limits of the law" is not explained.[22] The language of Article 14 is in the same vein:

> In accordance with the sacred verse "God does not forbid you to deal kindly and justly with those who have not fought against you because of your religion and who have not expelled you from your homes" [60:8], the government of the Islamic Republic of Iran and all Muslims are duty-bound to treat non-Muslims in conformity with ethical norms and the principles of Islamic justice and equity, and to respect their human rights. This principle applies to all who refrain from engaging in conspiracy or activity against Islam and the Islamic Republic of Iran.

This would be more cheering if, like the Irish Constitution, the document had specified just what it meant "to treat non-Muslims in conformity with ethical norms and the principles of Islamic justice and equity, and to respect their human rights." It does not. Moreover, in interpreting such a sentence as "this principle applies to all who refrain from engaging in conspiracy or activity against Islam and the Islamic Republic of Iran," one must bear in mind that Shari'a has historically entertained an extremely broad and elastic conception of what counts as "activity against Islam." The way these various provisions work is to reduce non-Muslim citizens to a very severe second-class status, excluding them from full participation in public life. It is true that an early Qur'anic sura, from the early period before Muhammad had power, says "there is no compulsion in religion."[23] But in Islam, suras composed later take precedence over suras composed earlier, when Muhammad had no power—and a later sura admonishes, "Fight those who believe not in Allah nor the Last Day, nor hold that forbidden which hath been forbidden by Allah and His Messenger, nor acknowledge the religion of Truth, [even if they are] of the People of the Book, until they pay the jizya with willing submission, and feel themselves subdued."[24]

From a logical point of view, what these examples show is that what really determines whether the convictional basis of a regime will be enforced is not whether all its convictions are such that they can be held by persons of more than one religion but *what these convictions are.* What made the difference between Ireland and Iran was that Catholicism requires religious liberty, while as presently constituted, Islam requires jihad.

What about Liberalism, then? The problem is that the Liberal state masks coercion under the pretense of neutrality, of having no confession in the first place. It can say until the sun freezes that it does not believe in coercion; yet just because, being neutralist, it cannot recognize its coercion as coercion, it coerces more and more freely. Had the pretense of neutrality been merely an unfortunate choice of tactic, inessential to the Liberal approach to government, then Liberalism could be reformed. But contemporary Liberal thinkers do not view it as a tactic; they view it as the very definition of Liberalism. Just by doing so, they have made their movement irreformable. A movement can shed accidental traits it has picked up along the way, but it cannot shed its essence, except by coming to an end.

IV

Very well. We have seen in principle that a political community *could* associate itself confessionally with but a single religion and yet not coerce conscience. It depends on the religion. The religion itself might be of such a nature as to repudiate coercion of conscience. But there is quite a difference between saying that something is logically possible and saying that it is likely; and there is quite a difference between saying that it is likely and saying that it is a good idea.

How so? Suppose the religion at hand does happen to be one of those that are of such a nature as to repudiate coercion of conscience. Still, people often misunderstand the nature of their own religion. According to the Fathers of the Church, "God does not want unwilling worship, nor does He require a forced repentance," yet consider how often Christians have in fact demanded unwilling worship in His name! From a Christian point of view, such misunderstandings may even be strongly motivated, for Christians recognize that ever since the Fall, people have liked pushing other people around. Grace transforms us, but grace works little by little, and in this life its sanctifying work is not complete. Besides, there will always be wolves among the flock. This is not a cynical reflection upon Christian teaching; it *is* Christian teaching. Jesus admonishes, "Beware of false prophets, who come to you in sheep's clothing but inwardly are ravenous wolves. You will know them by their fruits." St. Peter warns, "There will be false teachers" who bring truth into disrepute. St. Paul speaks of "false brethren" who "spy out our freedom which we have in Christ Jesus, that they might bring us into bondage."[25]

One may think that the temptation to push people around arises only when the community is religiously fractured—that if only the community were religiously homogenous, the temptation would not arise. But such thinking is itself a temptation. Here is how this line of thought would develop:

First reflection: If there were fewer people to push around, the temptation to push them around would not arise so often.

Second reflection: If only there weren't so many people of other religions to push around!

Third reflection: We had better push out people of other religions, so we won't be so tempted to mistreat them.

In fact, the problem is even worse, for the line of thought I have just dramatized deals only with the community's domestic affairs. One must also reckon with the temptation to push around neighboring communities.

Why should one want to associate the political community with a single religion anyway? If one believes God commands it, as in Islam, then that is the end of the matter. One must. According to Christianity, however, God does not command it. Of course Christianity is a proselytizing religion, but it does not follow that the state must be a partner in evangelization. Yes, if one believes the Church to be the guardian of the truth about that which is worth the supreme and unconditional commitment of human beings, then obviously one will want people to adhere to the Church. But, given the teachings of the Church, one will want them to do so voluntarily. Patristic writers such as Gregory of Nazianzen explained that, for the age of the Church, the meaning of the Old Testament punishment of stoning for impiety was to suffer the refutation of one's arguments: "For to those who are like wild beasts true and sound discourses are stones" (*Second Theological Oration*, section 2). Does state patronage make voluntary adherence to the revealed faith more likely? On the contrary, it may make it less likely, because it adulterates the motive of faith with the motive of worldly advancement. England has an officially established religion, yet the fraction of Englishmen who set foot in a church in the course of a year is notoriously low.

These are prudential considerations, not arguments of principle, and of course prudential considerations can cut the other way too. It made sense to establish a homeland outside of Europe for the Jews, considering the Nazi attempts to exterminate them, and such a state naturally makes special accommodations for Judaism, even if many citizens are not observant. It does not take much imagination to think of other special cases in which a highly particularistic confessional regime might be justified. One suspects, though, that they will remain special cases.

Given the differences in their supreme and unconditional commitments, different religions will inevitably view matters differently. Within Christianity, however, there are not only prudential but theological reasons for expecting such special cases to be rare. Consider again the convictional basis of the American Founding. The Declaration of Independence was creational, monotheistic, moral in a Decalogical sense, providential, and committed to a high view of the intrinsic worth of man. Now it is true that these beliefs are held by Christianity; but Christianity does not say that one has to be Christian to hold them. At least Catholicism does not say so, and neither does what might be called High Protestantism. In fact, Catholics and High Protestants hold that every last one of these beliefs can be known to be true by the exercise of reason alone. The supreme example of such arguments is the *Summa Theologiae* of St. Thomas Aquinas, which, though thoroughly scriptural, advances essentially philosophical arguments for all of the points at issue: For the existence of God; for His creation and governance of the universe by eternal law; for the unique dignity of the rational creature that is man; and for the unique privilege of this man, that, rather than being jerked around by instincts, he participates in eternal law in his own finite way via natural law.

To be sure, in the Christian view there is more to be known than what can be known by reason alone. There is also Revelation. But even though it is rational to believe in Revelation (in the sense that there are good reasons for doing so), these good reasons are not demonstrations, like those of mathematics. They require faith, which is a gift of divine grace. Now is it not likely that, in most cases, the project of drawing people into the faith would be jeopardized not just by coercion but also by too strongly expecting of people a faith that they cannot attain without grace?

How then could such jeopardy be avoided? St. Paul offers the interesting remark that the Torah acted as a custodian (literally, boy-leader, *paidagogos*) to the people of Israel. Just as upper-class boys in his time were escorted to school by a servant, so the descendants of Abraham were escorted to the Messiah by the law of Moses.[26] This raises an interesting question. Could natural law play the same role for Americans that St. Paul thought the law of Moses played for the descendants of Abraham? Could it serve as an escort, leading the people of the nation to something that it cannot attain by itself?

If so, then Christians would have reason not merely to accept the relatively ecumenical character of the nation's confession but to prefer it to the alternative. Under the circumstances of the day (and perhaps of most days), a more ecumenical confession might be more conducive to the spread of Christian faith than one that was more specifically Christian.

V

So it is that, in the West, confessional states are experiencing a strange second life. Or shall we say a third one? For we have witnessed three waves of this sort of thing. The convictional basis of the old sort of regime was usually Lutheranism, Calvinism, or Catholicism. The convictional basis of the next sort was Classical

Theism, with its belief in natural law—an umbrella that sheltered not only the three religions just mentioned but also many others, and which, precisely for Classical Theist reasons, protected even the consciences of those who were not CT. The convictional basis of the present sort is Liberalism, which is also a coalition of religions rather than just one. But it is a different coalition. Confessionally speaking, what distinguishes the present Liberal confessional state from the previous confessional state is that the present one rejects Classical Theism, rejects natural law, refuses to acknowledge its commitments, violates conscience, and hides behind the cloak of supposed neutrality.

Because Liberalism itself seeks a confessional state, the question that Liberalism would have us frame—"Is the alternative to Liberalism a confessional state?"—is misleading. The real question for our day is whether we will have the kind of confessional state that we have historically enjoyed, the kind established at the American Founding, which is declaratory but not coercive—or the kind of confessional state that Liberal thinkers now propose for us, which is coercive but not declaratory.

To put the matter another way, the Liberal version of recent religious history is mistaken about two related contests: First regarding the nature of toleration, second regarding the nature of the state. As Liberal thinkers tell the first story, the contest lies between those who support toleration and those who oppose it, with liberal thinkers as the champions of toleration. There are, of course, real foes of toleration. But in the West, the real contest of our time lies between the classical and the neutralist views of toleration. The former view is grounded on a paradox: The reason we put up with some bad and false things is that the nature of the good and true demands doing so. The latter view is grounded on an incoherency: The reason we put up with some bad and false things is that we are indifferent among competing views of good. In a nutshell, proponents of the classical view try to judge wisely while proponents of the neutralist view claim falsely not to judge. By adopting the neutralist pretense—by disguising their judgments under the cloak of non-judgment—Liberals are able to present themselves as tolerant while in fact practicing bigotry.

And as Liberal thinkers tell the second story, the contest lies between a Type I and Type IV confessional state, with them as the champions of the former. There are, of course, real proponents of Type IV confessional states. But in the West, the real contest of our times lies between a Type II and a Type III confessional state, with them as the enforcers of the latter. By pretending that they have no confession, Liberals are able to use increasingly strong means to enforce what they deny having.

Even today, most people are still Classical Theists, though very confused ones. The Liberal state is able to rule them by one means alone: Obscuring its real nature. Can this continue?

NOTES

Note: With permission, portions of this chapter are taken from my book *The Line Through the Heart: Natural Law as Fact, Theory, and Sign of Contradiction* (Wilmington, DE: ISI Books, 2009).

1. *McCreary County, Kentucky v. American Civil Liberties Union of Kentucky*, 545 U.S. 844 (2005), at 876.

2. See especially Budziszewski, *Line Through the Heart*, chapter 10, "The Illiberal Liberal Religion." The first two sections of this essay rework the argument of that chapter; the rest of the essay carries the argument further.

3. Compare Reinhold Niebuhr, "The Christian Church in a Secular Age," in *Christianity and Power Politics* (New York: Charles Scribner's Sons, 1940), 204–5: "Strictly speaking, there is no such thing as secularism. An explicit denial of the sacred always contains some implied affirmation of a holy sphere. . . . Consequently the avowedly secular culture of today turns out on close examination to be either a pantheistic religion which identifies existence in its totality with holiness, or a rationalistic humanism for which human reason is essentially god or a vitalistic humanism which worships some unique or particular vital force in the individual or the community as its god, that is, as the object of its unconditioned loyalty." Compare also Paul Tillich, *Systematic Theology* (Chicago: University of Chicago Press, 1951), 1:211: "'God' is the answer to the question implied in man's finitude; he is the name for that which concerns man ultimately. This does not mean that first there is a being called God and then the demand that man should be ultimately concerned with Him. It means that whatever concerns a man ultimately becomes god for him, and, conversely, it means that a man can be concerned ultimately only about that which is god for him."

4. Aristotle, *Nicomachean Ethics*, book 1.

5. Romans 3:8.

6. *Lemon v. Kurtzman*, 403 U.S. 602 (1971), at 612–13.

7. See Paul Kurtz, *Humanist Manifestos I and II* (New York: Prometheus Books, 1973), and "Humanist Manifesto 2000: A Call for a New Planetary Humanism," *Free Inquiry* 19.4 (Fall 1999).

8. Hilary of Poitiers, "To Constantius," quoted in Lord Acton, "Political Thoughts on the Church," in *Essays in Religion, Politics, and Morality*, ed. J. Rufus Fears, vol. 3 of *Selected Writings of Lord Acton* (Indianapolis: Liberty Classics, 1988), p. 24; Isidore of Pelusium, *Epistles*, 2.129, quoted in Margaret A. Schatkin and Paul W. Harkins, trans., *Apologist, Saint John Chrysostom*, vol. 73 of *The Fathers of the Church* (Washington, D.C.: Catholic University of America Press, 1985), p. 83, note 30; Lactantius, *Divine Institutes*, 5.20, trans. William Fletcher (public domain, www.newadvent.org/fathers).

9. Second Vatican Council, Declaration on Religious Freedom, *Dignitatis Humanae*, "On the Right of the Person and of Communities to Social and Civil Freedom in Matters Religious," 7 December 1965.

10. Ahmad ibn Naqib al-Misri, *Reliance of the Traveller*, rev. ed. (Beltsville, MD: Amana, 1994, 1997). This is a collaborative work; only a small part comes from the original manual by Ahmad ibn Naqib al-Misri. The quotation from 'Umar Barakat is found in sec o9.0, p. 599.

11. Al-Baqarah (Qur'an 2), 216, and An-Nisa' (Qur'an 4), 89. Here and throughout my discussion of *The Reliance of the Traveller*, I am using the translations of Qur'an and *hadith* provided in the English version of the work itself.

12. The Arabic plural is actually *ahadith*, but it is often rendered as *haditha* or *hadiths* in English.

13. The speaker is Muhammad. 'Umar Barakat remarks that this hadith is recorded by Sahih al-Bukhari and Muslim ibn al-Hajjaj.

14. John Rawls, *Political Liberalism* (New York: Columbia University Press, 1993).

15. "*First, the statute must have a secular legislative purpose*; second, its principal or primary effect must be one that neither advances nor inhibits religion; finally, the statute must not foster 'an excessive government entanglement with religion.'" *Lemon v. Kurtzman*, 403 U.S. 602 (1971), at 612–13; emphasis added.

16. There have been apparent exceptions to the tendency of our courts to treat secular ideologies as nonreligious. See, for example, *Torcaso v. Watkins*, 367 U.S. 488 (1961), at 495: "We repeat and again reaffirm that neither a State nor the Federal Government can constitutionally force a person 'to profess a belief or disbelief in any religion.' Neither [of them] can constitutionally pass laws or impose requirements which aid all religions as against nonbelievers, and neither [of them] can aid those religions based on a belief in the existence of God as against those religions founded on different beliefs." Ibid., note 11: "Among religions in this country which do not teach what would generally be considered a belief in the existence of God are Buddhism, Taoism, Ethical Culture, Secular Humanism and others." For the general pattern, however, see *Alvarado v. City of San Jose*, 94 F.3d 1223 (1996), note 2 (internal citations removed):

> In *Torcaso*, in the context of ruling on a state statute requiring notaries to profess belief in God as a condition of office, the Supreme Court assumed without deciding that certain non-theistic beliefs could be deemed "religious" for First Amendment purposes. . . . Much has been made of this footnote, which has been explained as follows by Judge Canby, concurring in *Grove*: "The apparent breadth of the reference to 'Secular Humanism' . . . is entirely dependent upon viewing the term out of context. In context, it is clear that the Court meant 'no more than a reference to the group seeking an exemption, which, although non-Theist in belief, also met weekly on Sundays and functioned much like a church. . . . Thus *Torcaso* does not stand for the proposition that "humanism" is a religion, although an organized group of "Secular Humanists" may be.'"

See also *Peloza v. Capistrano School District*, 37 F.3d 517 (9th Cir. 1994), cert. denied, 515 U.S. 1173 (1995): "neither the Supreme Court, nor this circuit, has ever held that evolutionism or secular humanism are 'religions' for Establishment Clause purposes." I thank Professor David K. DeWolf, Gonzaga University Law School, for calling my attention to these passages.

17. Had the document's chief draftsman, Thomas Jefferson, been writing for himself alone, he might well have written differently; indeed, its references to Providence were added by the

Continental Congress. In a republic, however, the "authors" of a document are not its draftsmen but those who give it authority—in this case, the delegates assembled.

18. A qualification is in order: perhaps enough has been said, provided that one includes previous publications. The fact that I have written about these matters before allows me to move more quickly in the present essay, zeroing in on what has hitherto been the most tentative aspect of the argument and fleshing it out a little further.

19. The current text of the Constitution of the Republic of Ireland may be found online at http://www.taoiseach.gov.ie/eng/Youth_Zone/About_the_Constitution,_Flag,_Anthem_Harp/Constitution_of_Ireland_March_20. An unofficial variorum text, valid through 1999, showing the original language that was subsequently removed, may be found at www.johnpghall.pwp.blueyonder.co.uk/constit.htm .

20. *Dignitatis Humanae*, section 2. The document goes on to specify the juridical implications of these principles in some detail.

21. Islam is divided between Sunnis and Shi'ites. The most numerous branch of the latter division is Twelver Shi'a, so-called because it adheres to the Twelve Imams, the twelfth of whom is expected to return as the Mahdi. The Ja'fari school is the dominant Shi'a school of Islamic jurisprudence, as contrasted with the four main Sunni schools. Ja'fari is distinguished by its reliance on *ijtihad*, which is the "independent" exercise of *aql*, a general term for the faculty of reason. Though suspicious of *ijtihad*, the Sunni schools of jurisprudence do allow a role to analogical reasoning, which they call *qiyas*.

22. Text taken from www.servat.unibe.ch/icl/ir00000_.html, a website maintained by the University of Bern, Switzerland.

23. Al-Baqarah (Qur'an 2), 256.

24. At-Taubah (Qur'an 9), 29–30.

25. Matthew 7:15–16a, 2 Peter 2:1, Galatians 2:4 (RSV).

26. Galatians 3:23–26.

5

DEFENDING THE PERSONAL LOGOS TODAY

Peter Augustine Lawler

Few sophisticated people deny the reality of free persons these days. Nor do they deny that the significance of the free person is the "bottom line" when it comes to moral reasoning and public policy choices. The feminist may, in her proud atheism, say that Darwin explains it all, but she also proudly refuses to be determined by her biology, to be a reproductive machine for her country or her species. Our theorists tend to be relativists or non-foundationalists, saying that there's no "truth" that can authoritatively guide us. But what they really mean is that there's no metaphysics or theology or national identity or science that trumps our devotion to the flourishing of particular personal lives. The premise of non-foundationalism is that the person is the "bottom line," and there's no need to explain why.

Consider that even our eugenics have become personal. We uniformly condemn the monstrously tyrannical and yet quaintly wacky schemes to improve citizens or the species that are found, for example, in Plato's *Republic*, or among the Nazis, or even among the turn-of-the-twentieth-century Progressives. Our transhumanists promise that biotechnology will extend indefinitely the existence of particular persons—and even that the limits of the person's imprisonment in his or her body will be simply overcome. After many missteps we can say that our science is all about serving the person these days, even among those scientists who know that there's no natural evidence for personal significance at all.[1]

My purpose here is to show that our devotion to the unique and irreplaceable significance of particular persons is Christian. It remains Christian, in fact, even in its modern, seemingly post-Christian form in the work of our country's founding philosopher—John Locke. What distinguishes the person most truthfully is that Logos itself is necessarily personal, and so we can make sense of our personal devotion, as our philosopher-pope emeritus has reminded us, only by taking seriously the possibility of a personal science of theology. The West—and America in particular—can't and shouldn't dispense with its distinctively Christian and deeply truthful roots.

THE DISCOVERY OF THE PERSONAL LOGOS

We begin, with the help of our philosopher-pope emeritus, with the first words about the relationship between Greek philosophy or science and Christianity spoken during the period of Hellenic Christianity.[2] Then, the Greeks and the Christians agreed that we're hardwired as beings with minds to think about who or what God must be and that we're animated by Eros, or love, to seek the truth about God. The idea that God is Logos is what allowed the Greeks and the Christians to use both argument and mockery to collaborate against those religions that are man-made and obviously unreasonable.

God is neither cruel nor arbitrary, and the truth about God must correspond to what we can know about ourselves and the rest of nature according to our best lights. Both the Greeks and the Christians contributed to genuine enlightenment, to the liberation of human beings from a world where the word of God both was used as a weapon and justified the use of weapons. Before the philosophers and the Christians, the name of God or the names of the gods were thought to be for the justification of all kinds of force and fraud by those shameless and cunning enough to know what to do with them.

Through reflection, Aristotle attempted to grasp God as a kind of magnet moving human desire or longing. He understood God only as the *object* of love, as a wholly self-sufficient or unerotic or unmovable being, not as a person at all. God didn't love back, and mortals certainly couldn't have God as a friend. Aristotle's God is certainly not a "relational" God, one who cares or even knows about the existence of particular human beings. According to Aristotle, our pursuit of divine knowledge, or what God knows, becomes progressively more impersonal. The pursuit of philosophic or scientific truth requires that the individual philosopher die to himself. The Socratic drama of the pursuit of wisdom is the particular being losing himself in his apprehension of anonymous or impersonal truth.

From this classical view, we approach divinity, or what is best in us, through our perception of the Logos or rational causality that governs all things. We see past every anthropomorphic claim for personal intervention or personal causation that would disrupt that Logos. The idea of a personal God or a personal Logos is an oxymoron. True theology—authentically natural theology—must correspond to what we really know about the insignificance of persons and a divine "law" that has no place for them.

The Christian criticism of Aristotelian theology is that it doesn't account for what we really know about the human person. For the Greek philosophers the realm of personal freedom, finally, is a mythical idea, one that must be rhetorically supported but for which there's no scientific evidence. The only true freedom is the freedom of the human mind from anthropomorphic delusions about natural causation. The Christians respond that human longings and human action exhibit evidence of personal freedom, and the person must have some actual foundation in Being itself. What we really do know, they say, points in the direction of the creative activity of a personal God. The personalities of God and humans can't be wholly or irredeemably unrelated. The possibility of the free and rational being open to the truth depends upon the corresponding possibility of a personal, rational science of theology.

The classical philosophers were, of course, perfectly aware that human beings are "manly," that they need to feel important. Such self-confidence is required to make self-conscious life endurable and great human deeds possible. But according to their science, all assertions of human importance are unrealistic exaggerations, and the philosopher gently mocks without obviously undermining the aspirations of particular individuals to self-sufficiency. For the Christians, however, even science depends upon the possibility of personal significance, and Christian theology criticizes both the civil theology and the natural theology of the Greeks and Romans for their inability to account for personal freedom, for the being who is not fundamentally merely part of a city or part of some necessitarian natural whole.

According to the Christians, not only do particular men and women need to feel important; they are, in fact, important. The Christians add that the unrealistic exaggerations of their magnanimous pretensions need, in fact, the chastening of the truthful virtue of humility, the virtue of ineradicably relational and lovingly dependent beings. For Aristotle, the pride of the magnanimous depends on his inability to wonder about the mystery of his own being or his place in some cosmos. For the Christian, nothing is more worthy of wonder than the unique and irreplaceable significance of every person's existence. So as genuinely magnanimous humans, we acknowledge our own being as a gift and our undeniably significant and excellent accomplishments as dependent on a personal, relational context beyond our complete control and comprehension.

PHYSICS AND PHILOSOPHY AND THE PHYSICIST AND THE PHILOSOPHER

That there's a somewhat mysterious ground for personal freedom—for the only being we know in which Logos resides—in an otherwise seemingly necessitarian cosmos does, in some ways, offend the mind. But to understand all that exists in terms of impersonal causation suggests that Being itself is constituted by an intelligence that is incapable of comprehending itself. The being who is open to the truth about Being, the human person, can seem to be a chance occurrence in a cosmos that has no particular need for and is seemingly distorted by his or her existence. The appearance of the human person, even the philosopher with the name Socrates, offends the human mind precisely because the person called Socrates is much more than a mind. As far as we know, the human mind can only appear or function in a whole person.

The real existence of the whole philosopher or physicist can't be accounted for in any mathematical or certainly necessitarian physics. The physicist (as the Christian philosopher Walker Percy wrote)[3] is a leftover in the world described by his theory, and so he has to struggle, with uneven and always incomplete success, to locate himself in that world. The being he understands as essentially mind—himself— has no place in a world that he understands as essentially composed of bodies. So physicists, and other scientists and materialistic philosophers, might seem to spend much of their lives diverted from who they are through unrealistically impersonal thought, only to attempt to reenter the world of real human beings from time to time through losing themselves in a different way through bodily enjoyment.

The world, the contemporary classical philosopher Leo Strauss wrote, is the home of the human mind.[4] That means, of course, that it's not quite the home of the human person. The personal being who wonders is necessarily a wanderer in the cosmos. Minds and bodies, we can say, can be fully at home in the world described by natural theology—whether that theology is inspired by Aristotle or Darwin or some other "naturalism" or (as Heidegger said) "biologism." Our experiences of alienation or "homelessness" are deeply unnatural and so deeply unreal.

From the view of the personal Logos, the homelessness in that world we all share comes from being neither minds nor bodies or even just an incoherent mixture of the two. Persons are distinguished by joys, responsibilities, and miseries that come from being self-conscious, relational, incomplete, and troubled in ways impossible for pure mind and pure body. Neither minds nor bodies—considered as wholes— are animated by love, which turns out, for persons, to be personal love all the way down. Our deepest longing is to be transparent before another, a person who knows and loves me "just as I am." The longing for the transparency of the heart—or one's inward, irreducible personal disposition—has no place in either Aristotelian or Darwinian psychology or ethics.

Aristotle, following Socrates, says we're most deeply moved by wonder, and the Bible says we're most deeply wanderers or pilgrims in this world. Surely the truth is that because we wonder we wander or because we can wander we wonder. It's because of our personal detachment that we're open to the truth and we always fall short of integrating ourselves into the nature our physicists and biologists so perfectly describe. This doesn't mean that being personal means we're nothing but absurdly purposeless leftovers or miserable aliens stuck inside our puny, particular selves. Sure, we have miseries not given to the others species that flow from our contingency as wanderers, but we're also given joys (such as wonder and deeply personal love) and responsibilities (such as those that flow from being open to the truth and taking responsibility for the very future of life on our planet) not given to the other species.

In some ways it might offend the person's reason less to affirm an account of the precondition and ground of all being to be creative and truly conscious—or erotic and rational—thinking. In the final analysis, the world is more love than mathematics, and the particular human person is more significant and wonderful than the stars. Nobody wonders but the wanderer, and nothing is more worthy of wonder than the wanderer. As Percy and our popes and other leading Catholic thinkers have emphasized, this conclusion is perfectly compatible with what we really know about natural evolution.

The evolution of nature, we can't help but see, produces ontological differences or different kinds of beings. Being changed when the plant emerged from the rock, as biology emerged from physics. How life—and so the distinction between life and death and life and nonlife—emerged from inanimate nature remains a mystery to us. Being changed again when the animal emerged from the plant; all the capabilities and behavior turned the distinction from life and death into birth and death. Being changed again when the social, rational, free, or technological animal emerged who can raise the question of being, take things personally, love personally, be aware of, reflect on, and rebel against personal contingency and mortality.

The personal rebellion against a nature seemingly indifferent to personal being is reflected in the fact there's no dolphin technology worth talking about. Not only do the dolphins lack the "hardwiring" to invent their way ingeniously out of much of what they've been given by nature, as far as we can tell they're fine with the world nature has given them. But it's not only technology, of course, that distinguishes us. Neither are there dolphin physicists, priests or preachers, presidents or princes, poets, or philosophers, and even dolphin parents aren't that much like our parents. And of course there's no dolphin safe sex. Because particular dolphins aren't moved by the prospect of personal extinction that comes with one's own death, they can't conceive of projects to disconnect erotic enjoyment from birth and death.

The last ontological difference that emerged naturally, of course, is easily the most important one. Arguably there's more significance to the distance between each person and each dolphin than between a dolphin and a rock. The questions that surround the mystery of being—including who we are, what we are, and who or what God is—couldn't be raised without us. Actually, we really know that the "what" questions couldn't be raised by anyone but a "who," a being with a name who can name. (Certain other animals have names and even know them, but we give them their names to personalize them, with very limited success, in our own image.) And so despite the best efforts of many philosophers and scientists, we've never been able to reduce the "who" to a "what," the human person to some impersonal, wholly necessitarian natural process. The "who" is the being open to the "what," and the mystery of the "who"—the person—is much more wonderful than the famous "why is there being rather than nothing at all?" issue.

Perhaps the physicists are right that impersonal nature would be perfectly explicable without us, at least if one doesn't dwell too much on the mystery of being or the mystery of life. But everyone knows that physics can't explain the physicist. Perhaps physics, for all I know, can explain the correspondence between the physicist's mind and the invincible laws of nature. But the physicist isn't a mind; he's a whole human being—a person—who can't be reduced to a body or a mind or even some incoherent mixture of the two. The physicist can't explain the uniqueness of the scientific effort of human beings to deny the uniqueness of our species—and especially particular members of our species—in the cosmos. We don't look to the physicist to explain the undeniably truthful and undeniably personal and undeniably wonderful experience of the particular human being existing for a moment between two abysses. We can look to penetrating psychologists from Aristophanes to Pascal to Nietzsche to Percy to remind us that the physicist's attempt to lose himself in an impersonal account of nature is really, in part, an always partly failed attempt to divert himself from what he really knows about himself, the "who," the particular being with a name who can name.

ETERNITY, CREATIVITY, AND TIME

The Greeks' focus on eternity is on the "what" that necessarily is; the Christians' focus on the loving creativity of God is on "who" exists in time—for a moment—in this world. The eternal God, for Aristotle, has no concern for ephemeral beings, each of whom exists contingently or by chance. The idea of eternity, for philosophers, protected the impersonal intelligibility of nature. That idea is at the foundation of a world that is the home of the human mind.

For the contemporary classical thinker Strauss, the deepest distinction is between identifying being with eternity or being with creativity. If being (including each of our beings) is caused by some personal creativity—then each of us is finally free from natural necessity. And this means that the philosopher's claim for wisdom through the rational apprehension of necessity can't be justified. This also means that the philosopher's claim that human Eros finally points away from persons in the direction of ideas is mistaken. For Strauss, as for the Christians, the deep question is whether God is a "who" or a "what." For Strauss, the Platonic truth is that being that being is nothing personal, and so those who pursue eternal truth (the philosophers) have no deep attachment to the pursuit of personal freedom—a pursuit based on illusions the philosopher himself doesn't share.

The classical philosophic or scientific understanding of the world in terms of impersonal necessity or eternity alone can't account for the real existence of persons, of beings open to the truth and defined in this world by time. If time and eternity really are infinitely distant from one another, then we can't understand why human beings can know God or anything eternal. The Creator and the creatures made in his image—as persons with Logos—can't be captured by the radical distinction between time and eternity, because they are created to be more than temporal beings and open to much more than the incomplete truth about themselves in time. Our understanding of being can't dispense with persons, because as far as we know, Logos is only a property of persons. We are open to eternity only in time, and so in some sense our personal identities are hardwired into the order of Being itself.

Classical monotheism, in truth, denies the real relationships between God and humans and between eternity and time. Greek philosophers clearly distinguished the personal illusion of religion from the philosophic science of theology, showing that, for the most part, at least the lives of particular men are as unreal or as insignificant as the personal gods they invent. For the Greeks, religion was useful for the regulation of lives, but it had nothing to do with the truth.

From the Greek view, the early Christians seemed like atheists. They rejected the whole world of ancient religion and its gods as nothing but empty custom or contrary to what we can really know. That's because the Christians agreed with the Greek philosophers that traditional myth must be rejected in favor of the truth about Being, and the Christians added that all human beings are called to regulate their lives in light of what they can really know. Only from the perspective of a personal Logos can the truth affirm and guide human freedom. The Christians, by discovering a transformed understanding of the Logos at the ground of Being, showed God to be a person concerned with persons. The Christians show why divine truth can't be separated from personal morality.

Sin flows from the denial of the truth about our relational, loving freedom, from the madness that flows from the aspiration to be as autonomous or self-sufficient as some thinkers imagine God to be. The sin described in Genesis flows from the false separation of divine wisdom from personal or "relational" morality. The key Christian doctrine of the Trinity reconciles monotheism with a God who is personal, relational, living, and loving. From a Christian view, the Deistic denial of the Trinity obliterates both the possibilities of both God's personal and providential love and personal sin.

CHRISTIAN PERSONAL LIBERATION

The modern, non-Trinitarian, non-relational narrative of the person often presents Christianity as a decline, as Jefferson wrote, into "monkish ignorance and superstition" from the urbane and humane enlightenment of the classical Greeks and Romans. But from any personal view, that could hardly be true. For a helpfully extreme corrective to this misleading view, we can turn to David Bentley Hart's *Atheistic Delusions.*[5] The Christian idea of the person was, from its beginning, the source of much of the liberation we so cherish today. Hart describes a pre-Christian world that was cruel and capricious—reminding us forcefully of the torture and murder that ancient paganism tolerated as a matter of course, precisely because it regarded particular persons as unreal. The impersonal truth was best seen by the philosopher who became dead to himself, who resigned himself to the ephemeral insignificance of his particular existence.

Christianity was, in a way, the slave revolt Nietzsche described, a cosmic rebellion against the enslavement of each of us to natural and political necessity. Christ, the Christians claimed, freed us from the limitations of our merely biological nature through his perfect reconciliation of God's nature and human nature. He was, the Nicene fathers concluded, fully God and fully human. This means that a personal being is somehow natural being yet not defined by the natural limitations and direction given to the members of all the other species. A person isn't a "species being" but has a unique and irreplaceable personal destiny.

The coming of Christ, it is barely too strong to say, transformed each of us from being nobody to being somebody—a somebody of infinite value. Maybe more precisely: Christ taught each one of us who he or she truly is. None of us is destined to be a slave, and death has been overcome. We are no longer defined by our merely biological nature, because our nature is now to be both human and divine. From one view, there is no empirical evidence that death has been overcome for each particular human being. From another, there's abundant evidence in the unprecedented virtue flowing from the unconditional love present among the early Christians and that virtue's indirect, historical transformation of the broader social and political world. The change in understanding of who each of us is is the result of a deepened human inwardness or self-consciousness: Christ made each of us irreducibly deeper by infusing divinity into every nook and cranny of our nature. In our loving relationships with other persons and the personal God, we don't surrender what we know about our own irreducible personal identity.

Many of the features of the personal liberation praised by American Lockeans, Hart observes, came into the world in Christian communities. Even the Stoics did not approach the Christians in their indifference to a person's social status. The Christians were the first to be completely opposed to slavery; the first for raising women to equality in marriage and elsewhere; the first for faithfulness in monogamous marriage; the first for the egalitarian brotherhood of all men. For the Christians, the community of personal love wasn't some otherworldly hope. Rather, that community was formed by obligations given to personal, relational beings made in God's image here and now.

So, as St. Augustine made most clear, personal liberation is most of all about a theological revolution. Christianity freed the person from the enslavement of *civil theology* (which understood each human being to be most fundamentally a citizen or merely part of a city) and the enslavement of *natural theology* (which understood each human being to be merely a part of nature fundamentally indifferent to personal existence). Christianity freed us from the lies that we're meant to be either "city fodder" or, as we say today, "species fodder." It has also protected us—witness the anticommunist dissidents Solzhenitsyn and Havel—from the more recent lie that we're "history fodder." Only the personal theology of the Christians can account for the longings of the whole human person, the free, relational, and truthful being who preserves his or her personal identity in loving relationship with a personal God.

There's nothing in Augustine that corresponds to the Socratic image of the cave. The wise philosopher-king—in touch with the whole truth about nature—constructs civil theological images with which he perfectly controls the lives of the citizens for whom he has taken responsibility. The exceedingly rare perfect liberation of the philosopher becomes the condition of the "cave" (or the civil-theological fantasy in which most people necessarily live) being his creation. The free mind—unencumbered, apparently, by any bodily or other limitations—takes charge of the world that citizens mistake for freedom. That mind, of course, views ruling as an unpleasant necessity that has nothing do with any care or concern—much less love—for his fellow citizens or fellow persons.

Augustine's good, empirical news about personal liberation begins with the thought that the cave—the city or regime—itself is a vain philosophic illusion, and personal, relational (and so not autonomous) freedom is equally the destiny of us all under a personal, loving God. There's not a word in Augustine's truthful teaching that suggests that God is personally concerned with the fate of any particular city, but God is equally concerned with the fate of every particular person. The truth about God is accessible to each of us, and it is so morally elevating that it can be conveyed without noble lies.

THE MEDIEVAL DIFFERENCE

The difference between the leading medieval Christian thinker Thomas Aquinas and the best of the medieval Jewish and Muslim thinkers (particularly Maimonides) continues to be about the truth concerning true or "essential" divinity—and so, true or "essential" humanity.[6] Both Thomas and Maimonides seem to contend that divine providence pertains to particular human beings, and not "humanity" or the species. This means that each human creature exists for his or her own sake and not merely as part of a part of a political community or a species. Each of us is an end, not a means, as God himself is an end and not a means.

For Maimonides, however, the existence of particular human beings—separate and distinguishable individuals—appears to fade away when we are what we are most truly, what each of us is as an intellectual being or mind. At that level, individuation no longer exists, and the lawful divinity that truthfully characterizes the world is revealed as being for the mind as such. The truth is not for or about anyone in particular. Brague, following Leo Strauss, claims that the close reader of the great Jewish philosopher eventually discovers that the idea of personal or particular providence turns out to be a fantasy or at least deeply problematic. The pretensions of particular persons have no real foundation, and the source of true divine law—or true natural law—could not be a person.

This means that the divine revelation at the foundation of moral/political legislation depends on personal premises—on premises about human individuation—that don't correspond to what minds can really know about what a human is. Divine revelation as found in the Bible doesn't correspond to the true law of nature. So it's the necessities connected with the body and not those connected with the mind that are the cause of revealed moral/political law. The source of divine moral/political law, officially, is a radically mysterious, capriciously willful God who's incredible to the mind. The will of the God of revelation, as Strauss always says, is incompatible with the divine/natural law known through reason alone. God is either willful and personal or rational and impersonal. The incredible synthesis that is the claim of personal Logos of the Christian undermines the "truth claims" of both revelation and reason. This alleged synthesis denies the truth about both moral/political and intellectual necessity, of what we are as enslaved bodies and liberated minds.

In the best case, however, the true source of divine moral/political revelation isn't mysterious at all, according to Maimonides. It is the product of the will operating in the service of the mind's freedom. The free mind, or the philosopher, determines what opinions—and so what legislation—are "healthy." This legislation for moral/political health (what beings with bodies need in order to flourish) flows from an impersonal truth that has no room for either the free person or the God of revelation. When Strauss and Straussians talk of rehabilitating the wisdom of

Maimonides and defending healthy civic opinion, they assume the untruth of such opinion and the desirability of the rule of philosophers or the wise over the ignorant. The Straussian effort is on behalf of nothing personal. It is on behalf of civic theology and natural theology, on behalf of citizens (and statesmen) and philosophers. That effort, thank God, is mission impossible.

Thomas disagrees with Maimonides on the truth we can see with our own eyes about what or (better) *who* we are. The intellect does not have some abstract existence detached from its existence in a particular individual, and that person cannot be reduced to mind or body or even some incoherent mixture of the two. There is no intellect, but intellects; and intellects have a place only in the context of a uniquely personal reality. So there is no "what" called humanity or "the species," but only "whos" or irreducibly particular, unique, and irreplaceable persons.

For Thomas (unlike the Platonists ancient, medieval, and contemporary), the fundamental choice is not between the reason of the liberated mind and willful subordination to divine revelation. It is between the impersonal Logos of the philosophers and scientists (defended in his time by Maimonides and other "Averroeists") and the personal Logos that does justice to what we can really see about who we are.

THE MODERN VIEW OF PERSONAL FREEDOM

Some Christians, of course, had reasonable objections—not unlike those of Maimonides—to the idea of God as personal Logos. This idea might be understood to bind God by natural laws that weren't his creation. The emphasis on either God's love or God's reason can easily seem to compromise the freedom of his will and so the omnipotence on which rest our hopes for personal salvation. So a characteristic Protestant form of nominalism is about securing the freedom of the God on whom we can rely with certainty for personal salvation from what would otherwise be our natural/biological destiny. God's personal will overcomes impersonal necessity; God saves us from who we otherwise are as fallen or otherwise hopelessly corrupt and vainly deceived natural beings.

The more characteristically modern form of nominalism was about freeing up the will of persons made in God's image. The limiting of the willful God with either Logos or love seems to undermine his personal significance, and so ours. As free persons, in fact, we are not limited by an order of nature not of our making and have no inclination or duty to limit our personal freedom in love with other persons— even the love of God. As free persons we don't orient our will in love of God or with charitable concern for those he made in his loving image but only in terms of our own personal being or identity.

The modern form of liberation of the person from the chains of Logos and love is most strikingly displayed by our founding philosopher John Locke. Locke's freeing of the person from both erotic and Logos-based limitation and direction was, it's important to emphasize, almost the opposite of some return to Platonic political philosophy. He intended to produce both empirical confirmation and a kind of radicalization of the unprecedented Christian insight into personal freedom.[7]

For Locke, words—our capacity for reasonable speech or Logos—don't give us any access to the truth about nature or God. There is, in fact, no science of theology or science of nature that incorporates the truth about who we are as freely willing and insistently particular beings. Words are the weapons we use to secure our being against nature and without a providential God. Words are the weapons we use to make ourselves progressively freer or progressively more real.

Locke's state of nature, for example, was not meant to be an empirical account of the way human beings are. It is a tool used by Locke to liberate the individual from nature and from other individuals. It was a potent phrase, like all words well used, that allows us to add to our personal significance by becoming less dependent on our natural environment—an environment that includes our own bodies and corresponding natural, social instincts.

Locke denies that human individuals are, most fundamentally, loving or relational beings. And so he denies that God is loving or relational or providential. We shouldn't rely on his love, just as we shouldn't rely on the love of any other person. Locke's Deistic or "Socinian" denial of the truth of the mystery of the Trinity was really a denial that God is relational, and so a denial that any person could be fundamentally connected with or dependent on other persons. The free person—divine or human—is an intellectual and emotional whole. For the Christians, both personhood and Logos are necessarily relational, and so personal monotheism—without, of course, the mystery of the Trinity—is an oxymoron. Locke's individualistic idea of the person is the assertion (without, as Rousseau complained, real evidence) that personal, non-relational monotheism is possible.

For Locke, God remains a free person with an irreducible personal identity, and so does each of us. This means that Locke sides with the Christians against the classical claims of civil and natural theology. The Lockean "law of nature" is all about persons—being both rational and industrious—employing their freedom to escape from their miserable natural condition and to remake the world in the image of their freedom. Nature's indifference to persons is to be inventively displaced by free assertions of personal significance. As a person, for Locke, I don't exist for my species or my country (as a citizen), I exist for myself. My body is my own property—to be employed for my own security and convenience. The Lockean radicalizes—on a Christian foundation—the claim for personal freedom. I'm not a part of some whole greater than myself. I'm not bound to others—including God—through love.

God doesn't simply disappear in Locke because the mystery of the human person—irreducibly self-conscious and relentlessly particular personal identity—remains. So there's some connection, at least, between Locke and Pascal on the mysterious hiddenness of the Being who is the source of our self-consciousness, our freedom, and our uneasiness or restlessness in his absence. For all practical purposes, Locke teaches, that mysterious God is dead to us, and the good and bad news is that he left us free persons on our own. He encouraged us, in that way, to think of ourselves as on the way to replacing him.

That mystery of personal freedom, in fact, becomes greater than it ever was for the Christians who claimed to have discovered the personal Logos. The human person is a mysterious exception to the laws of nature that govern the other species and nature as a whole. And the human mind is not for understanding the "essences" at the foundation of natural regularities. It is a weapon—in the hands of persons—for reconstructing nature, for replacing, we say today, impersonal (and so random and cruel) natural evolution with conscious and volitional evolution. Personal human thought and will identify Being itself with personal being. There is no impersonal Logos and no personal love that limits what persons can do for themselves. Like the Christians, Locke holds that there is no "humanity" or human species but only particular personal identities—each of which is unique and irreplaceable, especially to itself.

We're the beings with enough self-consciousness or self-ownership to have a relatively stable and clear sense of who we are as particular, vulnerable, mortal (or embodied) beings. By thinking through all that is implied in self-ownership, Locke believed he could see what Plato and Aristotle could not—the irreducible inward world of subjectivity, the world of conscience. Locke believed he relocated Being itself in the particular experiences of personal identity.

Locke knew he couldn't have grasped that true insight about the true inwardness of each of us without knowledge of the Bible. He thought of himself, in fact, as providing empirical confirmation of the basic biblical insight about who we are—a confirmation superior to anything found in Plato and Aristotle. According to Locke, it is the freely creating human who created the freely creating God. That's the opposite, of course, of what the Bible tells us. But the Bible—unlike other premodern texts—still shows *who* God should be if truly created in our human image. We are, alone among the animals, partly and indefinitely free from nature through our own activity or creativity. We aren't, as they say today and the Christians first said, defined by our biology.

Locke sides with the Christians against the classical thinkers and the Darwinians concerning free personal identity. From this personal view, even philosophy is not learning how to die; it's not forgetting about one's personal needs or personal contingency and mortality. For Locke, like the Christians, we can say that our deepest longings are in some sense personal, for a sort of happiness compatible with the real experiences of personal identity. For Locke, like the Christians, the being most worthy of wonder is the free person, and Locke adds that the rest of nature is worth little or nothing unless both wonderfully and methodically transformed by personal efforts. Everything worth knowing—and every form of security we can truthfully believe in—is a personal creation.

THE CHRISTIAN FOUNDATION OF THE SEPARATION OF CHURCH AND STATE

A form of American pride is that the separation of church and state—or the freedom of mind or conscience—had to be won against Christian tyranny, against the tyranny of established churches, inquisitions, and Puritanical fanaticism. That freedom, we can even think, was won by an enlightened or classical war of the philosophers against monkish ignorance and superstition and the despotic craftiness of priests. Without, of course, denying the many forms of corruption of Christianity by the temptations of political power, we can see that the separation of church and state depends on the personal liberation discovered by the Christians. We can add that Locke himself knew this.

Brague explains better than anyone why the separation of church and state—or the separation of divine law and human law—necessarily depends on this Christian view of personal freedom.[8] If, according to the pre-Christian or classical philosophers, the truth about the impersonal Logos of nature is equivalent to divinity truthfully understood, then human beings need illusions about providential divinity to sustain their illusions about their own freedom or personal significance. And then the task of the political philosopher is to protect the tension between the truth about impersonal divine "law" and the moral/political dogmas that support human law. This means that civil theology is indispensable but merely salutary, and true or natural religion is philosophical liberation from personal concerns.

Insofar as our Darwinians share that view of the impersonal, species-oriented truth about the Logos of nature, then religion still makes sense as a way of supporting those same beneficial communal illusions. Neither Aristotelians nor Darwinians can, however, make sense of the freedom from political/divine law that we all believe human beings to possess. Freedom from political/divine law must be for personal/divine law, for beings who can know that they are in some sense created in the image of a personal God.

The limitation of government must be for both personal freedom and freedom of the church. The church—not the state—is the institutional embodiment of the relational, personal truth about who we are. The state is limited by that personal, social truth. We are not most fundamentally political beings, even if, as St. Thomas says, we are also made to be citizens of some particular country. We are more social than political beings because we are most fundamentally free and relational persons under a transpolitical God.

It is Christianity that discredited the idea of civil theology, as Locke agrees. Before the Christian discovery of personal freedom, political control of religion was thought to be both natural and normal. The ancient philosophers approved of the pagan reduction of religion to superstition and empty ritual in order to support the city and its laws. Locke stands with the Christians in openly proclaiming that every civil religion is untrue and personally degrading.

Locke's teaching, as Ward notes, really means to hold that "it is only with the coming of Christ that the principle of separating of religion and politics first appeared."[9] So it's only with the coming of Christ, as St. Augustine claimed, that popular religion can become something other than civil or political theology—or an instrument of the "cave" or "regime." It's only with the coming of Christianity that popular religion could make a serious claim to be true religion. It's only with the coming of Christianity that ordinary people could make the claim for freedom that was formerly reserved for the philosophers.

It is, similarly, only with the coming of Christianity that religion also can't be reduced to natural theology—or a way of expressing the impersonal truth about nature discovered by the philosophers. Because the human difference is freedom, religion that does justice to who each of us is as a person must understand each of us as more than merely or even essentially a citizen or part of nature. Religion must do justice to what each of us can know about our irreducible interiority or personal identity. Religion must be in some sense personal.

No Christian, Locke is right to say, sounds properly Christian when speaking of religion established by civil law. Locke's attack on using political coercion to enforce religious belief and practice is aimed at both pagan and premodern Christian religious practice. Both, we might say, can be criticized as being a violation of natural rights and genuinely biblical personal insight. Tocqueville, we remember, seemed to criticize the Puritans for being too Christian, for violating personal conscientious freedom by criminalizing every sin. But his criticism, not unlike Locke's, was actually that the Puritans weren't Christian enough. They attempt to legislate based on Exodus, Leviticus, and Deuteronomy, on the basis of nothing actually found in the words of Jesus or the New Testament. The Puritans—by mixing up divine and moral/political law—weren't Christian enough.[10]

Both Locke and true Christians are about articulating a universal ethics available to all free persons, and both agree that to be free, and moral, is not to be fundamentally political or deeply or merely philosophical. And so sin—or, for Locke, what a free person can know independently of government about his or her moral duties—

has a binding status that depends not at all on criminal law. Personal identity doesn't depend on political formation, and totalizing or regime-based political legislation is always an offense against what we can know on our own (or free from government interference) about who we are. The personal ethics of Christianity and Locke are equally, if not identically, cosmopolitan—or available to person as person wherever he or she might be located in the world.

Ward has identified two indispensable roles the churches will fill in any free society.[11] They will support a common morality that is more than self-interest, because they will inevitably understand persons to be more relational and so dutiful than will legislation based on a wholly Lockean or individualistic view of the free person. And as autonomous institutions churches would serve as strong counterweights to the always imperial and comprehensive claims made by the state. The churches will resist, in other words, the political tendency to make totalizing claims on personal beings.

The solitary person can't resist the power of the state alone—either in thought or in action. Inwardness or subjectivity, to be real and genuinely democratic, can't be too lonely. This means that Locke doesn't actually share the anti-ecclesiasticism of Madison's *Memorial and Remonstrance*, which is very extreme in portraying one's conscientious right to discovering one's duty to one's creator as a solitary or lonely activity. The true difference between the revolutionary American and French Constitutions, John Courtney Murray points out, is that our freedom for the exercise of religion is, in part, freedom of the church, an indispensable condition of the effectual exercise of the inward or conscientious freedom of the more-than-political person. It's the revolutionary French who, by denying the autonomy of the churches, made democracy "totalitarian" and religion merely civil theological.[12]

The trouble is that Madison's anti-ecclesiastical *Memorial* actually corresponds better to the nominalism or radical individualism of Locke's post-Christian account of the person. The churches, to be an effective counterweight, must be understood to correspond to the truth about personal freedom. We are free from government and nature to be who we are as relational, social beings open, in common, to the truth about who we are as free persons.

The churches can't have counter-political or counter-cultural weight if words are merely weapons. For Locke, words exist to secure the solitary individual's survival and identity, but we can't, after all, have personal identity all alone. As Tocqueville pointed out, the intellectual withdrawal and emotional withdrawal—both in the name of avoiding being suckered—of democratic pop Cartesianism, which could just as easily be pop Lockeanism (the skeptical rejection of every form of personal authority), makes stable personal identity too difficult to sustain. It results in the surrender of any personal point of view to the impersonal forces that surround us— to public opinion (determined by no one in particular), to the objective expertise of science, to the imperatives of technology, to inevitable historical progress or drift.[13]

DEFENDING PERSONAL FREEDOM THESE DAYS

We can conclude that Locke's view of personal identity depends on the Christian view of personal liberation, on Christian support that's not merely salutary. The relationship between the indispensable churches and the secular state in even a Lockean or insistently personal society shouldn't really be tensionless. The churches should be relatively counterweighty or countercultural proponents of a more deeply social and so more genuinely personal account of who we are, one that generates generous and charitable duties that go far beyond the domain of rights.

Locke's attempt to turn God into a past-tense, unprovidential, unjudgmental, uncaring, yet somehow still personal being is at odds with his project of securing a free society based on secure personal identity. His attempt is also at odds, perhaps, with what he recognizes as true about the free, willful, and caring biblical Creator— a "who" and not some natural "what." Nobody can really explain how personal identity couldn't be social and relational; the solitary "I" of Locke or Descartes is impossible to sustain or even fully imagine. That's why authentically personal effort to limit government depends on the freedom of the church—an organized body of thought and action—to be a truthful reflection of who we are as truthful, social, personal, and relational beings under God.

Locke's nominalism—to a point—can easily be defended as a weapon that has freed us so successfully from traditional structures of oppression, beginning with kings and other tyrants and including the quite un-Christian ecclesiastical deformation of political life. Much of this liberation can be affirmed by a Christian as authentically personal. This means that the liberation of women to be free persons, the liberation of ordinary people from drudgery through technology, the universal recognition of human rights all are achievements that are authentically personal from both a fully Christian and Lockean view. A Christian has to add, of course, that some of the most remarkable egalitarian movements for liberation—such as abolitionism and the civil-rights movement—were, in their way, more Christian than merely Lockean, insofar as they were animated by the kind of personal love that leads to courage, charity, and the other virtues that a consistent Lockean would regard as being for suckers.[14]

So honest reflection on what's undeniably good about modern personal liberation reminds us that personal significance has to be more than for mere personal survival or not-not-being in order to secure our personal identities as unique and irreplaceable beings. The great danger in our immediate future might be surrendering the liberty imprecisely called autonomy in the name of the indefinite extension of personal life.

Our biotechnological lurching in the direction of indefinite longevity is in the service of an intensely personal goal, but at the expense of the loving, relational dimensions of personal existence that make life worth living. It's surely too hard—and surely self-destructive—to believe that one's personal being is entirely in one's own hands, just as it's too hard to believe that Being itself is extinguished with the end of one's own biological (the indispensable condition of one's personal) existence.

For most of our country's history, our authentic Christians and our Lockeans allied to defend the free person against various modern efforts to reduce persons to being mere parts of some whole. These Christians and Lockeans united against scientific efforts to reduce free persons to slaves based on their biological or racial differences from other persons. They united against eugenics schemes that aimed to eradicate or degrade persons for the benefit of the race, the nation, or the species. They united against Marxist and Nazi efforts to turn persons into fodder for History or the Fatherland. Strauss is a bit imprecise when he says they united for "natural right" and against "History."[15] They weren't about defending some classical or Aristotelian understanding of nature at all; they were about defending the equality of free persons under God.

But today our libertarians—or Lockeans on steroids—are about reconstructing every human institution in the service of the free or self-sufficient individual. So they're mistaken—even from Locke's view—about deconstructing the social or relational institutions in which we as free persons can learn the whole truth about who we are. This means, for one thing, that they're all about a kind of nihilism, which denies that Logos is personal. And for another, they're all about making genuine personal identity too lonely to be sustainable. For these reasons alone, we have to follow our philosopher-pope emeritus and take seriously, once again, the possibility of the science of personal theology. We have to recover the true foundation of who we are and what we're supposed to do.

NOTES

1. For more on how "personal" our current situation is, see my "Being Personal These Days," *A Second Look at First Things: The Hadley Arkes Festschrift*, ed. Francis J. Beckwith, Robert P. George, and Susan McWilliams (South Bend, IN: St. Augustine's Press, 2012), 297–328. This chapter as a whole attempts to sketch out a kind of history of being personal in the context of the fundamental alternatives of Logos being either personal or impersonal. I bring together much of what I've written for more particular purposes, and this is really no more than the beginning of a sketch. So I've deliberately been light on the notes.

2. The articulation of the alternative of the personal Logos here is almost entirely indebted to the various writings of Joseph Ratzinger, Pope Benedict XVI. For more, see chapter 7 of my *Modern and American Dignity* (Wilmington, DE: ISI Books, 2010). I'm especially indebted to his Regensburg Lecture, his encyclical on love, his *Introduction to Christianity* (San Francisco: Igna-

tius Press, 1994), his *In the Beginning . . .* (Grand Rapids, MI: Eerdmans, 2005), and a number of the chapters in *The Essential Pope Benedict XVI* (New York: Harper/Collins, 2007).

3. Everything you need to know about the "theory" of the philosopher-novelist-physician Walker Percy is found in *Lost in the Cosmos* (New York: Farrar, Straus, and Giroux, 1983). For my early attempt to ground "postmodernism rightly understood" as moral and metaphysical realism in that theory, see *Postmodernism Rightly Understood* (Lanham, MD: Rowman and Littlefield, 1999). Percy's twentieth-century Thomism can be understood to flesh out much of our philosopher-pope emeritus's intimations in the direction of a science of theology that incorporates what's true about Anglo-American empiricism and what's true about European existentialism, while showing that a realistic account of the personal Logos could bring those two partial truths together in the realistic truth about who each of us is as a being hardwired to both wonder and wander.

4. On everything that's said about Leo Strauss here, see his *What Is Political Philosophy?* and my "What Is Straussianism (according to Strauss)?" *Society* (December 2010), 50–57.

5. David Bentley Hart, *Atheistic Delusions: The Christian Revolution and Its Fashionable Enemies* (New Haven, CT: Yale University Press, 2009).

6. In this medieval interlude I am almost entirely indebted to Remi Brague, *The Law of God: The Philosophical History of an Idea* (Chicago: University of Chicago Press, 2008). I am also indebted to my reading of Leo Strauss's reading of Maimonides, but even then it's Brague who's shown me what Strauss had in mind. For more, see my "The Logos in Western Thought," *Modern Age* 51, no. 1 (Winter 2009): 42–46.

7. My view of Locke here comes through reading his *Second Treatise*, especially the chapter on property, in light of his more abstract analysis of being and human being in *An Essay Concerning Human Understanding.* I learned the most from Lee Ward's version of this approach to understanding Locke on self-ownership and personal identity. See Lee Ward, *John Locke and Modern Life* (Cambridge: Cambridge University Press, 2010). Ward notices that "for Locke, the human 'Person' has property in his or her actions because they are the products of rational choice—the primary property is the self. . . . Locke's account of property in the state of nature thus presupposes the concept of personal identity . . . in the *Essay*" (94). Ward is greatly indebted—as am I—to the path-breaking work on Locke by Michael P. Zuckert. See especially Zuckert's essays on Locke collected in *Launching Liberalism* (Lawrence: University Press of Kansas, 2002). I understand that what I say here is controversial and could be better supported by a more detailed textual analysis than I'm able to give here. On Locke's nominalism, I'm also indebted to some basic insights found in John Courtney Murray, *We Hold These Truths: Catholic Reflections on the American Proposition* (Kansas City, MO: Sheed and Ward, 1960).

8. Brague, *The Law of God.*

9. Ward, *John Locke and Modern Life*, 229.

10. On this interpretation of Tocqueville, see my "Tocqueville on How to Praise the Puritans Today," in *Alexis de Tocqueville and the Art of Democratic Statesmanship*, ed. B. Danoff and L. J. Herbert Jr. (Lanham, MD: Lexington Books, 2011), chapter 11.

11. See Ward, *John Locke and Modern Life*, chapter 6.

12. In my analysis of American constitutionalism here—including my view of Madison's "Memorial and Remonstrance"—I am almost entirely indebted to Murray, particularly to his *We Hold These Truths*. For more, see my *Modern and American Dignity* (Wilmington, DE: ISI Books, 2010), chapter 8.

13. Alexis de Tocqueville, *Democracy in America*, trans., ed., and introduced by Harvey C. Mansfield and Delba Winthrop (Chicago: University of Chicago Press, 2000), vol. 2, parts 1 and 2.

14. Important here are the efforts of neo-Puritanical recovery by the excellent novelist-essayist Marilynne Robinson. See, for example, her "A Great Amnesia," *Harper's Magazine* (May 2008): 17–21. See also my "Tocqueville on How to Praise the Puritans Today."

15. Leo Strauss, *Natural Right and History* (Chicago: University of Chicago Press, 1953). My point here is to say that the Straussian dichotomy between "nature" (good) and "History" (bad), although a useful polemical tool during the Cold War, fundamentally misconceives the political situation today.

PIERRE MANENT

BETWEEN NATURE AND HISTORY

Ralph C. Hancock

Pierre Manent (b. 1949) has been praised very plausibly as the greatest living political philosopher. Raised in a committed communist family, he converted to Catholic Christianity in his youth. In his intellectual formation he benefited richly from the French national educational meritocracy and from that system's then still robust commitment to classical educational ideals. Raymond Aron, perhaps the greatest social scientist of his century (though shamefully almost ignored in the contemporary academy), late in his remarkable career hired the young Manent as his assistant. Manent credits Aron with saving him from the fashionable contempt of intellectuals for politics (including, especially, those intellectuals who fancy themselves politically "engagés") and showing him the high price in study and reflection that must be paid for real political knowledge.

It was Aron who referred Manent to the writings of Leo Strauss. In a poignant passage of his memoir-interview, Manent recalls that it was Aron himself who, in a way, redirected Manent's inquiries toward Strauss. Manent explains that he longed for some intellectual measure beyond politics that Aron, a perfect gentleman apparently perfectly at home in a world without a transcendent measure, could not supply. Recognizing his assistant's irrepressible interest in the transcendent dimension of political questions, and having not the slightest taste for cultivating disciples, "Aron," Manent says, "led me to Strauss knowing that to go towards Strauss was to distance myself from him [Aron]."

This is not at all to say that Manent in any way left behind Aron's remarkable political discernment and judgment, or for that matter, that he was to find in Strauss's works fully satisfactory guidance in his quest for a "measure" of political judgment. On the contrary, the Parisian author, while acknowledging a great debt of gratitude to the great German émigré, is also quite capable (which for some reason is rare among American "Straussians") of criticizing him both candidly and trenchantly. One notable point of difference between Manent and Strauss concerns precisely the question that will concern us here—of the status of Christianity in the interpretation of modernity, as we shall see.

CHRISTIANITY AND MODERNITY

The question of the relation between Christianity and the modern project is by no means narrowly historical or hermeneutical, since it bears on the very coherence and legitimacy of the modern project and thus on the ideas and ideals that frame our perceptions and deliberations and profoundly condition our lives. If modernity in some way derives from and depends upon Christianity and does not know it, then it risks being blind to its own deepest motives. Likewise, if profoundly Christian assumptions or motives issue into the modern project in ways that Christians ignore, then Christians are subject to a blindness that mirrors that of (other) moderns.

Even if he has not simply dismissed it, Pierre Manent has been careful to keep his distance from the argument that modernity was somehow generated by Christianity, or from Christianity, the notion that modern ideas or ideals are Christian commitments in "secularized" form. This is an argument that has been favored, in one form or another, by authors ranging from Hegel and Constant in the aftermath of the French Revolution to Marcel Gauchet and Charles Taylor in our own time. But one has only to mention the name of Friedrich Nietzsche to be reminded that the secularization theory has by no means always been understood to be favorable to the honor of modern "rationalism" and its associated moral horizon. Hans Blumenberg thought it necessary to refute the secularization thesis in order to defend *The Legitimacy of the Modern Age.*[1] Indeed it is far from obvious how a Christian pedigree can be good news for a modernity that understands itself as the emancipation of humanity from any authority supposed to be above or beyond it.

To be sure, Manent by no means denies that Christianity is involved in the genesis of modernity. Indeed, one might say, the whole point of his most important philosophical book *The City of Man* is to uncover the Christian factor in this genesis, or more precisely, to "interpret the movement of modernity, the condition of modern humanity, according to a triangulation that takes equally seriously the ancient, the modern, and the Christian poles." It is "by taking seriously the Christian pole" that Manent proposes to "escape the alternative of Straussian 'naturalism' and Heideggerian 'historicism.'"[2] The Christian pole is involved not only negatively or polemically, that is, as the obvious adversary of modern rationalism, the *infâme* (infamous, despicable) entity that Voltaire and so many others resolved to *écraser* (crush). Although Manent is often at pains to emphasize this polemical opposition between modernity and Christianity, in fact his deeper and more original thesis is that it was the reciprocal critique of classical nature and Christian grace—the erosion of both natural and supernatural substance effected by this critique—that produced modernity, a denaturalized nature that yields waves of radicalization, that is, History.

Now, what makes Manent's view particularly challenging and even elusive is that he does not finally deny the pertinence or legitimacy of either side of this eroding process. Grace undermines the pretensions of nature to self-sufficiency, and nature debunks the claim to order human life by some supernatural light. Grace critiques nature, and nature, grace; each thus erodes the other—and both are, in a way, right. The outcome, or the resulting process, is modern man, a being who is always running away from the good, is empty and blind—but each of the reciprocal critiques from which this process springs is in a way compelling.

Notwithstanding his Catholic faith, then, Manent is wary of the believer's tendency to presume more understanding, and thus more authority, than he possesses. On the other hand, Manent does not—despite his very high regard for Aristotle—simply affirm the stability, the adequacy, the truth of the classical understanding of nature. This is where he parts company with Leo Strauss, as is clear, for example, in his reflections on Strauss's *Natural Right and History*.[3] In these remarks, Manent casts doubt on the classical philosophical espousal of the prideful virtue, or "virtuous" pride of the gentleman. He regards the Christian and therefore the modern critique of classical pride as philosophically pertinent, from the standpoint of self-knowledge as well as that of justice. He cannot finally regard the classical self-understanding as a stable standpoint from which to stand in judgment on the historical-philosophical process set in motion by the Christian and modern critiques of classical magnanimity. On the contrary, Manent appears to accept the core of the modern philosophical critique of the particularity of the city, a critique that builds upon the church's own critique. According to Manent, the (modern) philosopher is "with the Christian against the citizen because he is with the universal against the particular. [Philosophy] affirms . . . the universality of the Church against the particularity of the city; it criticizes the pride of this particularity; it takes a skeptical position above every human self-affirmation that remains particular."[4] In another text, however, Manent seems to come down firmly on the side of classical political philosophy. Against the modern pretension to have passed from a condition of heteronomy to one of autonomy, Manent counters that "the human condition continues to be determined by the relation that obtains between nature and law; and mankind has not ceased to obey a law. . . . [M]odern experience itself attests to the fact that the Greek understanding of the law was superior to the modern understanding."[5] In other words, we may think we have escaped the human condition of being ruled by something understood to be higher than ourselves, but our very ruling idea of freedom cannot help but be itself transformed into an authoritative regime—thus the superiority of the ancients. But note that Manent does not go so far in his approval of the classical understanding of regime as to accept the idea of the best regime as the rule of the wise, classically understood. His regime analysis remains open-ended and fluid and therefore historical, if not strictly historicist.

What, then, is Manent's stable standpoint of interpretation? He expressly repudiates the Hegelian claim to stand satisfied at the end of history. He has expressed the wish to do justice to Strauss's appeal to nature and at the same time to Heidegger's experience of "history"—but how can he avoid being swept up in the eroding process he attempts to describe? Manent agrees with Strauss that modern rationalism cannot give a satisfactory account of itself, that it is not stable, that it generates successive waves of history. Indeed he presses Strauss on the question of the anthropological ground of the power of these historicizing waves, a power that Strauss's articulation of modern rationalism does not seem fully to account for. But from what philosophical standpoint might it be possible to account for this historical power? Manent strives to give a full hearing to the claims of classical, Christian, and modern authors, but he lands in no camp, and it is not clear that his triangulation achieves stability.

There are passages in his work where Manent seems to be inviting us to consider actual, authoritative historical Christianity as a viable ground for an understanding of Western history. The real question, the question covered over by loose talk about "secularization," Manent is keen to remind us, is the question between modern atheistic rationalists, on the one hand, and on the other not some vague ideal of "Christianity" but the real, established, authoritative, commanding idea of Christendom that preceded and was the object of the modern revolt. The real issue, it appears, is between rationalist revolutionaries and reactionary defenders of an established church. But it is clear that Manent adopts neither of these partisan viewpoints. The fact that moderate friends (neither reactionary nor revolutionary) of modernity (Constant, Tocqueville) judged that the revolutionary doctrine of rights had exposed a moral void, which in some way had to be filled, is therefore not, as Manent sometimes seems to suggest, merely an accidental episode in the career of modernity. Rather, this fact must be taken seriously as an indication concerning modernity's essence, or lack thereof. It points up the possibility that modernity may fail to be defined by itself, that it may be essentially derivative of Christianity, despite the anti-Christian intention modernity sometimes reveals.[6]

If modernity is a blind process unleashed by a reciprocal critique that is in some way valid, then the question again arises how Manent is able to secure a stable ground from which to understand and assess this process. The closest thing in Manent's thought to a firm standpoint from which the historical dynamic might be understood and assessed is a broadly Thomistic understanding of the relation of nature and grace: "Grace has meaning only if it presupposes nature: it corrects and perfects nature, without destroying it."[7] This broadly Thomist standpoint seems to be closely connected to Manent's repeated and emphatic insistence on Christianity as a church established authoritatively in this world as the real rival of—and therefore, apparently, the real alternative to—modern rationalistic emancipation: as opposed to vague, modern, privatized, Christian "ideals" or "values," there was once, at least, "a real universal community."[8] And yet Manent, in *The City of Man*, is quite candid regarding the fragility, even the makeshift quality, of Thomas's "synthesis." He also reminds us from time to time that this established political "inscription" of Christianity was of necessity imperfect—that there is no adequate worldly representation of the universal communion that forms the horizon of Christian hope. The "real" universal communion is never quite actual; it cannot therefore be simply identified with the Roman Catholic Church or any actual human community. The linkage between nature and grace, this world and the next, can never be finally determined. Manent recognizes that the practical effect of such an idea of a universal communion unobstructed or undistorted by human pride and vanity in fact contributes to the endless modern process of the negation of concrete authorities. It is hard to avoid the conclusion that Christianity tends heavily, if not inevitably, to become an "ideal" that contributes to the blind historical dynamic of emancipation from all law contaminated by human partisanship—that is, from all law. No one knows better than Manent the vulnerability and instability of modernity's attempt to affirm itself and its autonomy, without admitting any content or substance beyond itself. Still, it is not clear that he has identified a clear alternative to this process.

Manent wants to understand modernity "on its own terms," so as not to disguise or dilute the question of truth. Modern liberalism pretends to reserve a place for religious truth in the "private" realm, but Manent shows that this privatization cannot help but effectively put the question of truth in parentheses and eventually cause members of a liberal democratic community to forget altogether even the very possibility of a truth transcending plain human interests and political convenience.

The central question concerning Christianity and modernity in Manent's writing is not the status of the idea of secularization. On close examination, he clearly knows that this idea is largely true, if most often abused. Here Manent's position indeed follows or, perhaps, runs parallel to that of Leo Strauss. Just as Strauss clearly recognizes (and for his part, I think, deplores) the work of Christianity in the oblivion of classical political philosophy, and thus in the rise of the modern philosophical project, but still wishes to reserve to political philosophers the right to speak of nonphilosophical causes,[9] so Manent wishes to reserve to Christians—or at least to those who take seriously the question of the truth of Christianity—the right to praise Christian effects within modernity. The real question for Manent, or concerning Manent, then, is not that of "secularization" but, rather, that of the Roman Catholic Church as the authentic form of Christianity. He often suggests that the question of the relation between modernity and Christianity must be framed in terms of the actual, effectual Christianity that the authors of modernity actually opposed, namely, Catholic Christendom. Manent understands very well that, as Daniel Tanguay has written, "the Reformation merely aggravated and complicated a tension that already existed within the medieval church."[10] This is the inevitable tension between the invisible and the visible communion, between the church's otherworldly aspiration and its necessary engagement with this world. Although a Catholic or a political philosopher might well argue that the Protestant Reformers did not quite know what they were doing when they asserted the otherworldliness of the church against its worldly entanglements, Manent knows that, on Christian grounds, they were not simply wrong.

The hesitation or indeterminacy in Manent's apparent privileging of the authoritative Roman Catholic Church in his interpretation of the human, political reality of Christianity might be compared to his own reading of Chateaubriand's delicate position. Unlike our contemporary secularization theorists, Chateaubriand wrote at once as a believer and as a historian. Or at least he seems to write from such a position. "It is truly hard to decide whether Chateaubriand is in fact a believer, or whether 'Christianity' is for him only an 'idea,' the 'Christian idea' . . . whose fecundity was first manifest in a 'limited' [*entravée*] way by the church and the churches, but is now destined to regenerate actual human society" through the principles of "liberty, equality, and fraternity."[11] Certainly Manent cannot share Chateaubriand's confidence (if that is what it is) in the progressive realization in this world of "Christian" ideals. But he knows as well as anyone that the church's manifestation of Christian truth can only have been a "limited" manifestation. It is indeed "truly hard to decide" whether Christianity is a church or an idea—and not only for Chateaubriand.

Manent nowhere denies, in fact he affirms, that modernity is unthinkable without Christianity. If he does not settle into a recognizable "secularization thesis," this is because the insuperable interpenetration of Christianity and modernity is neither simply good news (in Constant's sense) nor bad news (in Nietzsche's). What he finds "quite troubling" is the fact that this interpretation is used not, as it might be, to provoke or press the question of the truth of Christianity, and therefore the question of truth, but rather, to suppress this question, indeed to reinforce a suppression of the question of truth to which the liberal world is already so expertly committed. "The more the role of religion shrinks in the life of modern man, the more it grows in modernity's interpretation of its past. The more atheistic we are as human beings, the more believing as historians."[12] Pierre Manent wishes us to be human beings before we are historians, and so to subordinate the question of the interpretation of modernity to that of the meaning of our very humanity. What is at stake, first and foremost, is not our history but our self-understanding and, therefore, our souls.

Manent's point is not, finally, that either the anticlerical modern rationalists or the reactionaries who rejected the secularization argument in the name of the concrete authority of Rome were right but, rather, that until we consider they might have been right, until we take their truth-claims seriously, we will not be alert to the truth at work in democracy and to its danger—the truth of this "total Humanity, without possible political inscription, that necessarily arises from democracy as the shadow of its light."[13] The truth of our human condition lies not in ancient, medieval, or modern thought but somehow in the shadow of the light of modern, universalizing democracy. Christianity is in a way the truth of democracy, not certainly as (1) a final and true articulation of nature and grace, nor (2) as a rational project intelligible on its own terms, nor (3) as an "ideal" subordinated in practice to late-modern subjectivity, but somehow as a question. Christianity/modernity is for Manent a question intended to engage not only the mind but the heart and the soul.

ORIGINARY GREEK DYNAMISM

Manent's exploration of *The Metamorphoses of the City* is a bold venture in the interpretation of the West,[14] and one the author regards as a significant departure from his earlier work including, notably, *The City of Man*. The fundamental innovation proposed in this new interpretation or exploration of Western civilization as a whole lies in Manent's emphasis on the dynamism, the apparently boundless transformational energy of this civilization, not primarily as a result (as Leo Strauss would emphasize) of the fruitful tension between Greek reason and biblical revelation, but in fact *from the very moment of its emergence in ancient Greece*. From this perspective, not only modernity but even Christian universalism as a human and political force appear as derivative of a political-spiritual matrix that comes to view centuries before Christ.

This most recent meditation on the *dynamic* of the West, as deriving from an ancient Greek matrix, is by no means a dispassionate historical survey; rather, in it the author continues to grapple at the most fundamental level with our modern predicament, our predicament as moderns. It seems to be our fate to wish to be, to *will* to be modern, Manent observes, but we find it impossible to arrive at our destination, or even—which is perhaps after all the same thing—to be able to say just what it would mean to arrive. The question of the meaning of this modern predicament continues to inform the author's brilliant new excavation of the Greek source of Western energy and of the Roman, Christian, and modern expressions of this dynamism.

A first question arises: Is this "we" pronounced by Manent in "we moderns" sincere, or is it ironic? Does the author intend to heal us of this modern willing that appears increasingly as an unintelligible commandment (as might be said of Leo Strauss, Manent's main interlocutor, and not only in this book)? Or does he intend to renew this project by exhibiting the deepest sources of its dynamic energy?

Certainly Manent agrees with Strauss that modernity is a *project*, a purposive human undertaking. Its beginnings are marked by a stupendous faith in the human capacity to transform the human condition (Bacon, Descartes). But Manent insists that the scientific ambitions of the modern project must be understood as ancillary to what is primarily and fundamentally a *political* project.

If the modern project is a human and political project, however, then why does it seem to escape human control? Why does our modern will appear as a fate toward which we are driven? In order to overcome the fatality of modernity, Manent proposes that we understand the modern project as political and thus as fundamentally continuous with the original political project, that is, with the Greek polis. "If we wish to understand the modern project, we must understand it on the basis of this first complete mobilizing of human action, that is, the city."[15]

To see this continuity between the ancient city and the modern project it is necessary to open oneself to the transformative radicality and dynamism of the human political project in its Greek beginnings: the modern will to transform derives from the original capacity to act, a capacity the new and terrifying character of which informed the great Greek tragedies. This capacity is terrifying because it is most fundamentally the production (and not the discovery) of the common. By emphasizing the dynamic productive quality of our Greek beginnings, Manent proposes to repent at least a little for having once exaggerated the modern difference. (Here he was led astray by Tocqueville, he notes—and surely also by Strauss.) To overcome this exaggeration is to see that the history of the metamorphoses of political forms must be traced back far beyond or behind the articulation of the modern project to the "original conflagration" that the Greeks set off.[16] The dynamic of history is not a product of modernity but of our Greek origins: the "movement of the city" was already apparent to the Greeks, and "subsequent history appears overall as the ever renewed search for the political form that might make it possible to gather again the energies of the city while escaping the city's fate as free but destined to internal and external enmity."[17]

Manent shares with Strauss the conviction that the most acute self-understanding and therefore the most fundamental way of knowing is a political knowing. A science of politics is not some regional science, of interest merely to practitioners or specialists, but the only path to "the things themselves." The deepest stratum of the constitution of our Western humanity (the most human humanity there is, it seems clear) must therefore be sought in the birth of the polis in ancient Greece. It would be hard to attach more importance to understanding the polis than Manent does here. In this he might appear as very much a student of Strauss or as even more Straussian than Strauss.

Soon we begin to see, however, more clearly in *Les Metamorphoses* than in Manent's earlier work, that his recourse to the Greeks has a very different meaning than it does in Strauss's—perhaps indeed an opposite meaning. Strauss proposed a conception of the city *as understood by classical political philosophy* (that is, by Plato and Aristotle) as a definite and limited model that could serve as a natural (and thus fixed) standard of political judgment and evaluation. Manent, on the contrary, draws our attention to the energy and dynamism of the city, to its historical fecundity. To understand Manent's departure from Strauss we must attend to the phrase "as understood by classical political philosophy." It is not so much, for Strauss, the ancient city in itself that provides a fixed and definite standard of political and ethical judgment, but the position the political philosopher assumes in relation to the city. The philosopher proposes himself—his own philosophic activity—as the definitive fulfillment of the city's emulation of serene self-sufficiency. The philosopher is posited as "beyond" the city, but this "beyond" appears within the perspective of the city's own proposition of excellence; the city is therefore interpreted as fundamentally aristocratic, and so is the "philosopher" who stands above it but not really altogether beyond it. The philosopher anchors the city's striving, while limiting it, and at the same time grounds (and defines) the activity of philosophy in the highest aspirations of what is taken to be human nature more generally, that is, in the hierarchy of the city. Strauss's "political philosophy" is in this sense deeply political, political all the way down, or all the way up—up, that is, to his praise of the lofty, supposedly apolitical serenity of the philosopher.[18]

Manent casts away this Straussian philosophic anchor of the city (and this political anchor of philosophy) by problematizing the relation between the philosopher and the city. That is, by setting aside the philosopher's interpretation of the city he exposes both the city and philosophy to the dynamism of History. But if nature understood politically is movement, then this political science must be a science of movement; Manent seeks, not a science of History, but a science of *movement* as a *political* science.[19] For Manent, the polis is somehow at once the touchstone of true science and a moving target. In taking leave of Strauss he now declares, more clearly than ever, anchors away! But, unlike Heidegger, he is not resigned to our ship's being rudderless.

Manent hopes that an examination of the history of the political forms that flowed from the originary Greek production of the polis can help address the present exhaustion of political forms. The first moderns suffered and benefited from a profusion, an accumulation of forms, but now our political imagination has become sterile. Whereas Strauss seeks to reground political and ethical judgment by directing modern readers to a science of regimes within the classical form of the ancient polis, Manent hopes to nourish our political imagination through a science of the movement or metamorphosis of political forms.

This turn from philosophically anchored regime to the metamorphosis of forms involves a partial rehabilitation of poetry in relation to philosophy. As politics and war are prior to "nature," so is poetry prior to philosophy. Mythical man ignores clear distinctions between gods and men and beasts; his poetry is poetry of metamorphosis. Myth becomes poetry proper, and perhaps Western man is born, in the Homeric articulation of man as mortal. (Both Homer and Christianity present us with the death of a young man; from this point of view, Jesus might appear as the synthesis of Hector and Patrocles. But Socrates is old, and he leaves no remains to raise the question of burial rites.) Classical philosophy suppresses the awareness of humanity as tragic mortality by turning attention away from human individuality and toward an impersonal eternity. Christianity seeks instead to assume our tragic mortality within a larger divine comedy, in which transcendence of our mortal divisions and enmities is somehow compatible with personal immortality. Modern philosophy in a way assumes the Christian program of overcoming death but in another sense furthers the classical philosophical suppression of mortality by diverting man's attention to the conquest of death, as if the ongoing attempt to make us a little "less mortal" could really solve our problem.

When we contemplate the history of political forms thus set in the context of the question of mortality, we can see that, whereas Strauss wishes to temper the modern conquer-death project by drawing upon the ancient ignore-death project, Manent would perhaps temper the philosophical non-death project as a whole, ancient as well as modern, by drawing upon a Christian hope tempered by a classical poetic or tragic sensibility. To put this another way: Manent wishes to temper Christian and post-Christian universalism by confronting us with the insuperability of the political dimension of the human condition. He conceives this political dimension, however, not through the aristocratic lens of political philosophy but through the democratic movement of its history.

Through readings of great finesse of Homer, Aristotle, Cicero, Augustine, and dialogue with moderns such as Montesquieu and Rousseau, Manent articulates our political humanity as structured by number, that is, by the primordial political dialectic between the few and the many, and by the emergence of the alternative structuring of the Western political horizon in terms of the complementarity between the One and the all. Our Western political history can be reduced to this: the war-ridden tension between the few and the many is partially superseded by the project of peace of all under One. But this project of perpetual, universal peace cannot succeed, and so pacification is always accompanied by the exacerbation, the radicalization of war.

Manent reveals these articulations already at work within the camp of the Greeks in the *Iliad*. He then reminds us of the classic presentation of the conflict between oligarchy and democracy in Aristotle's *Politics*, but he questions Aristotle's attempt to settle this conflict theoretically by appealing to the reflective choice of a noble happiness. In fact such a settlement reflects the unseen authority of a philosophic One who effectively takes the side of the few who are thus charged with educating the many for citizenship.

The fragility of this aristocratic strategy of classical political philosophy is apparent, Manent thinks, in the "incomparable tact" with which Aristotle treats the tension between the few and the many. Aristotle's idea of "reflective choice" strives to master "the amplitude of political possibilities" but cannot really do so. Politics is inherently democratizing, but Aristotle strives valiantly to give a stable aristocratic look to the dynamic political phenomena.[20]

The limitations of the Greek philosophic strategy become apparent in the core of Manent's book, which, with the help of Cicero, Augustine, Machiavelli, and Montesquieu, treats the science of Rome. We need a science of Rome because Greek political science (and Leo Strauss's political philosophy) fails to see clearly beyond the bounds of the experience of the Greek city, that is, the experience of the dialectic of the few and the many. *There is no Greek One.* The most telling evidence of this is that, as Montesquieu had already noticed, a full account of monarchy never emerges from Aristotle's study of regimes. Greek reason was enmeshed in the tension between aristocracy and democracy and never clearly envisioned the possibility of unity, that is, of a unified people under a king or a Caesar or of a unified humanity under a God. Only the science of Rome can give us access to the problem of *form* that is more powerful and more fundamental than that of *regime*, to an awareness of the human *condition* that extends further than a knowledge of our political *natures*, to the perspective in which the universality of the One and the All overcomes the tension between the few and the many. And for Manent the significance of the emergence of this Roman science is far from simply political: "Thus," he states, "the most delicate questions of morality, and even the most difficult questions of ontology (such as the status of individuality) are seen to be bound up with the question of political form." And since the decisive breakthrough in political form was an accomplishment of pagan Rome, Manent does not shrink from concluding that "the transition from Ancients to Moderns already happened in Rome at the end of the republican period."[21]

We learn from Montesquieu that the rise of Caesarism cannot be adequately understood as a response to the corruption of the classical republic. The empire did not only respond to the vices but more fundamentally inherited the energies of the city, energies that could no longer be contained within the city. Whereas Strauss endorses the Aristotelian judgment of excess as vice, Manent accepts Montesquieu's view that the human spirit exceeds the bounds of the city. The decisive evidence of the power and the elusive meaning of Rome is that the Romans were always willing to die for something that meant more to them than life. The city and the soul cannot be contained within the "natural" boundaries posited by Strauss and by his classical political philosophers.

For the classics, only philosophers transcended the city; philosophers articulated their own transcendence on the basis of the city's dialectic of few and many; therefore, no one really transcended the city. Rome was constantly agitated and driven to expansion by passions that exceeded its boundaries and by its willingness to die for some glory that eluded it. Christianity attributed this glory to a fully transcendent God, and for the first time proposed to all mankind a fellowship in a truly universal and eternal city, the City of God.

Manent's discussion of Augustine's engagement with Rome hinges on the problem of glory. The Roman passion for glory is at once nearest to and furthest from Christian humility. A powerful contradiction lies at the heart of the passion for glory: this passion seeks to transcend our humanity, yet it depends on the opinion of humanity. Glory is the greatest intensification of sinful pride and selfishness and yet lies at the threshold of a movement beyond the sinful self. Christian conversion can be seen as the antithesis of pagan glory or as its only true fulfillment. Christianity proposes to root out the human dependence on human opinion and yet also to fulfill the movement of human opinion toward something above it.

But can Christianity even conceive of an "above" without confirming its dependence on human opinion? Can a human being conceive a universal orientation to a divine One beyond the city without taking his bearings from the elevation configured by the city's tension between the few and the many? Manent deftly shows the presence of this problem in Augustine: the Christian rejection of Roman glory always runs the risk of collapsing into a complacent preoccupation with security and comfort. Max Weber's Calvinist capitalists already begin to rear their heads in Augustine's critique of the vanity of Roman glory.

Can Christian Rome definitively transcend pagan Rome? Can the perspective of the One/All represent a concrete and meaningful humanity to itself without drawing upon the substantial but theoretically and morally limited claim of the few over the many? Can there be conscience without honor?

Christianity proposes to purify and unify the whole soul, affective as well as intellectual, the heart as well as the mind (as Augustine argues, against Porphyry's Platonic elitism). A true salvation must be a universal salvation, at least in principle— that is, a salvation that addresses all humanity because it addresses the whole human being and not only (as is the case for the Platonists) the intellectual part. Manent observes that the Christian idea of the soul could not even have been formulated without the philosophic proposition of a distinction between soul and body. But can this distinction be sustained when wholly severed from perspective of the few versus the many, that is, from the aristocratic configuration of the classical city and the classical soul? Can the height of the One avoid collapsing into the width of universalist democracy without drawing upon an Aristocratic and Aristotelian pride? Is the effectual, political or post-political truth of rigorous transcendence a flat and relativistic subjectivism, or "equality by default?"[22]

Two things prevent the height of the City of God from collapsing into the width of a formless humanism or equality by default. One is the remnants of the classical, hierarchical city and soul within Christianity. The other is the inheritance of the particularism, the plain Jewish positivity of law and revelation.

Pierre Manent provides us with a wealth of new insight into the relation of Christianity to modernity and the antecedents of both in the political dynamics of the ancient world. Still, in the last analysis, I am not sure he has distanced himself from Leo Strauss or from Tocqueville as much as he seems to imply. By tracing Christian and modern universalism back, through Rome, to the original Greek emergence of politics itself, Manent seems to reground the legitimacy of the modern age. Yet he seems fully aware of the blindness of this universalism (the One/All configuration of transcendence) in its endless critique of all concrete and inherently particularist and aristocratic affirmations of human meaning (the few/many axis).

Insofar as the modern project puts the full authority of "reason" behind this endless critique, it seems reasonable and indeed wise, contrary to Manent's latest approach, to emphasize the peculiar force, the blind but resilient power of modernity as distinct from the spiritual power of Roman transcendence (both pagan and Christian). Leo Strauss, I have argued, did not ignore the spirit of Rome but chose deliberately, if perhaps quixotically, to ground "reason" in "nature" as articulated by the classical political philosophers. Tocqueville, for his part, sees clearly the implication of Christianity in the modern passion for equality but does not see this as automatically mitigating the radical and destructive power of the idea of *le semblable* (the same).

In this latest, profoundly original and insightful exploration of the metamorphoses of the city, Manent's political-philosophical perspective and rhetorical position appear still to be evolving. Profoundly concerned with the complacent apolitical drift of the West (and of Europe, in particular), he endeavors to uncover the *political* antecedents of Christian and modern universalism. He declines, however, to adopt Strauss's strategy of anchoring politics in nature (or, one might say, "nature" in politics), and so "the political" itself proves to be vulnerable to the historical force of the One/All. At the same time, the Christian critique of classical, limited, and aristocratic transcendence is in a sense spiritually validated in Manent's account by its anticipations in Roman glory, but by this very validation Christianity risks being swept up in the endless history of equality. The promised benefits of seeing modernity as political, then, risk being undermined by the insight into the boundless historical fecundity of politics. To understand Christianity as a human act of communion cannot rescue the human—and therefore political—meaning of Christianity if action itself is then understood apart from any natural ends or limits. We are left with new insight into the relation of Christianity to modernity.

If Christianity knows the "truth about man," as the young Pierre Manent concluded more than four decades ago, then this is because it knows that the form of universality (Roman-modern) cannot do without the content of the (Greek) city or without the command of the (Jewish) law. Leo Strauss insisted that we must reject the modern synthesis of law and reason and adhere either to one or to the other of the great alternatives. Manent recognizes the compelling and irreversible character of our interest in holding the Greek and Jewish elements of our humanity together. Indeed, if Strauss is right that both these alternatives are great, then the effectual truth of Strauss's counsel that we must strive to be either one or the other (either a believer or a philosopher, but not both) is in effect that we are condemned to be both and thus to be neither—that is, to manage our modernity as best we can by appealing to positive religion and to conventional nobility. Conscience needs both law and honor (and more concretely, their intersection in covenant and sacrament), or else it must collapse into subjective rights. And so I find that Manent's brilliant and penetrating tour of the history of political forms leads me back again into Tocqueville's camp: if reason must somehow assume practical, political responsibility for a transcendence it cannot master (by reducing it to a stable "nature"), this can only be by acknowledging the universality of justice without forgetting elevation or disdaining the support of revealed religion.[23]

NOTES

1. Hans Blumenberg, *The Legitimacy of the Modern Age*, trans. Robert M. Wallace (Cambridge: MIT Press, 1985).

2. Pierre Manent, "De la causalité historique," in *Enquête sur la démocratie* (Paris: Gallimard, 2007), 60 (all translations are mine). I say "his most important philosophical book *The City of Man*" meaning before the recent publication of *Les Métamorphoses de la cité*, discussed in the latter part of this essay.

3. Pierre Manent, "The Argument of *Natural Right and History*," unpublished paper presented at a conference, "Leo Strauss's *Natural Right and History:* A Reassessment," at Michigan State University, April 22, 2001.

4. Manent, "De la causalité historique," 60–61.

5. Ibid., 81.

6. Compare "la raison des Lumières croit plus de choses qu'elle n'en sait" (The Enlightenment believes more than it knows). Pierre Manent, *Cité de l'homme* (Paris: Librairie Arthème Fayard, 1994), 26.

7. Pierre Manent, "Sur la notion de sécularisation," in *Enquête*, 430–31.

8. Ibid., 60.

9. Compare my reading of Strauss's resistance to the "secularization thesis" in *Calvin and the Foundations of Modern Politics* (South Bend, IN: St. Augustine Press, 2011), 165–77.

10. Daniel Tanguay, "Christianisme et modernité: Pierre Manent, critique de la thèse de la sécularisation," paper delivered at a symposium on Science, Reason, and Modern Democracy, Michigan State University, April 17–18, 2009. This first part of the present paper is adapted from remarks presented at this same conference.

11. Manent, "Sur la notion de sécularisation," in *Enquête*, 425. We are reminded of Tocqueville's puzzlement (perhaps interpreted too hastily by Manent, in *Tocqueville and the Nature of Democracy*, trans. John Waggoner (Lanham, MD: Rowman and Littlefield, 1996), as simple skepticism about the Americans' interest in truth) before the this-worldly faith of Americans.

12. Manent, "Sur la notion de sécularisation," 423.

13. Manent, "Christianisme et démocratie," in *Enquête*, 463–64.

14. Pierre Manent, *Les Métamorphoses de la cité: Essai sur la dynamique de l'Occident* (Paris: Flammarion 2010).

15. Ibid., 10.

16. Ibid., 22.

17. Ibid., 12.

18. This is the interpretation of Strauss that is developed in my "Leo Strauss and the Nobility of Philosophy," chapter 5 of *Responsibility of Reason* (Lanham, MD: Rowman and Littlefield, 2011).

19. Manent observes that nature has three meanings: the tragic (birth, or natality), the philosophic (finality, or teleology), and the political (movement).

20. Manent, *Les Métamorphoses de la cité*, 125, 123, 124.

21. Ibid., 180.

22. See Philippe Bénéton, *Equality by Default* (Wilmington, DE: ISI Books 2004).

23. See the last chapter in volume 2 of *Democracy in America*. This is the broadly Tocquevillean view I develop in *The Responsibility of Reason: Theory and Practice in a Liberal Democratic Age* (Lanham, MD: Rowman and Littlefield, 2011).

7

CATHOLICISM AND THE CONSTITUTION

James R. Stoner, Jr.

In January 1899, Pope Leo XIII issued an apostolic letter denouncing certain "new opinions" known under the name "Americanism." The gist of these opinions was that, in the pope's words, "in order to more easily attract those who differ from her, the Church should shape her teachings more in accord with the spirit of the age and relax some of her ancient severity and make some concessions to new opinions . . . not only in regard to ways of living, but even in regard to doctrines which belong to the deposit of the faith." Concerning the latter, as you might imagine, the Holy Father was unequivocal: "Let it be far from anyone's mind to suppress for any reason any doctrine that has been handed down." Concerning ways of living, the papal response was more nuanced, for so long as "the divine principle of morals [is] kept intact," the church can accommodate herself "to the exigencies of various times and places [and] to the character and genius of the nations which she embraces." But ways of living and ways of thinking are intertwined, and the pope made clear that what counted for liberty in the one was not to be confused with license in the other. The so-called Americanist mistake was to suppose that "the newly given civil freedom which is now the right and the foundation of almost every secular state" entailed a liberty for Catholics to ignore the moral and religious teaching of the church, allowing "each one to follow out more freely the leading of his own mind and the trend of his own activity . . . unmindful both of conscience and of duty." The natural virtues of men of action cannot be allowed to eclipse, much less dispense with, the virtues of faith, hope, and charity or the virtues associated with prayer, contemplation, and service. Modern industry and industriousness and modern science, wrote the pope, are to be welcomed as "widening [the] scope of public well-being" and as contributing "to the progress of learning and wisdom," but "only on the condition of recognizing the wisdom and authority of the Church."[1]

Now the archbishop of Baltimore, Cardinal Gibbons, to whom the letter was addressed, responded to the pope with the reassurance that the American clergy and laity did not hold any such "new opinions," and Leo XIII graciously accepted the reply. Moreover, the historian of the episode believes the Holy Father's chief target was not the Americans at all but some European theologians, particularly in France, who celebrated a translation of a biography of the New York–born founder of the Paulist Fathers, Isaac Hecker, with praise for his "Americanism," meaning by the term a Catholicism that dispensed with pious ceremony and medieval doctrine in favor of an unmediated engagement with the modern world and secular democratic society.[2] Indeed, in the 1899 letter, the pope himself had made plain that under the name "Americanism" he did not mean to condemn "certain endowments of mind which belong to the American people" (the American character, in other words) and especially not "your political condition and the laws and customs by which you are governed."[3] Four years before, in another encyclical, he had praised "the young and vigorous American nation" and acknowledged "the equity of the laws which obtain in America and . . . the customs of the well-ordered republic. For the Church amongst you," he continued, "unopposed by the Constitution and government of your nation, fettered by no hostile legislation, protected against violence by the common laws and the impartiality of the tribunals, is free to live and act without hindrance," and he was clearly aware of the explosive expansion of Catholicism in America during the nineteenth century. The Holy Father praised as well the man he called "the great Washington," a man "of genius and statesmanship," especially for the words of his Farewell Address proclaiming that "without morality the State cannot endure . . . [and that] the best and strongest support of morality is religion."[4]

This forgotten quarrel between Catholicism and Americanism, then, was resolved amicably enough at the moment, and its terms were anyway a bit misleading, but I call attention to the episode because I think it indicates a larger tension between Catholics and the Constitution of the United States that is always under the surface of American politics and that sometimes erupts in political controversy. On the one hand, the Constitution forbids religious tests for office, prohibits religious establishment, and protects religious liberty, thereby insuring the freedom of the church from political interference and the equal citizenship of Catholics—so different in every respect from England in the decades before the Constitution was written. On the other hand, Catholics and non-Catholics have often distrusted one another over the course of our constitutional history and have wondered how deeply compatible are their respective ends. While aware of the blessings accruing to the church from religious liberty, Pope Leo added that "she would bring forth more abundant fruits if, in addition to liberty, she enjoyed the favor of the laws and the patronage of public authority."[5] But to this the Constitution is an obstacle. Today, the church often seems to receive from the law both disfavor and a withdrawal of patronage—sometimes in the name of the Constitution itself. Can a good Catholic today be a loyal friend to the Constitution? Can a loyal constitutionalist welcome or accept faithful Catholics as fellow citizens? Can American Catholics combine in their own lives and practice two seemingly opposite principles of authority: in political life, government by consent and the sovereignty of the people; in moral and religious life, the doctrine of the Magisterium and the sovereignty of Christ the King? I want to answer all these questions with "Yes," but I do not want to say it is easy. To explain my confidence, but also my hesitation, I discuss four moments in American constitutional development as they relate to what one might call, for lack of a better phrase, the Catholic question—not claiming to give a comprehensive treatment of the subject but hoping to shed some light on both our constitutional history and our predicament in the present. These four moments are the Founding, the aftermath of the Americanist controversy, the aftermath of World War II, and our present age.

CATHOLICS AND THE FOUNDING

Beginning with the Founding is familiar to constitutional originalists, and it makes sense in any study of the Constitution for two reasons. First, it is a standard maxim that the law should be interpreted in light of the intention of the lawmakers, and not merely their bare words, because laws are made to achieve some end or good. Second, it is evident that, whatever their limitations, the American Founders were men of political wisdom. Meeting in a provincial town on the edge of European-Atlantic civilization, they self-consciously designed a form of government meant to institute a "new order of the ages" and to revive self-government or republicanism, a form discredited since the fall of the Roman republic almost two millennia before—and they succeeded in this extraordinary ambition, not only creating the most powerful political entity since ancient Rome but changing the terms of world politics, all in the short space of two hundred years. Regarding the Catholic question, the critical figures among the Founders are the Carrolls of Maryland.[6] Charles Carroll of Carrollton was a signer of the Declaration of Independence, a wealthy financier of the American Revolution, an architect of the Maryland Senate, and later a confidant of Alexis de Tocqueville when Charles Carroll was in his final year of life and Tocqueville was on his youthful tour of America. Daniel Carroll was Charles's elder cousin, who took his place in the Philadelphia Convention in

1787 when Charles was detained by business in the Maryland Senate. He signed the Constitution and later sat on the commission that laid out Washington, DC. John Carroll was Daniel's younger brother and Charles's schoolmate in Belgium who became a Jesuit priest. He joined the unsuccessful diplomatic expedition to Quebec in 1776, was appointed the first bishop in the young United States (and was later made its first archbishop), founded Georgetown University, and was a friend of George Washington (Daniel and John's sister having married the owner of the plantation across the Potomac from Mount Vernon).

The Carrolls were patriotic supporters of the Revolution, the Declaration of Independence, and the Constitution—and thus of republican self-government. At the same time, they seem clearly to have adhered faithfully to Catholic orthodoxy. The evidence is, as one would imagine, strongest in the case of Archbishop John, not only in his life's work but also in his occasional publications, for example an early pamphlet written before his bishopric, refuting a former priest who renounced transubstantiation.[7] In that essay, Fr. Carroll agrees with his opponent that liberty of conscience is central to Christian life but assures his readers that such liberty is entirely consistent with Catholic doctrine. Church dogma is meant as a guide to the formation of conscience and is a better and surer guide than mere individual effort, a host of minds and witnesses providing a more secure foundation for an individual wagering the eternal fate of his soul (pace John Locke, who says to trust no one else except oneself with such a prize at stake).[8] Bishop Carroll endorsed George Washington's idea that all religions who taught good citizenship were equally welcome in America—Catholics, Jews, as well as Protestants, even Quakers (who were good citizens in Washington's view in most, though not all, respects as the Quakers refused to bear arms).[9] Under a pseudonym, Carroll wrote a letter to John Fenno's *Gazette of the United States* to denounce a Protestant minister's claim that the American Revolution was part of the progress of Protestant liberty, pointing out that Catholics fought for the patriot cause, which was itself in opposition to a Protestant throne.[10] Indeed, as Charles Carroll discovered in practice, the revolution removed the old collusion of (Episcopal) church and state in Maryland, where Catholics had been disenfranchised in colonial times and liberated only when the English left. Simultaneously, John Carroll, by coincidence one of three Jesuits in Rome when the pope suspended the Society of Jesus under pressure from the French king, likewise bet on separation of church and state as better for the freedom of the church.

Generalizing from the thinking of the Carrolls, as shared by Washington, here is what I conclude from the Founding: Being a good American requires loyalty to the Constitution and an unfeigned willingness to abide by its procedures and principles—but the reasons any individual or any group of individuals, even any church, have for their loyalty and willingness are matters of conscience that must be settled by minds according to what they understand to be the truth. This liberty of conscience is the true "new order of the ages" embodied in the Constitution. Unlike the ancient polis, whose republican government supposed a common mind-set in the people (a civic religion, if you will), American constitutionalism leaves citizens free to follow the truth as they understand it, respecting one another's differences and agreeing to abide by constitutional forms in the use of public power. Respecting one another does not mean ignoring each other's claims. Argument must be free and vital if truth is to be discovered and held as truth by those who are able; and since conversion is possible, even desirable, the way must always be left open to it. The Constitution and its principles themselves need defense, which will be differently made to different constituencies—to Catholics on the basis of natural law, to Protestants by biblical reference or private light, to secularists by history or ideas about individual self-development, and so forth. Not every set of fundamental interests or first principles can support taking the constitutional oath in good faith: not a Marxist's or a Nazi's, no longer a slaveholder's (after the Thirteenth Amendment), not a jihadist's. But whether the Constitution can be justified by reference to truly first things is something that each tradition or interest or community must work out for itself. My point is that American constitutionalism does not require any single creed but, rather, an agreement. It is in this sense a compromise and based on the morality of compromise: a promise to keep one's word in the performance of duties considered licit by an uncompromised faith. The Carrolls and the Catholics were not the only indicators of this understanding, but they were critical exemplars, as members of a religious minority then widely distrusted by the dominant faith. They were, a fact no one can gainsay, loyal players from the start. At the same time, since the political culture and the society underlying American constitutionalism were open to change (and indeed, encouraged by the Constitution to grow and develop), the constitutional agreement was itself dynamic rather than static in design. Human nature itself was thought by the Founders to thrive upon such dynamism, to welcome growth.

FATHER JOHN RYAN AND THE WELFARE STATE

Fast forward, now, across the nineteenth century, with its often bitter disputes between Protestants and Catholics, to the second moment I would like to examine: the aftermath of the Americanist controversy. In May 1891, eight years before the issue came to a head, Pope Leo XIII published *Rerum Novarum*, the encyclical that launched the modern teaching of the Roman Catholic Church on social justice.[11] In the intervening years, the new encyclical was assigned to a young American seminary student in St. Paul, Minnesota, who discovered in it his life's work. John Ryan was born to a large farm family in Minnesota, and he went on to become a professor of moral theology at the Catholic University of America in Washington and the most influential member of the clergy on the formulation of social policy in the first half of the twentieth century.[12] Sent to Catholic University by Archbishop Ireland after his ordination, Fr. Ryan studied moral theology and produced as his dissertation what would become his first book, *A Living Wage*.[13] Picking up from Pope Leo's comment in *Rerum Novarum* that the "great and principal duty [of employers] is to give every one what is just" in terms of wage, Ryan argued that government should insist that every workingman be paid enough at least to support himself and his family decently, and that every unmarried woman have a wage sufficient to support herself during her single life.[14] Ryan's argument was based on three factors: "first, that God made the earth for all human beings; second, that men must get their livelihood from the earth by labor; and third, that it is possible for a part of the people of any country to get possession of the earth—it follows that the laborer has a right against the masters of the earth to a decent livelihood, [since] every person has a right of access to the earth, an equal right with everybody else."[15] It is not sufficient to leave the determination of wages to the market, where unequal bargaining power can make a man willing to contract for less than the cost of subsistence. "Since God has imposed upon [man] the obligation of attaining his eternal end, his eternal salvation, God wishes him to have the means which are adequate to that purpose. . . . Therefore the persons in control of the goods of the earth have no more right to exclude the man who performs a reasonable amount of labor from this measure of the good things of life than they have to deprive him of his liberty, or to compel him to work as a slave." This is "self-evident," states Fr. Ryan. "The right to a living wage is one of the natural rights."[16]

Fr. Ryan did not study with a major economist at Catholic University, but he cites as a major influence on his thinking the Progressive economist Richard T. Ely, whose many books he read.[17] In fact he developed a sufficient relation with Ely that the latter wrote an introduction to his *Living Wage*. Ely was dean of the Progressive economists. He was a founder of the American Economic Association, who had earned his Ph.D. in Germany and began his teaching career at the Johns Hopkins University (where he counted among his first students Woodrow Wilson, on whose Ph.D. committee he sat) before moving to the University of Wisconsin for most of his long career. Ely took a historical approach to economics. In Ely's view Adam Smith's *Wealth of Nations* may have described what was needed for economic growth in his own age, but the so-called system of natural liberty had nothing permanent about it; in the industrial age, economic growth depended upon organization, and the wastefulness of free-market competition had become irrational, begging for national supervision of economic life. Ely rejected socialism as itself dogmatic, but he accepted the socialists' premise that economic life was socially organized, just not their conclusion that all ownership should be in the state.[18] Inequalities are natural, he wrote, but this meant that the state was justified in interfering with "liberty of contract," which would only exploit those inequalities. True freedom is a positive freedom that society achieves with the help of social legislation. Ely's economics is secular in itself, but coming from a background in Puritan New England, he is also described as a founder of the Social Gospel movement and in fact wrote a book on the subject.[19] One gets a flavor of this in an article he published on "Industrial Liberty" in 1902, which concludes: "We have, then, among others, three goals of industrial evolution—liberty, equality and fraternity—but the greatest of these is fraternity."[20] The echo of St. Paul is unmistakable. The theological virtues of Aquinas have yielded to the slogan of *la Révolution française.*

From different premises, then, the Catholic theologian and the Progressive economist reached a harmony of sentiment or maybe just happened to live in circumstances where their shared ideas were in the forefront and their implicit differences suppressed. Fr. Ryan promoted not only a minimum wage law but also legislatively supported social insurance for unemployment and old age, public housing, labor participation in industrial management, and more generally, the recognition of labor unions, vocational education, and an end to child labor in factories and the like. In the aftermath of World War I, he worked with the American bishops to devise and promote a document called "The Bishops' Program on Social Reconstruction," published in a book that includes a series of lectures on the various topics just listed given by Ryan at Fordham University in 1919. Although many of the reforms resemble ideas promoted by Sidney Webb's Fabian Socialist Society in England, the bishops note, they firmly reject the aims of socialism:

> It seems clear that the present industrial system is destined to last for a long time in its main outlines. That is to say, private ownership of capital is not likely to be supplanted by a collectivist organization of industry at a date sufficiently near to justify any present action based on the hypothesis of its arrival. This forecast we recognize as not only extremely probable, but as highly desirable for, other objections apart, Socialism would mean bureaucracy, political tyranny, the helplessness of the individual as a factor in the ordering of his own life, and in general, social inefficiency and decadence.[21>]

Like Leo XIII, even as they denounce socialism, they would reform capitalism in the name of social solidarity: "The present system stands in grievous need of considerable modifications and improvement," principally reducing inefficiency and waste, providing sufficient incomes for most, and preventing excessive incomes for a few. Not that every proposed reform needs to be dominated by the state.[22] To Fr. Ryan, for example, the state has a role to play in social insurance but only until the worker receives a sufficient wage to save and buy insurance on his own, the more responsible solution since it makes him an owner not a mere beneficiary.[23] The human person, his moral virtue, and his eternal destiny remain the Catholic's anchor in nature—but it is a person for whom submission to moral law is not a lifestyle choice but an obligation: "Thou shalt not covet," "thou shalt not steal."

What is the meaning of this confluence of Catholic social teaching and Progressivism for the rise of the welfare state in America and for the constitutional changes, not to say "Constitutional Revolution," that ensued?[24] At least this: We need to be cautious in thinking of the Progressives as the sole architects of the American welfare state. We all know, after all, that that system at the federal level was the achievement of the New Deal and not the Progressive Era, which made only initial reforms. The major pieces of New Deal legislation that remain in place today—the Social Security Act, the National Labor Relations Act, and the Fair Labor Standards Act—enact critical elements of Fr. Ryan's program: respectively, social insurance, the recognition of unions, and the minimum wage. Even considering the electoral politics of the 1920s and 1930s, it is clear that enactment of the New Deal depended on incorporating the Catholic vote into the coalition, and I think it bears reflection what this means for the thought implicit in the policies enacted. Progressivism emerged from Protestant America, sometimes directly in the form of Social Gospel, sometimes through secularized thought in the emerging academic social sciences. What put Progressives' reforms over the top, however, was their commingling with Catholics and Jews, people adhering to or at least raised in traditions of law and morality that antedated by some time the philosophy of John Stuart Mill and antedated even the Constitution of the United States and its Enlightenment forebears. The social solidarity and moral duty these traditions promoted had theoretical foundations in the philosophy of Aristotle, amplified for Catholics in the theology of Thomas Aquinas and the medieval scholastics. And while it is an interesting question (and much too complex for an aside) how Catholic natural law and modern natural rights relate to one another, it is no accident that—in the era when, as James Ceaser has explained, Progressive intellectuals had discarded the natural-rights foundation of American constitutionalism—Catholics like John Ryan confidently asserted the reality of natural rights, if in an obviously non-Lockean way.[25] As Franklin Roosevelt discarded the Progressives' audacity in critiquing the Constitution, following instead Felix Frankfurter's policy of claiming the mantle of John Marshall and Alexander Hamilton's liberal interpretation of the power of the federal government to justify unprecedented policy innovations,[26] so Catholics like Ryan anchored their policy arguments in timeless principles and thus signaled permanent standards of judgment by which the results of those policies might be evaluated and reassessed. This gave gravity, I think, to the vague optimism of the Progressives and gave policy choice the equilibrium of common sense. My point is not that the welfare state and its policies are unassailable today, only that their entrenchment in public opinion is not a mere accident but because they have deep roots.

FATHER JOHN COURTNEY MURRAY AND *DIGNITATIS HUMANAE*

The third moment, which I will describe more briefly, grows out of World War II and the scandalous acquiescence of some Catholic conservatives on the European continent to Fascist, Nazi, and Pétainist rule. My point is not to review that history but to discuss the consequent movement within certain Catholic circles and eventually throughout the church to look more favorably on democracy and human rights, indeed to ground Catholic political teaching increasingly in the language of human rights. Here two critical intellectual figures are Jacques Maritain, a French philosopher and convert to Catholicism, and Fr. John Courtney Murray, an American Jesuit priest. While Maritain played a role in drafting the United Nations' Declaration of Human Rights, which included social and economic claims in addition to the familiar "negative freedoms" of Anglo-American constitutionalism, Murray's importance was in reviving and generalizing the Carrolls' understanding that American constitutionalism was fully compatible with a Catholic life in a condition of underlying social and religious pluralism. The church had taken the position, as we saw in Pope Leo's comments quoted above, that the American arrangement of separation of church and state was only second-best, inferior to an explicitly confessional state on the model, say, of Malta—and in fact, for a brief while in the 1950s, Fr. Murray was disciplined by his religious superiors for arguing the opposite. But he persisted in thinking such an approach to be utopian in most countries of the modern world. "Religious pluralism is against the will of God," Murray wrote. "But it is the human condition; it is written into the script of history. It will not somehow cease to trouble the City."[27] In this context, Murray thought, support for religious liberty as a human right was essential to securing the liberty of the church itself in an always hostile world.

Murray referred to the principles of American constitutionalism as "articles of peace" rather than "articles of faith," but in fact he found the concord of Catholic and American principles to run deep, despite the limited involvement of Catholics in the establishment of the United States. Speaking of the Bill of Rights, for example, he wrote that it is

> not a piece of eighteenth century rationalist theory; it is far more the product of Christian history. Behind it one can see, not the philosophy of the Enlightenment but the older philosophy that had been the matrix of the common law. The "man" whose rights are guaranteed in the

face of law and government is, whether he knows it or not, the Christian man, who had learned to know his own personal dignity in the school of Christian faith.[28]

This was something the Carrolls knew and didn't have to say: Bishop Carroll could endorse George Washington's insistence on morality as a support of good government because the two friends understood by morality largely the same rules of human conduct, the same virtues more or less. Pluralism was, according to my argument, accepted in principle by the liberty of conscience constitutive of the American political order, but it was not originally put to the test because of the widespread moral consensus that Americans shared in that day, whether Catholic, Protestant, Jew, or Deist. In Murray's time this had begun to change, as he knew; it was happy that the articles of peace had as their authors men of faith.

Except in playing a minor role advising the first (and to date the only) Catholic to have been elected president of the United States, Fr. Murray was not influential on constitutional developments in the 1950s and 1960s before his untimely death at the end of that decade, a time when the Supreme Court deepened the separation of church and state or, rather, erected a wall between them. But he is thought to have been influential in the drafting of the Vatican II document "Dignitatis Humanae," the Declaration on Religious Freedom.[29] Here the church renounced any claim it may earlier have made to the special favor of the laws, declaring instead that religious freedom is grounded in the dignity of the human person. The church did not yield on its claim to be custodian of the one true religion but only denied that true religion could be imposed by coercion rather than embraced by conscience. Without reference to any particular country, the Declaration spoke of "the inviolable rights of the human person and . . . the constitutional order of society," adding that the "protection and promotion of the inviolable rights of man ranks among the essential duties of government. Therefore, government is to assume the safeguard of the religious freedom of all its citizens, in an effective manner, by just laws and by other appropriate means."[30] Although the document includes the phrase "free exercise of religion," which of course appears in the First Amendment to our Constitution, there is no mention of the prohibition against religious establishment, Fr. Murray explaining in a footnote that there are respectable opinions on both sides of the question whether religious establishment is consistent with religious freedom; nevertheless, the document does insist that "the equality of citizens before the law . . . never [be] violated for religious reasons." In short, the Vatican II Declaration aligns closely if not exactly with the First Amendment, at least if the No Establishment Clause in the latter is given an accommodationist rather than a separationist reading. After all, while insisting on the primacy of religious liberty and the injustice of religious discrimination, the church adds:

Government is also to help create conditions favorable to the fostering of religious life, in order that the people may be truly enabled to exercise their religious rights and to fulfill their religious duties, and also in order that society itself may profit by the moral qualities of justice and peace which have their origin in men's faithfulness to God and to his holy will.[31]

Although human dignity demands that people not be "driven by coercion but motivated by a sense of duty," law and government can use their coercive powers to promote responsibility and freedom, rather than yield to wantonness and license.[32] Washington's morality, in other words, and Carroll's endorsement of it, need not be abandoned even though religious liberty comes to be seen even by the Universal Church as a fundamental right.

THE PREDICAMENT OF THE CHURCH IN AMERICA TODAY

In retrospect, the mid-1960s seem to have been a high point in reconciliation between Catholics and the Constitution, as the Roman Catholic Church seemed to accept the American settlement as the best for most cases, if not simply ideal. But it quickly became the worst of times as well, as the U.S. Supreme Court began—first in the matter of contraception and in restrictions on suppression of obscenity, then by *Roe v. Wade* and *Lawrence v. Texas*—to establish constitutional rights to do acts held by the church to be deeply immoral.[33] With these cases, we enter the fourth and final moment I discuss: our present age. Fr. Ryan had been an opponent of the Supreme Court's decisions in *Lochner v. New York* and *Adkins v. Children's Hospital*, which struck down as violations of a purported constitutional liberty of contract maximum hours and minimum wage legislation, respectively.[34] Ryan saw the decisions as erecting constitutional barriers to just social policy, idolizing individualism, and breaching social solidarity. It could still be argued by Catholic friends of the free market, however, that the question of structuring the workplace was one on which societies might legitimately differ, however unjust it was universally for a prosperous society to pay only a bare subsistence wage. Now, however, the Supreme Court was licensing, in the name of the Constitution, direct and unmitigated moral evils. How does this affect the question of Catholics and the Constitution, then, today? Let me offer three concluding observations, without trying to settle the issue as a whole.

First, the church found its voice on the abortion issue and has probably influenced public thinking more clearly than in any previous instance in American history. True, it was only after the decision in *Roe v. Wade* that Catholic witness was widely taken to heart by other Christians and by thoughtful citizens—but taken to heart it has been. The decision in *Roe* and the subsequent cases built upon it have not been reversed, even though, in the right-to-die cases, they were not extended.[35] The salience of these social issues and the clarity of Catholic teaching in a wavering postmodern world have surely played a role in judicial appointments, with nominal Catholics now for the first time in American history a majority on the U.S. Supreme Court. While the *Roe* decision has not been reversed, recurring 5–4 votes suggest it has not been fully entrenched. Still, this situation of ambivalence perhaps indicates the absence of a jurisprudence that can marry principles of Catholic thinking with principles of American constitutionalism. Not a constitutional right to life but a lack of judicial power to countermand the legislature is for several justices still the basis of their opposition to *Roe*—or at least their professed jurisprudential basis—and this is weak in relation to arguments (first for abortion, now for homosexual marriage) based on equality, the principle of democracy itself.

Second, as threatening to Catholics as a jurisprudence that declares constitutional rights against Christian morality is the philosophical notion of "public reason" that would exclude from public debate arguments that are peremptorily said to be inaccessible to neutral citizens who are not committed to a particular faith.[36] It is an early lesson most politicians learn in America that invoking the authority of any denomination quickly excludes and thus alienates voters one may someday need, but this claim from the university (the doctrine was formulated by Harvard professor John Rawls) goes much further in disallowing any argument that secular professors deem unconvincing to secular people like themselves. Rawls's "overlapping consensus" is already censored and exclusionary, not consensual. The pluralism I consider implicit in the Constitution allows every kind of argument to make its case and trusts the political process in any generation to define the boundaries of ordinary political discourse. If George Washington was right that, for most people, morality is anchored in religious faith, to exclude religious witness is to upset any chance at moral consensus, substituting instead a moral vacuum filled only by a morality of individual fulfillment, which knows no limit it can never cross.

Finally, the hostility that appears to have arisen between what Catholics believe and what judges say is the Constitution tempts many Catholics and other Christians (especially younger ones) to withdraw and give up on American politics and constitutionalism in general. Indeed, in the age of self-expression and indignation, not only Catholics but American society at large both seem tempted away from constitutionalism, with all its compromises and procedures, privileges and immunities, terms and rights. This, I think, is an error, unwarranted in principle and imprudent in practice. While there are times when the best that can be done is conscientious objection (for example, for nurses and nursing students who would otherwise be forced to assist in abortions, perhaps for religious institutions being forced to provide health insurance plans that include contraception and maybe even abortion), it seems to me too soon for people of faith to give up upon their claim to equal citizenship in the constitutional order and their full freedom of speech in public debate. The Constitution was not an instrument designed to promote a Christian America, but from the beginning it was open to any form of light, whether its source be in reason, or in faith, or in that compound of the two that is Catholicism. Catholicism has contributed in the past to the growth of American constitutionalism—and perhaps the latter, too, has contributed to the development of Catholic doctrine. Who would want this healthy dynamic to come to an end?

NOTES

1. Leo XIII, "Testem Benevolentiae Nostrae," 22 January 1899, available online at http://www.papalencyclicals.net/Leo13/l13teste.htm (accessed 24 July 2012).

2. Thomas T. McAvoy, *The Americanist Heresy in Roman Catholicism, 1895–1900* (Notre Dame, IN: Notre Dame University Press, 1963).

3. Leo XIII, "Testem Benevolentiae Nostrae," 22 January 1899.

4. Leo XIII, "Longinqua," 6 January 1895, in Claudia Carlen IHM, ed., *The Papal Encyclicals, 1878–1903* (Raleigh, NC: McGrath, 1981), 363–70; available online at http://www.vatican.va/holy_father/leo_xiii/encyclicals/documents/hf_l-xiii_enc_06011895_longinqua_en.html (accessed 24 July 2012). Cf. "George Washington's Farewell Address," in *The Sacred Rights of Conscience*, ed. Daniel L. Dreisbach and Mark David Hall (Indianapolis, IN: Liberty Fund, 2009), 468–70.

5. Leo XIII, "Longinqua," 6 January 1895.

6. The following discussion draws on my essay, "Catholic Politics and Religious Liberty in America: The Carrolls of Maryland," in *The Founders on God and Government*, ed. Daniel L. Dreisbach, Mark D. Hall, and Jeffrey H. Morrison (Lanham, MD: Rowman and Littlefield, 2004), 251–71.

7. "An Address to the Roman Catholics of the United States of American by a Catholic Clergyman" (1784), *The John Carroll Papers*, vol. 1, ed. Thomas O'Brien Hanley (1755–1791), 82–144.

8. Locke, *A Letter Concerning Toleration*, ed. James H. Tully (1689; Indianapolis, IN: Hackett, 1983).

9. See Washington's letters to Quakers, to various Hebrew Congregations, and to Roman Catholics in W. B. Allen, ed., *George Washington: A Collection* (Indianapolis, IN: Liberty Fund, 1988), selections 182, 188–91; see Carroll's "Address from the Roman Catholics of America to George Washington," in *John Carroll Papers*, 1:409–11.

10. Reprinted in *The Founders on God and Government*, 266–69; also *John Carroll Papers*, 1: 365–68.

11. The author is grateful to the Center for Political and Economic Thought at St. Vincent College for permission to use, in this and the three succeeding paragraphs, material from a paper in the process of publication.

12. For the details of Fr. Ryan's life and intellectual development, I am relying on his autobiography. John A. Ryan, *Social Doctrine in Action: A Personal History* (New York: Harper and Brothers, 1941).

13. John Augustine Ryan, *A Living Wage: Its Ethical and Economic Aspects* (New York: Macmillan, 1906).

14. Leo XIII, *Rerum Novarum*, 15 May 1891, in Carlen, *Papal Encyclicals, 1878–1903*, 363–70, para. 20; available online at http://www.vatican.va/holy_father/leo_xiii/encyclicals/documents/hf_l-xiii_enc_15051891_rerum-novarum_en.html (accessed 24 July 2012).

15. John A. Ryan, *Social Reconstruction* (New York: Macmillan, 1920), 67.

16. Ibid., 69, 70, 75.

17. See Ryan, *Social Doctrine in Action*, 49–54. See also Clifford F. Thies and Gary M. Pecquet, "The Shaping of a Future President's Economic Thought: Richard T. Ely and Woodrow Wilson at 'The Hopkins,'" *Independent Review* 15, no. 2 (Fall 2010): 257–77; Luigi Bradizza, *Richard T. Ely's Critique of Capitalism* (New York: Palgrave Macmillan, 2013).

18. See Richard T. Ely, *Socialism: An Examination of Its Nature, Its Strength and Its Weakness, with Suggestions for Social Reform* (New York: Thomas Y. Crowell, 1894).

19. Richard T. Ely, *Social Aspects of Christianity, and Other Essays* (New York: Thomas Y. Crowell, 1889).

20. Richard T. Ely, "Industrial Liberty," Publications of the American Economic Association, 3rd series, vol. 3, no. 1 (Feb. 1902), 79.

21. "Appendix: The Bishop's Program," in Ryan, *Social Reconstruction*, 234–35; cf. ibid., 218, on Sidney Webb.

22. Ibid., 235.

23. Ibid., 93.

24. The phrase is from Edward S. Corwin, *Constitutional Revolution, Ltd.* (Claremont, CA: The Claremont Colleges, 1941).

25. James W. Ceaser, "The Progressive Attack on Natural Rights," at a conference sponsored by the Center for Political and Economic Thought at St. Vincent College, in the volume of proceedings edited by Bradley C. S. Watson, now under review.

26. See Felix Frankfurter, *The Commerce Clause under Marshall, Taney, and Waite* (Chapel Hill: University of North Carolina Press, 1937).

27. John Courney Murray, SJ, *We Hold These Truths: Catholic Reflections on the American Proposition* (Kansas City, MO: Sheed and Ward, 1960), 23.

28. Ibid., 39.

29. See Walter M. Abbott, SJ, ed., *The Documents of Vatican II* (New York: Guild Press, 1966). Fr. Murray wrote the introduction to the Declaration, ibid., 672–74.

30. Ibid., 677, 684–85.

31. Ibid., 685. See Murray's note 17 in the margins of the Declaration.

32. Ibid., 675.

33. *Griswold v. Connecticut,* 381 U.S. 479 (1965); *Memoirs v. Massachusetts,* 383 U.S. 413 (1966); *Roe v. Wade,* 410 U.S. 113 (1973); *Lawrence v. Texas,* 539 U.S. 558 (2003).

34. *Lochner v. New York,* 198 U.S. 45 (1905); *Adkins v. Children's Hospital,* 261 U.S. 525 (1923).

35. See *Washington v. Glucksberg,* 521 U.S. 702 (1997).

36. See John Rawls, *Political Liberalism,* expanded edition (New York: Columbia University Press, 2005; orig. 1993), 212–54.

PART III

FAITH AND CONTEMPORARY POLITICAL THOUGHT

BEHOLDEN TO REVELATION?

SCRIPTURE'S ROLE AS PUBLIC KNOWLEDGE AND MORAL AUTHORITY

Micah Watson

EVANGELICALS IN SEARCH OF POLITICAL THOUGHT

Few would doubt that evangelicals play an important role in American politics and culture. Less certain is how to understand, measure, and predict that role. From an external point of view, serious questions about what constitutes an evangelical complicate attempts to draw politically salient conclusions about a self-identifying group of between sixty and one hundred million Americans.[1] The difficulties of determining what such a vast number of citizens hold in common other than self-identification as evangelicals or membership in an "evangelical" denomination have led some to reject the meaningfulness of *evangelical* as a category entirely.[2]

One way to think about evangelicals and American politics is to bypass or bracket the external view and adopt instead an internal perspective.[3] For whatever the difficulties associated with establishing a comprehensive framework that would neatly identify the borders of evangelicalism and the doctrines of those who live therein, there can be no doubt that there are untold but significant numbers of American Christians who not only understand themselves *as evangelicals* but are also active politically. By adopting an internal point of view in thinking about these Christians, we can shift from descriptive questions of measurement and impact to normative questions as to how *should* an evangelical approach politics. Given two thousand years of church history and the legion of divisions among Christians, there are several approaches, or traditions, that an evangelical might subscribe to. This chapter considers whether evangelicals can embrace one particular school of natural law, the "new natural law" approach of Germain Grisez, John Finnis, Joseph Boyle, and others (hereafter referred to as NNL).

Rather than start with sociological attempts to define evangelicalism, a more personal hypothetical experiment may be more helpful. Let us consider Joshua and Sarah, a brother and sister who attend Wheaton College and Calvin College, respectively, two flagship institutions in the largely evangelical Council for Christian Colleges and Universities. Joshua and Sarah were raised in an evangelical Christian home and taught from a young age that their faith had implications for the world around them. Each of them made and later reaffirmed a personal decision to be a disciple of Jesus Christ. They believe that the Bible is their highest authority for understanding God's good character and his will, and they are committed to sharing the good news that Jesus Christ died on earth so we can live with him forever in heaven. At the same time, they believe that projects to provide clean water and medical attention to the poor complement the gospel message. Joshua is active in a chapter of International Justice Mission, and Sarah volunteers with Habitat for Humanity. While Sarah and Joshua may be fictional, they are typical of many flesh-and-blood evangelical college students.[4]

The questions that Sarah and Joshua will ask about evangelicals and politics are somewhat different from those asked by politics-and-religion scholars. For Sarah and Joshua want to know what they *should* think about politics and *how* to put those beliefs into practice. They will learn about and perhaps take pride in how their evangelical forebears lived out their faith in the abolition and civil-rights movements, and more recently in campaigns against abortion and human sex trafficking. They will perhaps be less enamored of the evangelical enthusiasm for prohibition in the last century or attempts to require the teaching of young-earth creationism in public schools. They will learn about other Christian approaches to political life—such as the Lutheran two-kingdoms approach or Roman Catholic social thought—and justifiably think that evangelicals have been rather ad hoc in their approach to political life.

How might their professors respond if Joshua and Sarah asked them to recommend an approach to political life that was consistent with their evangelical commitments? Answering this question well would require a great deal of careful thought about what any approach to politics must include, as well as how evangelical core distinctives would coalesce with some approaches and preclude others.[5] For the purposes of this chapter, I want to consider narrowly one particular evangelical distinctive and one particular philosophical approach to morality and politics.

The evangelical distinctive is a high priority on the centrality of scripture; this priority can be described as a cluster of claims. First, God speaks intelligibly through the Bible such that individual Christians can draw moral and political conclusions from scripture. Second, while the Bible does not address every political question nor provide unambiguous answers to every issue it does address, where scripture does seem to speak clearly it is the highest epistemic authority. As a result, and finally, any approach to politics (or any other subject) that would occlude the witness of scripture, cordon off biblical truths from the public square, or even contradict scriptural teaching would contradict evangelical convictions and thus fail to be a plausible option for evangelicals to adopt.

At the same time, my argument here assumes that scripture is not sufficient for an evangelical approach to politics. The evangelical political thinker who hopes to offer guidance to the Sarahs and Joshuas is faced with two monumental tasks. The first has to do with the insufficiency of scripture for addressing each and every political issue. If scripture is not enough, then evangelicals will have to think hard about what other resources should be mined for political wisdom and prescription. Hence my interest in what natural-law thinking can offer. The second monumental task is how to incorporate scriptural insights into political thinking responsibly. This is, to put it lightly, a rather delicate endeavor. Learning from Christianity's history will offer warnings as well as salutary insights, and one need not think too hard to come up with horrible examples of how scripture has been (mis)read and (mis)applied to politics (the parable of the great banquet in Luke 14 comes to mind). This task must be undertaken with a humble awareness of the reality that scripture can be misinterpreted while remaining committed to the evangelical conviction that God speaks through scripture and we can, to some extent, hear and understand rightly.

The new natural law approach I will describe is a variant of natural-law thinking. Natural-law theories have seen something of a renaissance recently.[6] Several scholars from various perspectives have suggested that Protestants in general and evangelicals in particular should consider the potential virtues of a natural-law ethic.[7] I argue that for all its many virtues, evangelicals cannot adopt NNL as a component of their political tradition because some aspects of NNL cannot be reconciled with evangelical beliefs about scripture.[8] I will describe NNL and then move to a narrowly tailored appraisal and critique before concluding with some virtues that scriptural revelation can bring to political philosophy.

THE NEW NATURAL LAW THEORY

New Natural Law theory is so named because "traditional" natural lawyers consider it a modern corruption that concedes too much to Hume, Kant, and other

Enlightenment thinkers. NNL proponents deny that their understanding is an in-novation. The debate between the two camps occurs on two levels. The first level of debate is over which account of morality and human action is true as such. The second level of debate concerns which account is most faithful to the thought of Thomas Aquinas. While these debates are connected, they are conceptually sep-arate. It's entirely possible that Grisez and Finnis have misinterpreted Aquinas while at the same time presented the true account of practical reason, and vice versa. (This is particularly true for Protestants, who have no formal ecclesial tie to Thomistic doctrine.)

While the academic genesis of the NNL project began with Germain Grisez's controversial reinterpretation of what Thomas meant by the first principle of prac-tical reason, the classic account of NNL is John Finnis's 1980 book *Natural Law and Natural Rights.* Shorter encapsulations of the basic philosophy can be found in several articles by Robert George, especially his *In Defense of Natural Law.* An ex-tremely helpful account of NNL that includes both the theory and its development has been written by philosopher Christopher Tollefsen.[9]

Grisez wrote his reinterpretation in 1965. We need not descend into the details of this debate, though the key contention of Grisez's article does illustrate one of the main points of dispute between traditional and NNL thinkers, and this dispute is also pertinent to evangelicals. Just as theoretical reasoning has as its first prin-ciple the law of noncontradiction, Aquinas identifies a first principle for practical, or moral, reasoning as well. That principle is found in the *Summa Theologiae* (I-II, 94, 2) and is stated rather simply: "Good is to be done and evil avoided."

Traditional natural-law theorists understand this principle in its seemingly straightforward sense. The terms *good* and *evil* here are morally laden terms and the task of the natural lawyer is to engage in theoretical inquiry so as to determine what constitutes good and evil and judge actions accordingly. Grisez's account challenges this interpretation and instead finds that the "good" that Aquinas writes of here is not morally laden but instead means a set of rational goods. Whereas the traditional natural lawyer attempted to derive his understanding of good from logically prior theoretical truths, NNL proponents think this violates the is/ought distinction and assert that the "good" of which Aquinas speaks is composed of a set of "premoral" goods that are underived and thus "basic."

NNL holds that human beings can identify reasons for acting and in doing so perform actions that can instantiate basic goods guided by a secondary set of moral principles. Decisions on specific moral issues—abortion, embryonic stem-cell re-search, lying, etc.—are derived from a reasoning process that incorporates respect for the basic goods and this secondary set of moral principles.

NNL proponents explain the basic goods as those ends that ultimately guide all rational human action. They are those reasons for action that do not need any further grounding and help us make rational (though not necessarily moral) sense of anything we might choose to do. For example, knowledge is one of the basic goods. When we try and understand a book, or a natural- law theory, we engage in an activity that needs no further explanation as to the point of what we're doing. We understand that deciding to pursue knowledge makes sense just in and of itself. This activity—the pursuit of knowledge—is described as "basic" because it needs no further ground beneath it, and it is a "good" because it is part of what makes a particular course of a human life valuable. Over the years during which the theory has developed, the list of basic goods has fluctuated somewhat, but the more or less settled list is as follows:[10]

> Knowledge: knowledge is worth pursuing for its own sake and not merely because of what it instrumentally might lead to.[11]
> Life: human life is valuable as are those goods or conditions that contribute to life, such as health, exercise, freedom from pain, and so on.
> Aesthetic appreciation: appreciation of beauty, whether in activity (see *play*, below), or contemplation of nature or art.
> Play: activities the point of which is just a good performance of the game, contest, run, and so on.
> Friendship: the weakest instantiation of this good is relative peace and coexistence, but the stronger version fits better with the widely understood use of the term, that is, a relationship in which the two or more members act for the other's good and well-being.
> Practical reasonableness: planning out one's life well and using intelligence to pursue goods in a flourishing way.
> Religion: thinking about and coming to terms with a reality greater than oneself, whether God, the gods, or some other articulation of a transcendent reality.
> Marriage: the biological, social and emotional matrix of a "one-flesh union" between a man and a woman.[12]

These goods are premoral in that they can guide human actions in both moral and immoral ways. Without the secondary set of moral guidelines (what NNL theorists call "modes of responsibility"), we cannot yet know whether an action that instantiates a basic good is moral. For example, a scientist on the verge of discovering a cure for cancer may be stymied by restrictions forbidding her from conducting human trials. Motivated by a desire to promote health and thus act for the basic good of life, she may decide to illegally test a group of homeless indigents. Such a course of action would indeed be immoral according to NNL (and not only NNL), but it would not be irrational. We can see the point of her action in that it is motivated by the basic goods of life and knowledge.

What does, then, help us understand why such a course of action is immoral? For this we need NNL's articulation of the modes of responsibility. Early on in the theory these modes seemed to "pop out of nowhere" and were admitted by Robert George to have been underdeveloped in the work of Finnis and Grisez.[13] The modes were seen as an intermediary set of rules that helped one move from basic goods to actual moral norms that might forbid or require particular acts. According to George, one of the most important developments in the theory has been the working out of the first principle of morality, from which the other "modes" follow. The first principle of morality (different from Thomas's first principle of practical reason) requires human beings to "choose and otherwise will those and only those possibilities whose willing is compatible with integral human fulfillment."[14]

The "how does this work" question is answered in part by looking at the actual modes or rules, which will be listed below. The first principle of morality enjoins human beings to engage in a life that respects the basic goods in a way that knowledge of the basic goods alone cannot do. In other words, because the basic goods make rational sense of action as such (both moral and immoral), another principle is needed to ground the human subject's responsibility to plan and live a life that rightly participates in those goods.[15] Morality has to be introduced somewhere. At any rate, the modes of responsibility are paraphrased from Finnis's original account as follows:[16]

> A Coherent Plan of Life: One should avoid drifting from moment to moment without any planning or aspirations to accomplish a flourishing life. A good life requires thought, care, and planning. The hardworking undergraduate students studying to prepare themselves for medical school fulfills this mode of responsibility better than the high-school dropouts who make no plans for the future and live from day to day, smoking marijuana and playing computer games in their mother's basement.
>
> No Arbitrary Preferences among Values: In pursuing a coherent plan of life, one ought not thereby to denigrate any of the basic goods. While a particular person will engage in some goods more than others, given different particular gifts and inclinations, one ought not to deny the intrinsic value of the other goods. Our hardworking pre-med students above violate this mode when, not having enough time or interest to enjoy their school's artistic offerings, they ridicule their art-major roommates for so doing.
>
> No Arbitrary Preferences among Persons: Do not unfairly prefer yourself over others; or, do unto others as you would have them do unto you. One must take care to look after one's own interests, if for no other reason than we are most directly responsible for our own well-being. But this is not a license to denigrate others' potential to engage in a flourishing life. For this example,

Finnis cites the analogy used by Nathan to indict King David for his adultery with Bathsheba and his murder of Uriah (2 Samuel 11). We grasp the unfairness of David's actions without having to look "beneath" the principle for a more fundamental ground.

Detachment: Do not become overly attached to any particular project or stage in one's own life. This mode might be considered a weight or a limit to the first mode. It is important to work out a coherent plan of life, but do not so commit oneself that in the course of the ups and downs of any human life one becomes fanatical about any one component of it. Avoid fanaticism. Our pre-med students would violate this mode if they became obsessed with getting into Harvard Medical School, and Harvard alone. As a result, they would neglect their friends and family and other aspects of their lives and, devastated by a Harvard rejection letter, turn down several other good opportunities to morph into another of our examples, and move into their mother's basement.

Commitment: The counterweight to detachment requires one not to give up a project or aspiration too quickly.

Efficiency, within Reason: Do not waste opportunities by pursuing them inefficiently. Take advantage of the best means available to achieve any given goal. There are many decisions in which the consequences should be a major factor. While Finnis is very careful to explicitly deny *consequentialism* in this mode, there are some decisions where the "more or less" comes into play.[17]

Respect for Every Basic Value in Every Act: While pursuit of one course of action will require a life more involved with some goods than others, one ought not take actions for the purpose of denigrating or violating any of the basic goods. NNL thinkers have also called this requirement the Pauline principle: evil ought not be done such that good may result. This mode is what allows NNL thinkers to defend human rights and eschew consequentialist moral reasoning that would sacrifice some lives for a purported greater good.

The Requirements of the Common Good: One ought to favor and promote the common good of the communities one belongs to.

Following One's Conscience: While one's conscience is not infallible, it is a moral duty to follow one's judgment on moral matters once one has come to a decision. In other words, even if it turns out that one was mistaken as to a moral judgment, to shirk what one takes to be one's moral duty is itself immoral.

With these two sets of ideas, basic goods that ground all rational actions and modes of responsibility that guide moral actions, NNL theorists can reason about specific norms for action. Some of these norms will be without exception, such as the norm against intentional killing of any sort.[18] Others, like keeping promises, may have exceptions. Some conclusions will be fairly straightforward in how one arrives at them and others will require a great deal of thought and consideration. It goes without saying that this is only a sketch of an intellectual project that has spanned decades and attracted several adherents as well as critics. At the same time, the good of explanation must in this case give way to the good of considerations of space. Now I will consider some of the attractions and difficulties that NNL poses for the evangelical trying to formulate a political tradition. If it is the case that a robust evangelical approach to political life requires an understanding of natural law (or something akin to it), might NNL be a good candidate?

TOWARD AN EVANGELICAL APPRAISAL OF NNL: SCRIPTURE AND DIVINE REVELATION

The most important consideration is whether what NNL posits about moral reality and human moral decision is true, and to what extent. Regardless of how useful and tempting such a theory may be for other considerations (as a common moral language with others, a translation device for biblical truths, a philosophically respectable framework, etc.), evangelicals must find the basic tenets of any natural-law theory persuasive on the merits.[19] What is immediately striking, and difficult, about this claim is that the NNL thinkers understand themselves to be articulating the very criteria by which we might judge the merits. In other words, because the basic goods and modes of responsibility are *per se nota* (self-evident), one has to apprehend their truth directly. *Self-evident* in this sense does not mean "obvious"; rather, it means that once one understands the terms involved in a proposition, one just "sees" that it is the case. Consider the transitive property in mathematics. If A=B, and B=C, then A=C. There is no further ground one can appeal to if a student does not understand this after it's been explained. NNL proponents claim that the premoral basic goods and the first principle of morality are self-evident in this way.[20]

How do evangelicals typically convince themselves that something is true? Typically, they revert to the witness of the Christian scriptures. Yet I've accepted the view that the scriptures by themselves are not an ethical answer book into which one can plug normative situations and from which one can then extract normative conclusions. The scriptures do not appear to be written with this sort of function in mind. At the same time, I take it as an evangelical given—albeit not self-evident—that scripture *does* speak with normative authority on some issues. Because scripture is not enough for a political tradition of thought, however, we need a supplementary theory of natural law that is accessible to our God-given reason. And because scripture does speak on at least some issues of moral import, a tradition of evangelical political thought will include a scriptural component in addition to a "natural law" theory of human nature and normative action.

Given these considerations, it is broadly the case that the primary tensions that arise between evangelical political thought and NNL have to do with the role of revelation and religion.[21] For however one understands Thomas's first principle of practical reason to do good and avoid evil, the evangelical will look first to scripture to determine what counts as good or evil.[22] I will now sketch out two related areas of disagreement. The first is a general disagreement on the status of scripture in our moral reasoning, and the second area concerns specific manifestations that might arise from the general disagreement.

The General Concern

One common misperception about the NNL theorists is that they do not value the role of faith and religion, that is, they have attempted to formulate an understanding of morality that eschews any sort of religious framework or commitment. While there are aspects of their theory that can invite such misperceptions, the NNL theorists do not understand themselves to be denigrating the role of religion.[23] Germain Grisez's opus, after all, is a multivolume work entitled *The Way of the Lord Jesus.* Nearly every NNL advocate is also a member of the Roman Catholic Church and often takes part in intra-Catholic disputes.[24] And Grisez, Finnis, George, and others have explicitly addressed in various works and speeches the role of faith and how it interacts with reason.[25]

Yet evangelicals have good reason to resist the NNL emphasis on the premoral basic goods and practical moral principles as the primary foundation of our reasoning about human actions and morality. Consider Finnis's statement that "the basic values, and the practical principles expressing them, are the only guides we have."[26] Even taking into account the context and knowing that Finnis is speaking of our natural reason, evangelicals do not need to accept that the schema described in NNL is the only moral guide we have. Instead, one can agree with Finnis et al. that human reason allows us to apprehend basic truths while also believing that our reason supports belief in the reasonableness and authority of divine revelation as expressed in scripture.

Robert George addresses this issue explicitly in two chapters in his *Clash of Orthodoxies,* "God's Reasons" and "On Fides et Ratio." In "God's Reasons," George notes that believers who understand God to forbid or require certain acts apart from any other supporting reason have an indefatigable reason to support that policy in public. These people might believe that God only expresses himself through divine revelation. George, contrariwise, believes that God himself has reasons to express the commands he has made and that these reasons are the very same reasons that are identified by philosophical reasoning. In this sense, God's revelation may be binding, but we cannot understand it without the aid of reason, and regardless, reason alone will give us enough to go on such that we can make our case to nonbelievers and believers alike without recourse to revelation.

In his commentary on Pope John Paul II's *Fides et Ratio*, George agrees that faith needs philosophy just as philosophy needs faith. He follows the late pope in disagreeing with "Biblicism," the view that only scripture can act as the sole criterion for truth. Just as the authority of the church is needed to combat various philosophical errors, so philosophy is needed to illuminate various theological concepts such as the Trinity, the status of the human person, and so on.

This is fine so far as it goes, yet there is something about the prioritizing of George and other NNL theorists that is problematic for the evangelical. Yes, reason can and should "flesh out" what we take to be normative truths expressed in scripture. Evangelicals who appreciate Thomas can agree wholeheartedly that our reason too comes from God, and that we are called to employ it whether we are interpreting scripture or thinking about what we can know about morality apart from divine revelation.

Nevertheless, even if one can accept that human beings can access truth both through reason via philosophy and reason via revelation, the evangelical must give priority to the latter in principle and in any potential conflicts between the two. Evangelicals, like other Christians, understand themselves to be subject to God's authority first and foremost. Contra George, evangelicals hold that the conveyance of a moral truth in scripture is itself a reason to believe it, and in doing so evangelicals ironically follow John Finnis's definition of authority:

> A person treats something (e.g., an opinion, a pronouncement, a map, an order, a rule . . .) as authoritative if and only if he treats it as giving him sufficient reason for believing or acting in accordance with it *notwithstanding* that he himself cannot otherwise see good reason for so believing or acting, or cannot evaluate the reasons he can see, or sees some countervailing reason(s), or would himself otherwise (i.e., in the absence of what he is treating as authoritative) have preferred not so to believe or act.[27]

Evangelicals believe God's authority is made most clear in scripture, and thus we are obliged to prioritize scripture above any other means of understanding moral norms. Yet this emphasis on scripture seems to be in serious tension with George and other NNL thinkers.[28] Indeed, they make the strong claim to have identified philosophically the very reasons that God has in holding that various acts—say infanticide—are unjust.[29] Moreover, such an approach seems to imply that it has only been in the last few decades that Christians have been able to adequately understand and defend what the Bible teaches about marriage.[30] While evangelicals can and should accept a stronger role for reason than they have historically, scripture cannot be relegated to a subordinate role as merely a confirmation of what reason finds on its own. Consider this description from George responding to a critic's charge that Judeo-Christian philosophy defends the value of human beings because they are made in God's image:

> Prof. Dever suggests that when Judeo-Christian philosophy confronts the [question of respecting human rights], it relies for an answer on the bare "scriptural assertion that humanity is created in God's image." But here, as elsewhere, *Jewish and Christian thinkers find in revelation the confirmation, but not the root*, of their philosophical affirmation of the nature and value of the human person—an affirmation found clearly (though not unmixed with error) in the philosophies of Plato and Aristotle, as well as in the thought of the great Roman jurists.[31]

To the contrary, I suspect most Jewish and Christian thinkers would not refer to revelation as a confirmation of a truth discoverable primarily through non-revelatory reason.[32] Rather, the fundamental truth held by (at least) Christian thinkers is that human beings have (a special) value, precisely because we are made in God's image, not to mention the profound implications the incarnation has for understanding God's love for us in that "while we were yet sinners, Christ died for us" (Romans 5:8) and we have been "bought with a price" (1 Corinthians 6:20). The evangelical will find the affirmation of human value among the virtuous pagans as praiseworthy at least in part because of the congruence with what the evangelical takes to be the most trustworthy source of moral truth: God's special revelation in scripture. I suspect many evangelicals have come to respect the insights of reason (from the Greeks and others) in part because these insights reinforce what scripture affirms. With NNL, the dynamic seems to be reversed.[33]

While it is undoubtedly wise to eschew "Biblicism" (understanding the Bible as the *only* source of truth), generally, and particularly in the public square when reasoning with non-Christians about why human beings are valuable, it is difficult to grasp how revelation plays a secondary role in explicating what *Christians* understand to be the true grounding of the dignity of human beings. Indeed, the premoral basic good of "life" and accompanying principles of morality, self-evident as they may be, seem a rather anemic grounding for the dignity of human beings when compared with what scripture tells us about human beings.

If I am correct in thinking evangelicals cannot concede scripture's pivotal relevance in ascertaining moral truth (as more than a supplement), then the NNL account, while not inaccurate so far as it goes, will be incomplete for the purposes of both public discourse and the truth of the matter. While the basic good of life and the modes of responsibility that flow from the first principle of morality may be apprehended as truly showing *that* human life is valuable and certain forms of it constitute genuine flourishing, such an account cannot say *why* human life is valuable. Evangelicals should insist that the "why" question cannot be fully answered without the help of revelation. This does not mean human beings who reject revelation will not value human life, but it does mean that the Christian political philosopher, as a *Christian* political philosopher, has more of a story to tell than the story afforded by philosophical reasoning alone.

These considerations encompass the general part of my first reservation about an evangelical rapprochement with NNL. Evangelicals do need to reconsider the role of reason as it pertains both to understanding scriptural truths and to conducting philosophical reasoning as such. But so long as evangelicals are identified by their adherence to the scripture as God's accessible revelation, they cannot accept an understanding of reason that reduces scripture to the mere handmaid of reason.

A Specific Concern: Lying

How might the general concern just discussed manifest itself in specific divergences when it comes to moral reasoning? After all, if God's wisdom/will/character is the ontological source for our moral knowledge, then we would expect our knowledge of morality to be consistent whether the avenue be the conclusions of practical reason or the more direct revelation of God through scripture. I would like to consider now an instance in which a conclusion of natural law reasoning *at least seems to* conflict with lessons drawn from passages of scripture.[34] John Finnis, citing an impressive record of Church Fathers and teachings, avers that lying is one of the few absolute moral prohibitions.[35] Following Augustine and Aquinas, Finnis does not shrink away from the hard cases that may arise from this injunction. Even if you were hiding Jews in Nazi Germany and the Gestapo was at the door asking about those in your charge, Finnis insists that you cannot lie. To be sure, you need not reveal the truth to the Nazis, and you ought not do so. The prohibition on lying does not entail a positive duty to disclose the whole truth to those who are not entitled to it. Nevertheless, the moral norm is absolute. To lie to the Gestapo agents at your front door is to slide into an unwarranted proportionalism and "enter . . . into the Nazis' politics of manipulation."[36]

Evangelicals may or may not find Finnis's arguments persuasive on their own. But their first recourse will be to consider if scripture has absolutely prohibited lying. Some passages do seem to reinforce this contention, such as Jesus naming Satan as the father of lies (John 8:44) and the commandment forbidding bearing false witness against neighbors (Exodus 20:16). Now, for argument's sake, consider how the following two passages might be interpreted to contest Finnis's claim. First is the account of the Hebrew midwives who disobeyed Pharaoh's order to kill all the male children:

> The king of Egypt said to the Hebrew midwives, whose names were Shiphrah and Puah, "When you help the Hebrew women in childbirth and observe them on the delivery stool, if it is a boy, kill him; but if it is a girl, let her live." The midwives, however, feared God and did not do what the king of Egypt had told them to do; they let the boys live. Then the king of Egypt summoned the midwives and asked them. "Why have you done this? Why have you let the boys live?" The midwives answered Pharaoh, "Hebrew women are not like the Egyptian women; they are vigorous and give birth before the midwives arrive." So God was kind to the midwives and the people increased and became even more numerous. And because the midwives feared God, he gave them families of their own. (Exodus 1:15–21, NIV)

The second passage is found in the book of Joshua (chapters 2 and 6), with the account of Rahab the prostitute and her protection of the Hebrew spies in the soon-to-be destroyed city of Jericho. After she has taken in the two spies, the king of the city orders her to turn them over and yet she does not:

> But the woman had taken the two men and hidden them. She said, "Yes, the men came to me, but I did not know where they had come from. At dusk, when it was time to close the city gate, the men left. I don't know which way they went. Go after them quickly. You may catch up with them." (But she had taken them up to the roof and hidden them under the stalks of flax she had laid out on the roof.) (Joshua 2:4–6)

The rest of the story is familiar. The two spies promise Rahab protection in exchange for their safe escape. The Hebrews march around the city and the walls are destroyed, leading to the sacking of the city. Joshua spares Rahab and her family because she protected the spies, and she was adopted among the Hebrews.

Should these two passages offer any pause to the evangelical considering whether there is truly an absolute prohibition on lying? After all, it seems clear that what took place in each instance were, in fact, lies. That is, the midwives and Rahab knowingly communicated information that they knew was not true. Moreover, Shiphrah and Puah are described by the author as being blessed by God. Their actions were motivated by the honorable fear of God, and there is no distinction recognized in the text between their choice not to kill the newborn

boys and their subsequent lie about this choice. Perhaps a familiarity with Hebrew would qualify this interpretation, but in the English rendering the blessing
of God (the "So God was kind to the midwives") follows immediately after their
lie to Pharaoh.

At first glance, Rahab's account does not seem nearly as strong. After all, God
blessed the midwives, but it is only Joshua—a mere man—who makes a deal with
the resourceful Rahab. While it is clear that Rahab lies, and things seem to work out
well for her and her family, it's not as clear from the Joshua passage that this is approved behavior. The Hebrew scriptures are replete with accounts in which actors
violate various norms wherein the actors seem to benefit, and no divine disapproval
is noted (Joshua 9 offers an instructive example of this).

Yet evangelicals believe scripture to be comprised not as isolated incidents but
as a connected story in which some passages can be illumined by others.[37] Rahab's
actions, while not explicitly affirmed in the book of Joshua, are explicitly affirmed
twice in the Christian scriptures of the New Testament. In the famous "faith" chapter in Hebrews 11, the author compiles a who's who list of exemplars of faith from
the Hebrew scriptures.[38] This list is divided into two components; the first is a list
of major figures with some description, and the second is a quick compilation of
figures whose actions cannot be described because of time constraints. This second
list includes Gideon, Barak, Samson, Jephthah, David, Samuel, the prophets. The
first list includes the patriarchs, plus one, who by faith did remarkable things: Abel,
Enoch, Abraham, Isaac, Jacob, Joseph, Moses, and . . . Rahab. "By faith the prostitute
Rahab, because she welcomed the spies, was not killed with those who were disobe-
dient" (Hebrews 11:31).

Even more explicit is James. In his famous passage in chapter 2 declaring that
faith without works is dead, he too chooses Abraham as an exemplar. And alongside
Abraham he highlights Rahab:

> And the scripture was fulfilled that says, "Abraham believed God, and it
> was credited to him as righteousness," and he was called God's friend.
> You see that a person is justified by what he does and not by faith alone.
> In the same way, was not even Rahab the prostitute considered righ-
> teous for what she did when she gave lodging to the spies *and sent them
> off in a different direction?* As the body without the spirit is dead, so faith
> without deeds is dead. (James 2:23–26; my emphasis)

This would seem to be an endorsement of her actions in full.[39] James declares
through a rhetorical question that her works—reasonably understood as her hiding the spies and lying to the authorities—give evidence of her faith and thus her
righteousness. There are still ways by which one could deny that this understanding

from Hebrews and James is authoritative, but the "commonsense" reading indicates that James at least considers her deceit as not only allowed but praiseworthy.

These two accounts in the Hebrew scriptures, and the commentary on them in the Christian scriptures, do not by any means settle the matter as to whether it is ever permissible to lie.[40] One would need to think about how such passages can be reconciled with others that might appear on first glance to support an absolute prohibition.[41] The point is that it is this debate that the evangelical will find preeminent; for if a biblical author inspired by God points to Rahab as an exemplar of faith and righteousness as illustrated by her deliberate misleading of others, *then* the evangelical will not be persuaded by the most sophisticated arguments from natural reason alone and have reason to reject any philosophical system that from the outset favors such arguments over scripture's witness.[42]

CONCLUSION

This incompatibility between evangelical convictions and certain aspects of NNL leaves much to be considered with regard to NNL, and the original query posed by our hypothetical evangelical college students, Joshua and Sarah. NNL authors understand themselves to be articulating an understanding of public reason that is universally accessible to the human being as such. Given this understanding, the criteria for judging their project a success might be found not only in its intellectual and philosophical coherence but also in its potential to attract people who are generally sympathetic to its normative claims and judgments. Evangelicals are a good test case, and if these observations are sound, there is some work to be done, either to persuade evangelicals that scripture does coincide seamlessly with the findings of practical reason (as in the case of lying), or that the evangelical conviction that biblical revelation is also publicly accessible and preeminently authoritative is unsound.

With regard to the plight of Joshua and Sarah, pointing out a tension with an alternative approach to political thought does not in itself supply a positive way forward. The issue is not whether evangelicals will use scripture in their thinking about political issues. In practice, this is already the case whether it be the quoting of poetry in the Psalms to support a pro-life stance or opposing George Bush's plans for social security because it would violate the commandment to honor our fathers and mothers.[43] Evangelicals can and should prioritize the place of scripture in their thinking about politics, but they must do so with integrity and care. I conclude with three ways that scripture might play a role in an evangelical political tradition.

First, scripture might call into question moral or political norms arrived at by a sequence of reason alone. This is the sort of negative exercise I've engaged in above with regard to lying. At the very least, if we believe that scripture has derivable meaning and can make a legitimate moral claim on us, then evangelicals would do well to consider how scripture would interact with philosophical claims. One need not stake out any particular political ideology to see how this might work. Can the evangelical reconcile the Anabaptist position on nonviolence with a responsible and careful reading of scripture? What about the tenets of just-war theory? Perhaps an easier example would be the difficulty an evangelical might have with reconciling a claim that all taxation is unjust (and hence should be avoided) with Jesus' words, and deeds, on that subject (Matthew 22:15–22). Scripture does not address every moral or political question, but it does address some, and evangelicals should consider how scripture might temper claims made by philosophical reason alone.

Second, evangelicals should accept that reason should work in tandem with scriptural revelation. Too often we speak as if the distinction is between reason and revelation when, in truth, we utilize our reason when considering the claims of philosophy alone *and* the claims we find in scripture. Evangelicals already do this, often without thinking about it. If a clear commandment from scripture alone was enough to warrant obedience, then evangelical women would not attend church without some sort of head covering. Paul (seems to) make it clear in 1 Corinthians 11 that women ought to cover their heads because woman is man's glory, and "because of the angels." While there are some congregations where women will wear hats in response to this injunction, the vast majority of evangelical women do not. Why? Is it not simply because we cannot make heads or tails of what Paul means by it?[44] Evangelicals should welcome attempts to clarify biblical concepts and ideas through the use of our reason. Philosophical reflection can help us think about marriage, equality, poverty, and other important issues that have significant moral and political application.

Finally, scripture can and should inform our public witness because scripture gives us a fuller picture of human reality than is afforded merely by reason alone. We can learn more about our purpose as human beings generally and Christians specifically. For example, any fair reading of scripture, with an eye toward careful hermeneutics, will support the contention that God has a special concern for the poor and underprivileged (Matthew 25). Many theologians and ethicists are entirely right to highlight the preponderance of verses and passages underscoring this concern.[45] Any natural law account of human flourishing that neglects or underplays a crucial role for positive and tangible charity for the least of these falls short of the biblical vision of human well-being. This biblical vision offers us both a more complete picture of our calling as human beings and a deeper motivation to pursue the calling. And at the core of evangelical identity is a belief that the biblical good news is accessible to human beings as such, and that evangelicals are called to proclaim that good news to all the nations, including their public squares. It may very well be epistemologically self-evident that we should respect the basic good of life and avoid an arbitrary preference of persons. But this is not the sort of sustenance that will fuel the human heart to act justly, and love mercy, and walk humbly with our God.

NOTES

1. *U.S. Religious Landscape Survey, Religious Affiliation: Diverse and Dynamic*, by the Pew Forum on Religion and Public Life (Washington D.C.: Pew Research Center, 2008), http://religions.pewforum.org (accessed January 5, 2011). The sixty million figure is by some measures a conservative estimate. Gallup polls have consistently numbered American evangelical adults between the high 30s and low 40s percentage mark. Wheaton's Institute for the Study of American Evangelicals estimates the number at 100 million. See "How many Evangelicals Are There?" Institute for the Study of American Evangelicals, at http://isae.wheaton.edu/defining-evangelicalism/how-many-evangelicals-are-there/ (accessed January 5, 2011).

2. See, for example, D. G. Hart's *Deconstructing Evangelicalism: Conservative Protestantism in the Age of Billy Graham* (Grand Rapids, MI: Baker Academic, 2004).

3. I am borrowing here, with some liberties, from H. L. A. Hart's distinction between the external and internal points of view with regard to judges. H. L. A. Hart, *The Concept of Law*, 2nd edition (Oxford: Oxford University Press, 1994), 89–91.

4. David Bebbington, *Evangelicalism in Modern Britain: A History from the 1730s to the 1980s* (London: Unwin Hyman, 1989), 1–17.

5. See J. Budziszewski's introduction to his *Evangelicals in the Public Square* (Grand Rapids, MI: Baker Books, 2006), 15–37.

6. See, for example, David VanDrunen, *A Biblical Case for Natural Law* (Grand Rapids, MI: Acton Institute, 2006); Stephen J. Grabill, *Rediscovering the Natural Law in Reformed Theological Ethics* (Grand Rapids, MI: Eerdmans, 2006); Daryl Charles, *Retrieving the Natural Law: A Return to Moral First Things* (Grand Rapids, MI: Eerdmans, 2008).

7. For example, Budziszewski, *Evangelicals in the Public Square*.

8. Thus this is not a comprehensive critique of NNL. For such a critique (albeit one I don't find particularly convincing), see Russell Hittinger, *A Critique of the New Natural Law Theory* (Notre Dame, IN: University of Notre Dame Press, 1987). For a more recent collection of interactions with NNL, see Nigel Biggar and Rufus Black, eds., *The Revival of Natural Law: Philosophical, Theological and Ethical Responses to the Finnis-Grisez School* (Burlington, VT: Ashgate, 2000).

9. Germain Grisez, "The First Principle of Practical Reason: A Commentary on the *Summa Theologiae*, 1–2 Question 94, Article 2," *Natural Law Forum* 10 (1965): 168–201; John Finnis, *Natural Law and Natural Rights* (Oxford: Oxford University Press, 1980; 2nd ed. 2011); Robert P. George, *In Defense of Natural Law* (Oxford: Oxford University Press, 1999), esp. 42–54; Christopher Tollefsen, "The New Natural Law Theory," *Lyceum* 10.1 (Fall 2008), at http://lyceumphilosophy.com/?q=node/97. Tollefsen's summary is a good one, though for a more comprehensive

and thick account, Grisez emphasizes the importance of a tri-authored piece from 1987: Germain Grisez, Joseph Boyle, and John Finnis, "Practical Principles, Moral Truth, and Ultimate Ends," *American Journal of Jurisprudence* 32 (1987): 99–151.

10. With the exception of marriage, I paraphrase the first edition of Finnis, *Natural Law and Natural Rights*, 59–75, 86–89, for these descriptions.

11. Finnis devotes chapter 3 in *Natural Law and Natural Rights* to the basic good of knowledge. His starting with knowledge is particularly strategic in that (1) the reader is engaged in pursuing that very good in attempting to understand the chapter, and (2) to deny the basic knowledge of good appears to be self-refuting. How would we come to *know* that knowledge is not intrinsically worth pursuing?

12. Marriage was not originally articulated as one of the basic goods (it was understood as a special subset of friendship), but as NNL developed, marriage came to be seen as a basic good. This understanding of marriage, as well as further implications drawn from it, has been controversial. See, for example, John Finnis, "Law, Morality, and 'Sexual Orientation,'" *Notre Dame Journal of Law, Ethics and Public Policy* 9 (1995): 11–39; John Finnis, "Is Natural Law Theory Compatible with Limited Government?" in *Natural Law, Liberalism, and Morality*, ed. Robert P. George (Oxford: Oxford University Press, 1997), 1–26.

13. George, *In Defense of Natural Law*, 50–51.

14. Ibid., 51. George is quoting from John Finnis, Joseph M. Boyle Jr., and Germain Grisez, *Nuclear Deterrence, Morality, and Realism* (Oxford: Clarendon Press, 1987), 283. In a relatively recent piece (*Theological Studies*, 2008) Grisez has changed his emphasis from integral human fulfillment to integral communal fulfillment, but that particular shift does not concern us here.

15. This first principle is, like the basic goods, underived and thus basic. As such, NNL proponents do not attempt to "argue" for it by appealing to underlying principles. Rather, they argue dialectically by attempting to show the flaws in competing theories of morality. The "basic" nature of the premoral goods as well as the first principle of morality explain why so much criticism is epistemological in nature.

16. Finnis, *Natural Law and Natural Rights*, 103–27. I should note here that NNL is an ongoing project with many iterations and participants, and thus formulations of the modes of responsibility have shifted somewhat since first introduced in the 1970s. Grisez's description in *The Way of the Lord Jesus*, vol. 1, *Christian Moral Principles* (Chicago: Franciscan Herald Press, 1983), 205–22, differs slightly from Finnis's account here and, indeed, from Grisez's account articulated in *The Way of the Lord Jesus*, vol. 3, *Difficult Moral Questions* (Quincy, IL: Franciscan Press, 1997), 858–70. Yet another brief account is found in Finnis, Boyle, and Grisez, *Nuclear Deterrence*, 284–87. I find Finnis's account—also repeated in *Natural Law and Natural Rights*, 2nd ed. (Oxford: Oxford University Press, 2012)—most helpful for the purposes of this chapter. The in-the-family differences that do exist between the various accounts do not affect my overall argument.

17. Finnis notes that generally, if a choice must be made, it's better to prefer human good to animal good, prefer a basic good (life) over an instrumental good (property), better to wound than to kill, to stun than to wound, and so on. Finnis, *Natural Law and Natural Rights*, 111.

18. See Gerald Bradley, "No Intentional Killing Whatsoever: The Case of Capital Punishment," in *Natural Law and Moral Inquiry: Ethics, Metaphysics, and Politics in the Work of Germain Grisez*, ed. Robert P. George (Georgetown: Georgetown University Press, 1998), 155–73; John Finnis, *Moral Absolutes: Tradition, Revision, and Truth* (Washington, D.C.: Catholic University of America Press, 1991).

19. Or at least persuasive in part. I do not think one need accept a theory in its entirety to find much of it persuasive. The rub here is the differences in opinion as to what criteria determine the "merits."

20. Any system of thought will include first principles that themselves cannot be proved. Otherwise the system would rest upon an infinite regress of reasons. George comments on how dialectical arguments can support claims about self-evident goods. George, *In Defense of Natural Law*, 61–63.

21. Some of this tension may result just from the different purposes of a given theory. NNL does not attempt to answer every question nor to address metaphysics or religious truth as such. The source of the disagreement, then, may very well be about what the proper reach of a moral theory and political theory ought to be.

22. This is the case whether the moral "good or evil" adheres directly in Thomas's first principle or in the NNL modes of responsibility.

23. Much has been made of the description of "religion" as one premoral basic good that is incommensurable with the other basic goods. For reasons I won't expound on here, I think Robert George has adequately responded to this charge in the second chapter of *In Defense of Natural Law*, 69–75.

24. See particularly George, *Clash of Orthodoxies*, 231–316.

25. For example, see Robert P. George's address at Union University on February 25, 2009, available (as of yet only in the audio) at http://www.uu.edu/audio/Detail.cfm?ID=381.

26. Finnis, *Natural Law and Natural Rights*, 119. I take Finnis here to be arguing that any meaningful action must fit into the framework of the basic goods (i.e., we won't find either the church or scripture directing us to actions that are somehow alien to the basic goods). I don't think he means here to purposefully exclude attaining knowledge of moral action through revelatory means, though given the emphasis on unaided reason through NNL his wording is unfortunate.

27. Ibid., 233–34; original emphasis.

28. I should caution that as with any "school" of thought there is some room for disagreement and development among the school's adherents. Finnis both defends the exclusion of divine causality from an account of human flourishing and explains how theological truths might fit into such an account. See John Finnis, "Telling the Truth about God and Man in a Pluralist Society: Economy or Explication," in *The Naked Public Square Revisited: Religion and Politics in the Twenty-First Century*, ed. Christopher Wolfe (Wilmington, DE: ISI Books, 2009), 111–25. This chapter basically explains why Finnis structured *Natural Law and Natural Rights* as he did.

29. "We also believe not only that there are reasons (apart from revelation) for these policy positions, but also that these reasons are (or, at least, are among) God's reasons for willing what

He wills. Indeed, it is our view that often the identification of these reasons by philosophical inquiry and analysis, supplemented sometimes by knowledge derived from the natural and/or social sciences, is critical to an accurate understanding of the content of revelation in, say, the Bible or Jewish or Christian tradition." George, *Clash of Orthodoxies*, 65.

30. "There are, I submit, answers to these questions [about why marriage is between a man and a woman]. But one cannot simply look up the answers in the Bible. To achieve an adequate understanding of the biblical teaching, one must advert to philosophical truths. . . . [George goes on to describe the NNL argument about one-flesh unions.] These are *philosophical* questions that cannot be evaded if we are to understand, much less defend, the biblical view of marriage." Ibid., 310–11.

31. Ibid., 37; my emphasis.

32. Nor do they need to hold that it is *only* in scripture that we find the dignity of the human person, but scripture's place is not subsidiary.

33. But see Finnis, "Telling the Truth," 118, 121–22, in which he describes a sort of reflective equilibrium between natural reason and revelation and defends the justifiably public nature of God's role in morality and human well-being. Consider the following passage in which revelation's role seems significantly stronger than in other NNL sources, though arguably here revelation is necessary mostly for the cultural instantiation of the truth of human equality as opposed to a *reason* to accept it as true simply:

> That human beings are radically equal in dignity is entailed by the revelation that we are all made in God's image, and are called as sons and daughters into his household in the transcendent Kingdom.[footnote omitted] Can we have much confidence that, without benefit of those revealed teachings, this radical equality would have been steadily understood and affirmed—practically, that is, precisely as ground for true entitlement of all to equality in basic rights—or much confidence that it will be long maintained if they are set aside?[footnote omitted] I do not think so.[footnote omitted] Without those revelatory insights, or confirmations of insight, into our nature and potential destiny, people . . . gravitate towards some version of views that treat dignity as variable, waxing, waning, predicable of us at some time after the start of one's existence as a human being.

34. The "at least seems to" here cannot be overestimated, and not just to cover myself from critical response (which I welcome). This section is meant to highlight what seems quite possible in principle: that what reason seems to say and what scripture seems to say can conflict or exist in tension. What to do in that case, for the evangelical, is what I'm after here regardless if the reader agrees with my particular interpretation of scripture.

35. See generally John Finnis, *Moral Absolutes: Tradition, Revision, and Truth* (Washington, D.C.: Catholic University Press, 1991). More specifically, see his elaboration in *Aquinas: Moral, Political, and Legal Theory* (Oxford: Oxford University Press, 1998), 154–63. See also the debate on *Public Discourse* sparked by the Live Action tactics used to expose Planned Parenthood,

at http://www.thepublicdiscourse.com/topics/lying.

36. Ibid., 159–60.

37. This is not to diminish the very real challenges in understanding scripture this way. See Richard Bauckham, "Reading Scripture as a Coherent Story," in *The Art of Reading Scripture*, ed. Ellen F. Davis and Richard B. Hays (Grand Rapids, MI: Eerdmans, 2003), 38–53.

38. Augustine is a crucial conversation partner for evangelicals on this issue and many others, for he shares with them the priority on scripture and yet comes to an absolutist position on the impermissibility of lying. Augustine dedicates two treatises to the subject, *De Mendacio* and *Contra Mendacium*, and both address the examples of the Hebrew midwives and Rahab. Augustine does not, however, address the New Testament commentary on either passage. Regardless, the salient point is not whether Augustine is right or wrong on the biblical witness about lying. The point is that the biblical witness is where evangelicals believe the debate should first take place. I have examined Augustine's specific arguments and hermeneutics in his two treatises in "Augustine Contra Lying: The Bible and Exception-less Rules," an address given at the 2012 Christians in Political Science meeting at Gordon College, Wenham, Massachusetts. On file with the author.

39. As an interesting side note, Rahab is also an ancestor of the House of David and thus she is listed in the genealogy of Joseph, Jesus' father (Mathew 1). She is listed as King David's great-great-grandmother.

40. To truly evaluate the exercise conducted above, we would want to ask several more questions. Did I properly take into account the context and the genre of the passages in question? Are they merely reporting, or do they include normative teaching? How do they interact with competing passages that seem to condemn lying? Should we emphasize Israel's political experience as normatively illuminating, as Oliver O'Donovan does? How has the ministry, crucifixion, and resurrection of Christ changed the reality of our world and our reading of the Hebrew scriptures? If there does seem to be a moral judgment made in the text, is it repeated elsewhere?

41. Joseph Boyle has dealt with some of these issues in his piece reviewing Augustine's and Aquinas's treatments of lying, "The Absolute Prohibition of Lying and the Origins of the Casuistry of Mental Reservation: Augustinian Arguments and Thomistic Developments," *American Journal of Jurisprudence* 44 (1999): 43–65. Christopher Tollefsen also has a forthcoming book that deals directly with these matters, *Truth, Lies, and the Natural Law: Why Lying, Even for a Good Cause, Is Always Wrong*. Each author raises important points that beg for a more substantial response, though there remains a gulf between an evangelical and a Catholic position on the centrality of scripture's role.

42. The death penalty is another good test case, though for lack of space I cannot pursue it here. NNL holds that the death penalty is intrinsically immoral and can thus never be applied. A very strong case can be made that Paul (Romans 13) and Jesus (Matthew 15) affirm the congruence of the death penalty with God's law.

43. Psalm 139 is often cited by pro-lifers. For the social security argument, see Jim Wallis's letter to members of Congress, at http://www.sojo.net/index.cfm?action=sojomail.

display&issue=050502#2.

    44. While there are speculations in various commentaries, most admit that they really have no idea what Paul means by the "angels" comment.

    45. Whether the means to that end identified by those same theologians and ethicists are equally supported by scripture is another question entirely (i.e., I have my doubts that the flat tax is mandated by scripture or that Jim Wallis is right to think that privatizing social security violates the fifth commandment).

FIDES, RATIO ET JURIS

HOW SOME COURTS AND SOME LEGAL THEORISTS MISREPRESENT THE RATIONAL STATUS OF RELIGIOUS BELIEFS

Francis J. Beckwith

Religious citizens, like their nonreligious compatriots, attempt to shape public policy in order to advance what they believe is the common good. Critics have suggested that there is something untoward with such activism, since the positions advocated by these citizens are informed by their religious beliefs. Some of these critics ground this judgment in the claim that religious beliefs are by their very nature not amenable to rational assessment and are thus irrational.

This view should not be confused with what is sometimes called Political Liberalism and often associated with the work of John Rawls and his numerous disciples.[1] According to that view, policies informed by religious or secular comprehensive doctrines that limit the fundamental liberties of citizens who do not share those comprehensive doctrines are justified if and only if the coerced citizens would be irrational in rejecting the coercion. Rawls himself concedes that many of these comprehensive doctrines, including the religious ones, are *reasonable*.[2] This is why Rawls distinguishes between reasonable comprehensive doctrines and the grounds by which the government may be justified in coercing its citizens.[3]

The focus of this chapter will be on those who eschew Rawls's modest approach and argue that *all* religious worldviews are at their core unreasonable, because they are dependent on beliefs not amenable to reason. The implication of this view—

that some, though not all, proponents of it explicitly acknowledge—is that religiously informed policy proposals have no place in a secular liberal democracy that requires the primacy of reason. Although this view of religion's rationality is found or implied in several U.S. Supreme Court opinions as well as among some legal and political theorists, it is far more controversial than its advocates portray.

I. FAITH, REASON, AND LAW

IA. The Courts

Historian James Hitchcock has carefully documented how modern U.S. courts treat the rational status of theological beliefs.[4] He concludes that "the incoherence of the modern jurisprudence of the Religious Clauses is the inescapable result of the Court's positing of religion as essentially irrational."[5] In what follows are some comments found in the cases Hitchcock cites, though there are many others that space constraints prevent me from presenting.

Some jurists seem to believe that the sine qua non of a rational belief is something akin to the type of empirical proof found in the natural sciences.[6] In *U.S. v. Ballard* (1944), for example, Justice William O. Douglas states:

> Men may believe what they cannot prove. They may not be put to the proof of their religious doctrines or beliefs. Religious experiences which are as real as life to some may be incomprehensible to others. Yet the fact that they may be beyond the ken of mortals does not mean that they can be made suspect before the law. Many take their gospel from the New Testament. But it would hardly be supposed that they could be tried before a jury charged with the duty of determining whether those teachings contained false representations. The miracles of the New Testament, the Divinity of Christ, life after death, the power of prayer are deep in the religious convictions of many. If one could be sent to jail because a jury in a hostile environment found those teachings false, little indeed would be left of religious freedom.[7]

Justice William Brennan asserts in a 1976 opinion in *Serbian Orthodox Diocese v. Milivojevich* that "it is the essence of religious faith that ecclesiastical decisions are to be reached and are to be accepted as matters of faith whether or not rational or measurable by objective criteria." He further argues that "constitutional concepts of due process, involving secular notions of 'fundamental fairness' . . . are therefore hardly relevant to such matters of ecclesiastical cognizance."[8] This would come as quite a shock to Moses.[9]

Relying on the "insights" of that great jurist Clarence Darrow, most well known for his role of defense attorney in the famous Scopes "Monkey Trial," Justice John Paul

Stevens wrote in a concurring opinion in *Wolman v. Walter* (1977) that "the distinction between the religious and the secular is a fundamental one. To quote from . . . Darrow's argument in the Scopes case: 'The realm of religion . . . is where knowledge leaves off, and where faith begins, and it never has needed the arm of the State for support, and wherever it has received it, it has harmed both the public and the religion that it would pretend to serve.'"[10] It seems that for Justice Stevens a religious belief cannot ever be an item of knowledge, for if it were it would no longer be a religious belief. The implication of this view is that religious beliefs ought to be of no concern to the state, unless their champions pretend that these beliefs are items of knowledge and mistakenly try to insert those beliefs into the public square. Thus, it is not surprising that Justice Stevens, in a dissenting opinion in *Webster v. Reproductive Health Services* (1989), calls the pro-life position on fetal personhood a "religious tenet" that cannot in principle rise to the level of knowledge so that it may be reflected in our laws.[11]

In *Engle v. Vitale* (1962), Justice Hugo Black explains why the First Amendment forbids the state from requiring its public-school students to open each day with the public recitation of a government-authored prayer: "The Establishment Clause thus stands as an expression of principle on the part of the Founders of our Constitution that religion is too personal, too sacred, too holy, to permit its 'unhallowed perversion' by a civil magistrate."[12] Thirty years later, in the case of *Lee v. Weisman* (1992), Justice Anthony Kennedy reinforced Black's understanding of religion when he wrote: "The design of the Constitution is that preservation and transmission of religious beliefs and worship is a responsibility and a choice committed to the private sphere, which itself is promised freedom to pursue that mission."[13] In his dissent, Justice Antonin Scalia wryly replied: "Church and state would not be such a difficult subject if religion were, as the Court apparently thinks it to be, some purely personal avocation that can be indulged entirely in secret, like pornography, in the privacy of one's room. For most believers it is *not* that, and has never been."[14]

The common thread in these opinions (Justice Scalia's excepted) is that religious beliefs and their attendant notions such as moral and metaphysical beliefs are epistemically akin to self-regarding private and personal matters of taste and thus not proper subjects of rational assessment. This is not to say that there are not justices like Scalia who disagree with this understanding. Rather, what I am suggesting is that the general tenor of the Court's opinions touching on the epistemic nature of religious beliefs and their attendant notions is that these beliefs are not amenable to reason.

IB. The Legal Theorists

One finds among some legal theorists an echoing of these juridical sentiments. The late Stephen Gey, for example, states that the separationist view of the Establishment Clause, which he and others embrace, is grounded on two primary assumptions about the nature of politics and religion. Concerning politics, "in a proper democracy, religion should be primarily a private phenomenon because religion and politics are simply incompatible." This is because, Gey says, "religion is particularly ill-suited to the sorts of pressures and influences that define the political process. Combining the typical political phenomena of personal greed, self-aggrandizement, duplicity, log-rolling, dealmaking, and unprincipled compromise, with the typical religious phenomena of theological certainty, absolute moral dictates, and the threat of eternal damnation, creates an especially dangerous cocktail." As for religion, Gey continues, the separationist assumes "it is no longer possible in the modern world to decide collectively matters that are by their nature nonrational, metaphysical, and impervious to both empirical analysis and logical proof or disproof." Given the large number of such irrational and unprovable religious perspectives embraced by citizens in our pluralistic society, "the separationist perspective is that it is best for society if everyone is permitted to follow their own faith where it leads, without having to worry about their safety in the company of others who are devoted to contradictory moral and theological absolutes."[15]

Offering an account similar to Gey's, Suzanna Sherry suggests that the relationship between church and state—as embodied in the Constitution's Free Exercise and Establishment Clauses—should be viewed as analogous to what she describes as the different and contrary epistemic commitments of faith and reason. Although she concedes that, "while it may be possible to envision a religion based wholly or partly on reason, most of the major religions in America are based on faith as the underlying epistemology." According to Sherry, "for the faithful, the ultimate authority and source of truth is extrahuman and evidence can—and in some religious traditions, must—be entirely personal to the individual." On the other hand, "for the reasonable [i.e., those who follow reason], both the source and evidence for the truth lie in common human observation, experience, and reasoning."[16]

A person operating under the epistemology of faith, according to Sherry, is "able to ignore contradictions, contrary evidence, and logical implications. Indeed, one test of faith is its capacity to resist the blandishments of rationality; the stronger the rational arguments against a belief, the more faith is needed to adhere to it. . . . [However,] secular science and liberal politics, both committed to the primacy of reason, necessarily deny that any truth is incontestable."[17]

Following along the same lines as Gey and Sherry, though in a clearly more philosophically sophisticated fashion, Brian Leiter contends that all religions have at their core two sorts of beliefs:

> (1) [At least some beliefs central to the religion] issue in *categorical* demands on action, demands that must be satisfied, no matter what an individual's antecedent desires and no matter what incentives or disincentives the world offers up;

(2) [At least some beliefs central to the religion] do not answer ultimately—
or at the limit—to *evidence* and *reasons* because evidence and reasons
are understood in other domains concerned with knowledge of the
world. Religious beliefs, in virtue of being based on "faith," are insulated from ordinary standards of evidence and rational justification, the
ones we employ in both common sense and science.[18]

Concerning (1), Leiter points out that because of the categorical nature of their
beliefs, some religious citizens have been in the forefront of many important movements for social justice, including the abolitionist movement, the American civil-
rights movement, and the cause to end apartheid in South Africa. On the other
hand, the categorical nature of their beliefs has led other religious citizens to engage
in all sorts of horrific mischief, such as supporting American racial segregation,
bombing abortion clinics, and flying airplanes into buildings.[19]

Leiter brings up two possible counters to (2). The first is what he calls "'intellectualist' traditions of religious thought." He offers up, without citation, Paley's
"natural theology," neo-Thomist arguments, and Intelligent Design as examples, and
promptly dismisses them as "insulated from the evidence," for two reasons. First,
writes Leiter, "it is dubious, to put the matter gently, that these positions are really
serious about following the evidence where it leads, as opposed to manipulating it
to fit preordained ends." And second, "in the case of the sciences, beliefs based on
evidence are also *revisable* in light of the evidence, but in the intellectualist traditions in religious thought just noted, there is no suggestion that the fundamental
beliefs will be revisable in light of new evidence."[20] The second possible counter to
(2) that Leiter brings up is Reformed Epistemology, but he promptly dismisses this
as well. After mentioning two of its most important philosophical advocates, William Alston and Alvin Plantinga, Leiter states that he is "going to assume—uncontroversially among most philosophers but controversially among reformed epistemologists—that 'reformed Epistemology' is nothing more than an effort to insulate
religious faith from ordinary standards of reasons and evidence in common sense
and the sciences, and thus religious belief is a culpable form of unwarranted belief
given those ordinary epistemic standards."[21]

There seems to be a common thread that connects the court opinions with the
views of Gey, Sherry, and Leiter. I will call this common thread, Secular Rationalism (SR). It is the view that religious beliefs are irrational because they are based
on (1) unprovable claims, in the sense that they are the sorts of belief that cannot
in principle be proven; (2) incontestable claims, in the sense that they are the sorts
of beliefs that can not in principle be falsified; and (3) claims that cannot change
or develop, because they are insulated from the ordinary standards of evidence and
rational justification.

II. DON'T KNOW MUCH ABOUT THEOLOGY

Anyone familiar with the literature in philosophy of religion, philosophy of science, metaphysics, and epistemology over the past fifty years would feel as if he or she has within grasp an embarrassment of riches by which to critique SR. Thus, given the space allotted to me, I cannot possibly offer the comprehensive critique that SR so richly deserves. For this reason, my focus will be on only three main points: (A) SR is Epistemically Suspect, (B) SR Begs Substantive Questions, and (C) SR Confuses Religion as Such with Particular Religions and the Beliefs Tethered to Them.

IIA. SR Is Epistemically Suspect

Foundationalism in epistemology is the view that for a belief to count as rational it must be either properly basic or inferable or derived from beliefs that are properly basic. Foundationalism comes in a variety of types.[22] SR seems to be a species of Narrow Foundationalism (NF), according to which we are rationally justified in holding our beliefs if and only if they are properly basic (i.e., foundational) or are based on those foundational beliefs. The only properly basic beliefs are those that are self-evident,[23] incorrigible,[24] and evident to the senses,[25] and all rational non-basic beliefs (i.e., those beliefs that are proper to hold but are not basic) must be inferable or derived from these properly basic beliefs.

It is, however, well-known that NF has been savaged in the philosophical literature because it is self-referentially incoherent.[26] That is, the claim that for a belief to be rational it must be self-evident, incorrigible, evident to the senses, or inferable, or derived from a self-evident belief, an incorrigible belief, or a belief evident to the senses is a belief that is not a self-evident belief, an incorrigible belief, or a belief evident to the senses, or inferable or derived from those beliefs. Thus, by its own standard, NF is not a rational belief and is therefore self-referentially incoherent.

SR falls prey to this same error. Take, for example, Sherry's claim that "secular science and liberal politics, both committed to the primacy of reason, necessarily deny that any truth is incontestable."[27] We can put the epistemic core of this claim in the form of a proposition:

A. Reason necessarily denies incontestable truths.

Is this an incontestable truth? If reason necessarily denies incontestable truths, and Sherry is offering *A* as a canon of reason, then *A* is not an incontestable truth. But in that case, it is not incontestable that reason necessarily denies incontestable truths. Thus, reason may in fact affirm incontestable truths. On the other hand, if *A* is an incontestable truth, and Sherry is offering *A* as a canon of reason, then it is not the case that reason necessarily denies incontestable truths. Consequently, reason requires that we believe at least one incontestable truth, namely, that reason necessarily denies incontestable truths. In that case, reason would be downright unreasonable.

But not only can one reject *A* because it is self-referentially incoherent, one can also reject it because it is simply false. Take, for example, these claims:

B. All bachelors are unmarried males.

C. 2 + 2 = 4

D. C = 2πr

B, *C*, and *D* are necessary truths. They are true in every possible world. But necessary truths are incontestable truths. If it is reasonable to believe in necessary truths (and it would seem to be so because they are in fact "truths"), then it is not only not true that reason necessarily denies incontestable truths but in some cases reason necessarily *affirms* incontestable truths.[28]

Now consider these claims:

E. It is morally wrong everywhere and always to torture children for fun.

F. The proper end of the human mind is the acquisition of wisdom.

G. Human persons are beings of immeasurable worth and dignity.

E, *F*, and *G* seem like perfectly rational beliefs for anyone to hold. They are, to be sure, not incontestable like *B*, *C*, and *D*. But they seem far less contestable than Einstein's Second Theory of Relativity, an established scientific theory if there ever was one. Nevertheless, one can easily imagine Einstein's theory being refuted, but it's difficult to imagine how one can ever be wrong about *E*, *F*, and *G*. Moreover, these beliefs are not self-evident, incorrigible, evident to the senses, or inferable or derivative from beliefs that are self-evident, incorrigible, or evident to the senses. They seem to be properly basic beliefs, perfectly rational to hold without the assistance of an argument or evidence. So, it seems that there are beliefs that one has no obligation to contest or prove that are nevertheless perfectly rational to hold. Although this should be enough to raise suspicions about SR's epistemic credentials, the SR advocate also completely ignores the facts. That is the focus of the next section.

IIB. SR Begs Substantive Questions

SR begs substantive questions by simply ignoring substantive examples of religious beliefs and defenses of them that are inconsistent with SR's definition of religion. In the writings of the legal theorists cited above, one does not find a hint that any of the authors has more than a superficial acquaintance with the vast literature produced by religious (and some nonreligious) thinkers who make a case for the rationality of beliefs on which religious worldviews often depend. Nevertheless, Leiter makes mention of "intellectualist traditions" and "reformed Epistemology," and Sherry concedes that "it might be possible to envision a religion based wholly or partly on reason."[29] Neither author goes any further than mention and dismissal. And in both cases, neither author (with the exception of Leiter's one citation of Plantinga's *Warranted Christian Belief*) connects his or her claims with any identifiable arguments or bodies of literature. To show how SR begs substantive questions, I will assess each of the three claims the SR advocate offers as support for his or her conclusion that religious beliefs are irrational: (1) religious claims are unprovable, (2) religious claims are incontestable, and (3) religious claims cannot change or develop because they are insulated from the ordinary standards of evidence and rational justification.

Because of space constraints, my analysis will focus on only one religion, Christianity, the theological tradition and its claims about which the courts and political theorists seem most concerned.[30] As should be obvious, Christianity, like virtually every religious tradition, is a complex, interconnected, and oftentimes interdependent tapestry of beliefs, practices, institutions, and ways of life that concern a variety of doctrinal, philosophical, moral, practical, liturgical, and ecclesiastical topics. Consequently, Christian theism, as is the case with every other secular or religious comprehensive worldview, entails and depends on certain beliefs, some of which are metaphysical, epistemological, historical, and moral. My analysis of SR will focus on these types of beliefs.

IIB.1. Religious Claims Are Unprovable. There are all sorts of ways that one can try to "prove" one's point of view, depending on the sort of claim one is making. If, for example, I were to claim that I am directly aware of certain universal, immutable, and abstract truths (e.g., "2 +2 = 4," "C = $2\pi r$"), it would be a fool's errand for me to try to "prove" this claim in the same way that I may try to prove that the New York Yankees beat the Boston Red Sox last night or that my wife is preparing Texas Chili in the kitchen. So, the fact that universal, immutable, and abstract truths cannot be "proven" by reading the sports section of the *Waco Tribune-Herald* or by sense of smell does not mean that they are not susceptible to demonstration.[31] For this reason, Christian thinkers offer different sorts of arguments for aspects of their worldview depending on the nature of the subject under discussion. If we look at just the literature produced over the past fifty years by serious Christian thinkers defending these metaphysical, epistemological, historical, and moral beliefs, the volume and quality of the work is impressive, even if one were to remain unconvinced by most or all of their arguments.[32]

As for the central philosophical claim of Christian theism (that there exists a self-existent, personal, necessary eternal being on which the universe depends for its existence), numerous arguments have been offered, including cosmological, moral, ontological, and teleological ones.[33] General defenses of the rationality of theism are plentiful.[34] The literature is also awash with sophisticated critiques of philosophical naturalism, Christian theism's chief intellectual rival.[35] One of the most influential arguments on that topic—Alvin Plantinga's "An Evolutionary Argument against Naturalism"—has been the subject of numerous critiques and defenses, including an entire academic tome dedicated to assessing it.[36] Metaphysical questions that have been addressed in a plethora of works concern moral realism,[37] the existence and nature of the soul,[38] and whether living organisms are substantial beings with real natures,[39] all of which many Christian thinkers see as deeply connected to their theological tradition. Some authors have argued that Christian Mystical Practice (CMP) is a doxastic practice analogous to sense perception, and thus a reliable means by which to perceive God.[40] Most religious believers and their critics consider the Problem of Evil as a possible defeater to Christian theism, and many Christian thinkers have offered a variety of responses.[41]

Christianity's central historical belief is that Jesus of Nazareth died and rose from the dead and thus vindicated his claim to be the Son of God. Numerous Christian scholars have critically assessed this belief, marshaling a case based on historical sources.[42] They have gladly engaged those who challenge it.[43] Consequently, when Sherry compares belief that Jesus is God's Son to Holocaust denial, she compounds her ignorance with irony.[44]

Leiter, to his credit, does concede that "there is a large literature in Anglophone philosophy devoted to defending the rationality of religious belief," but rather than engaging any of it, he dismisses the entirety of it in one fell swoop: "suffice it to observe that its proponents are uniformly religious believers and that much of it has the unpleasant appearance of post hoc, sometimes desperately post hoc, rationalization."[45] Remarkably, he offers virtually nothing in support of these controversial claims. Probably because it is irrelevant,[46] false,[47] and misleading,[48] he does not explain why the authors' being "uniformly religious believers" is relevant to assessing the quality and importance of their work. As for the "post hoc" accusation, he provides no actual examples but demurs by conscripting for his purposes a quote from a popular article authored by Alex Byrne, an accomplished MIT philosopher with no expertise in philosophy of religion.[49] It is not surprising that Byrne's article gets many things wrong about contemporary philosophy and its relation to the rationality of theistic belief.[50]

In one place Leiter does appear to critically assess an identifiable philosophical school of thought that supports the rationality of theism, Reformed Epistemology. But upon close inspection, one discovers that he actually does not assess it at all, let alone critically.[51] Leiter merely assumes as correct the negative judgment of Reformed Epistemology that he attributes to "most philosophers," even though he does not back up that claim with any data, does not explain why the thinking of "most philosophers" (most of whom are not experts in the appropriate philosophical specialties) provides sufficient warrant to discard by assumption an entire philosophical school of thought, and does not offer evidence that "most philoso-phers" have such an informed understanding of Reformed Epistemology that this *argumentum ad populum* is not just a fallacious appeal to authority.

IIB.2. Religious Claims Are Incontestable. This section will be very brief. First, as I have noted above, the idea that a belief must not be incontestable in order to be rationally held is self-referentially incoherent, and there are numerous beliefs that are rational to hold even though they are incontestable or nearly so (see IIA, above). In addition, much of the Christian philosophical and historical arguments surveyed above are driven by the fact that Christian beliefs are in fact contestable! Thus, the charge of incontestability is wildly off the mark.

IIB.3. Religious Claims Cannot Change or Develop Because They Are Insulated from the Ordinary Standards of Evidence and Rational Justification. What are the ordinary standards of evidence and rational justification? It depends (see IIB.1, above). Evidence and rational justification for metaphysics, history, epistemology, and ethics are different than they are for chemistry, physics, or medical pathology. Because religious claims rely more on the deliverances of the former group than the latter, it is a mystery why Leiter faults religious claims for being insulated from "standards of evidence and reasons in the sciences."[52] It's like blaming Major League Baseball for not having a twenty-four-second clock.

Claims in literature, morality, law, and philosophy are rarely within the purview of the natural sciences, but this hardly makes them irrational. For example, it seems perfectly rational (see IIA, above) to say that it is wrong always and everywhere to torture children for fun, even though it is not a belief established by any science. In fact, the claim that it is irrational to hold a belief insulated from "standards of evidence and reasons in the sciences" is itself not a deliverance of any science. Thus, on its own grounds it is irrational.

Moreover, in order for the sciences to even get off the ground they must assume certain presuppositions that are not themselves the deliverances of the sciences. As the philosopher John Kekes points out:

> Science is committed to several presuppositions: that nature exists, that it has discoverable order, that it is uniform, are existential presuppositions of science; the distinctions between space and time, cause and effect, the observer and the observed, real and apparent, orderly and chaotic, are classificatory presuppositions; while intersubjective testability, quantifiability, the public availability of data, are methodological presuppositions; some axiological presuppositions are the honest

reporting of results, the worthwhileness of getting the facts right, and scrupulousness in avoiding observational or experimental error. If any one of these presuppositions were abandoned, science, as we know it, could not be done. Yet the acceptance of the presuppositions cannot be a matter of course, for each has been challenged and alternatives are readily available.[53]

Consequently, if the sciences require presuppositions that cannot themselves be deliverances of the sciences and the sciences are rational enterprises, then we have another reason not to believe that the "standards of evidence and reasons in the sciences" are the only basis by which to assess the rationality of a belief.

There are, of course, standards of evidence and reasons that are proper to the sciences. So, perhaps what the SR advocate is claiming is that there are scientific beliefs held by some religious believers without proper regard to the standards of evidence and reasons in the sciences. Given the examples proffered by Sherry and Leiter, I suspect that this is what they mean.[54] But this is a criticism of the intellectual integrity of *the believer* and, ironically, only makes sense as a judgment of the believer's character if in fact the belief in question is *not* insulated from standards of evidence and reasons in the sciences.

But what's good for the goose is good for the gander. Remember, the SR advocate also claims to ground his position on "common sense,"[55] and that "the source and evidence for the truth lie in common human observation, experience, and reasoning,"[56] for he decries that which is "impervious to . . . empirical analysis."[57] But some views that claim to be consistent with SR and the deliverances of modern science seem not only inconsistent with common sense, experience, reasoning, and empirical analysis but also incapable of being refuted by such avenues of knowledge. Take, for example, thinkers such as Paul Churchland who maintain that modern science establishes the truth of philosophical materialism, and thus we have no grounds to believe in any immaterial realities. Churchland states, "The important point about the standard evolutionary story is that the human species and all of its features are the wholly physical outcome of a purely physical process. . . . If this is the correct account of our origins, then there seems neither need, nor room, to fit any nonphysical substances or properties into our theoretical account of ourselves. We are creatures of matter. And we should learn to live with that fact."[58] This seems to be obviously inconsistent with common sense, experience, and reasoning. For Churchland intends his statements to be about something, which means his powers of reasoning allow him to grasp ideas that provide warrant for the propositional content of his statements. But the relationship between these ideas is logical, not spatial or material, and the power to grasp and offer these ideas as reasons for a conclusion requires intentionality, an ofness or aboutness (e.g., "This thought is about materialism"), something that cannot be had by a physical state. For this reason, Churchland maintains that intentionality and all our mental states literally do not exist.[59]

Churchland also tells us that "we should learn to live" with materialism, implying that we intellectually err if we do not do what we *ought to* do. This advice seems to be grounded in the more primitive notion that our mental powers are ordered toward the acquisition of truth, and thus to frustrate that end is inconsistent with our good. But such a normative judgment—grounded in ends and goods—implies formal and final causality, which, like all our mental states, has no place in Churchland's materialism. Nevertheless, Churchland, like many other philosophical materialists who hold similar views, has not abandoned his materialism despite its apparent inconsistency with common sense, experience, and reasoning.

Does it follow from this that Churchland's unwavering posture—seeming to contravene common sense, experience, and reasoning—means that philosophical materialism, or at least Churchland's version of it, is insulated from the ordinary standards of evidence and rational justification and is therefore irrational? It depends. If one treats modern science as the measure of rationality and if one believes that modern science requires belief in philosophical materialism, and if philosophical materialism seems to be inconsistent with common sense, experience, and reasoning, then common sense, experience, and reasoning may not be rational. So, to be insulated from common sense, experience, and reasoning is not to be insulated from the ordinary standards of evidence and rational justification. And thus, Churchland's position is "rational." On the other hand, if one believes, as Gey, Sherry, and Leiter apparently do, that common sense, experience, and reasoning are of a piece with the standards and methods of modern science as well as the ordinary standards of evidence and rational justification, then philosophical materialism, or at least Churchland's version of it, may not be rational.

The point here is that there are just too many philosophical considerations that must be addressed before one can confidently suggest that a claim, religious or otherwise, is insulated from the ordinary standards of evidence and rational justification and thus cannot change or develop. Ironically then, by ignoring these considerations, the SR advocate insulates his position from just the sort of criticisms that may count against SR. But the Christian theist need not rely on this tu quoque, for as a matter of historical fact, the idea of doctrinal development—the progressive changing of beliefs over time in response to a variety of external and internal challenges and insights—is *integral* to the Christian faith as well as other faiths.[60] It is a mystery how Gey, Sherry, and Leiter could have missed this. Consider just four examples from the history of Christianity:

(1) One of the most important developments in Christian theology occurred as a consequence of its encounter with Greek philosophy. As some scholars have

noted, most Christian thinkers in the Church's first six centuries, rather than seeing pagan philosophical traditions as a threat, conscripted their insights to such an extent that the Early Church was able to formulate its most important creeds and resolve what otherwise would have been intractable theological issues.[61] Later on, as Christianity moved into the Middle Ages and into the modern period, the church's philosophical inheritance continued to play an important role in the development of dogmatic and moral theology.[62] Ironically, some writers, claiming to offer a more "scientific" understanding of theology, fault the church for *not* insulating itself from the influence of Greek philosophy.[63]

(2) St. Thomas Aquinas, relying almost exclusively on Aristotle's view of biology, held that the human fetus did not receive its rational soul until several weeks after conception.[64] It was for centuries the dominant view of the Catholic Church as well as for many non-Catholic Christians. But as the science of embryology discovered more about human development, and biology rejected Aristotle's views, the church, though never discarding Aquinas's metaphysics, embraced the view that an individual human being, with a rational soul, begins at conception.[65]

(3) Although the theory of evolution has been widely accepted in the academy, it has been rejected by some segments of the religious world, most notably among some (but by no means all) Fundamentalist and conservative Evangelical Protestants.[66] Nevertheless, the wider Christian world has engaged evolution rather impressively, showing respect for the deliverances of the natural sciences while pressing for philosophical modesty and rigor on the part of materialists who mistakenly believe that evolution is a defeater to theism.[67] The Catholic Church, for instance, has dealt with the creation/evolution question by making important and careful distinctions between science, metaphysics, and biblical hermeneutics.[68] Some Catholic authors, thoroughly committed to the church and its teachings, have made some valuable contributions in understanding the relationship between science and theology and why the proposals by certain segments of the Christian world (e.g., creationism and intelligent design) may not be fruitful approaches.[69] Other thinkers, from a variety of Christian traditions, have advanced similar efforts, though in some cases showing a bit more sympathy for intelligent design or at least the theoretical issues raised by it (while, however, engaging its critics).[70]

What this shows is that Christian thinkers—regardless of where they may stand on the intersection of theology and science—are having an important conversation among themselves and with various critics outside their communities, precisely because they do not believe that their theological beliefs are insulated from external challenges that may lead to true development and better understanding.

(4) The relationship between Christianity, its moral and political theologies, and the idea of religious liberty has clearly changed over time. As the late Avery Cardinal Dulles, SJ, pointed out: "The problem of religious freedom, as understood today, has emerged only since the Enlightenment. In the Middle Ages, no doubt, the Church tolerated or authorized practices that strike us today as inconsistent with due respect for religious freedom."[71] The changing cultural and political landscape of post-Reformation Western Europe called for Christians to reassess how they thought church and state should interact. But the Protestant and Catholic communities did not have the luxury of just affirming religious liberty by fiat. If they were to affirm it, it had to be consistent with scripture and (in the case of Catholics) tradition (including the church's prior authoritative pronouncements) and thus a legitimate development of doctrine. If theology is truly a knowledge tradition (and thus must take account of and not insulate itself from serious intellectual and cultural challenges), then thoughtful Christians had to proceed in this fashion. And they did. The Roman Catholic Church, for instance, grounds its defense of religious liberty in its rich theological anthropology, connecting this doctrinal development to the deliverances of its predecessors, while other Christians have made a different sort of case.[72]

IIC. SR Confuses Religion as Such with Particular Religions and Beliefs Tethered to Them

SR inhibits the critic of religion from getting his hands dirty. What I mean by this is that, rather than having to assess each case offered by religious believers for the policies they support, the SR advocate can simply offer his or her understanding of religion as irrational and then note that the policy defended by religious believers is tethered to that irrational tradition. This is precisely what I think Leiter does when he admits that there is a sense in which all commands of morality are categorical but nevertheless argues that the ones that issue from religious beliefs, unlike their secular counterparts, are insulated from "standards of evidence and reasons in the sciences."[73] In this way, SR functions as a sort of epistemic exclusionary rule, disallowing any arguments for public consideration if obtained without a secular warrant.

It is important to remind the reader of what we covered in IIIB. I noted there that the SR advocate ignores the voluminous number of arguments offered by religious believers, and in particular Christians, for the rationality of their theological beliefs (see IIB). But even if we set aside those arguments and concede to the SR advocate for the sake of argument that those theological beliefs are not amenable to reason, it does not follow that attendant beliefs tethered to those theological beliefs are not themselves amenable to reason. Consider, for example, Jesus' command that one ought to love one's neighbor as oneself, the Golden Rule. Suppose citizen X accepts that command because X believes that Jesus is God Incarnate and God should be obeyed because God can never be mistaken about his commands. On the other hand, citizen Y, an agnostic, also accepts the Golden Rule but not based on the authority of Jesus. Rather, Y maintains that the Golden Rule is simply a philosophical version of Immanuel Kant's Categorical Imperative that Y accepts on what he believes are reasonable arguments.[74] So, even though for the Christian the Golden Rule is tethered to Jesus' authority (a belief that the SR advocate holds is irrational), one need not accept Jesus' authority in order to be rational in accepting the Golden Rule. Moreover, some of the beliefs discussed in IIB, though embraced by religious believers, are not strictly dependent on the veracity of the believer's religion. The existence of the soul, for example, may be rationally defensible by philosophical argument even if it turns out that the believer's religion is false.[75]

Now let us consider a substantive policy question: abortion. As most everyone knows, opposition to legal abortion in the United States is disproportionally found among those who are theologically conservative religious believers, and a vast majority of those believers are Christians who identify themselves as Catholic or Evangelical Protestant. It is clear that the connection between their opposition to abortion and their religious beliefs is not merely tangential. As many pro-life advocates—as diverse as Pope John Paul II and Evangelical philosopher J. P. Moreland—have conceded, their pro-life convictions rely on a philosophical anthropology that arises from their theological beliefs about the nature of the human person.[76]

Justice John Paul Stevens dismissed the pro-life position on abortion because it is a "religious tenet" that cannot in principle rise to the level of knowledge so that it may be reflected in our laws (see section IA). There is a sense in which Justice Stevens is correct, insofar as pro-life advocates concede that their view is tethered to their theology of the human person. But there is a sense in which the justice is mistaken—not only because there are self-identified unbelievers who oppose abortion because they believe the unborn are human persons,[77] but because the case for fetal personhood offered by religious believers is based on real arguments that may be assessed independently from one accepting the theological tradition from which the belief in fetal personhood arises. Justice Stevens seems to believe that if a belief is a religious tenet it cannot in principle be the deliverance of, or supported by, rational argument. But why should anyone believe this is true, especially after one carefully examines the nature of the arguments in the abortion debate?

Those who support abortion rights—pro-choice advocates—offer arguments to establish that what they believe is the correct moral account of prenatal life. Pro-lifers, in response, offer contrary arguments for the purpose of showing that the pro-choice position is mistaken. Both sets of advocates typically zero in on one question: Is the unborn a moral subject? Pro-choicers answer this question in the negative, but the specificity of their answer depends on what they believe is the point in its development at which the unborn becomes a moral subject. Some argue for a moderate position, arguing that the fetus becomes a moral subject (or a "person") when it becomes sentient,[78] which occurs sometime between sixteen and eighteen weeks after conception. Others argue that the fetus becomes a moral subject later, at the onset of organized cortical brain activity,[79] which arises between twenty-five and thirty-two weeks after conception. Yet others locate this decisive moment at some time after birth, arguing that even newborns are not moral subjects.[80] This is why pro-choice advocates will refer to fetuses prior to whichever decisive moment they embrace as human beings that are *potential persons* but not actual persons.

Pro-lifers, with few exceptions,[81] argue that the unborn is a moral subject (i.e., a person) from the moment it comes into being at conception, because it is an individual human being and all human beings have a personal nature, even when they are not presently exercising the powers that flow from that nature's essential properties.[82] These essential properties include capacities for personal expression, rational thought, and moral agency. The maturation of these capacities are perfections of a human being's nature, and thus, contrary to what some pro-choice critics claim,[83] the human fetus can be wronged even before it can know it has been wronged.

To understand the pro-lifer's point, consider this example. Imagine that a pro-choice scientist wants to harvest human organs without at the same time harming human beings that are moral subjects, that is, persons. In order to accomplish this he first brings several embryos into being through in vitro fertilization. He then implants them in artificial wombs, and while they develop he obstructs their neural tubes so that they may never acquire higher brain functions, and thus they cannot become what the typical pro-choice advocate considers "persons."[84]

Suppose, upon hearing of this scientist's grisly undertaking, a group of pro-life radicals breaks into his laboratory and transports all the artificial wombs (with all the embryos intact) to another laboratory located in the basement of the Vatican. While there, several pro-life scientists inject the embryos with a drug that heals their neural tubes and allows for their brains to develop normally. After nine months, the former fetuses, now infants, are adopted by loving families.

If you think what the pro-life scientists did was not only good but an act that justice requires, it seems that you must believe that embryos are beings of a personal nature ordered toward certain perfections that when obstructed result in a wrong. This is why pro-life advocates would say that human embryos are not potential persons but, rather, that they are persons with potential. The point here is not to defend the pro-life position on abortion or even to make a case against the variety of pro-choice positions noted above. It is, rather, to show that the pro-life position, though tethered to the philosophical anthropology of particular theological traditions, may be defended by rational arguments independent of the veracity of any of the traditions from which it hails.

Abortion, however, is not the only public-policy issue about which religious citizens have offered rational arguments that seem to be informed by—but do not require belief in—their theological creeds. Other such public-policy issues include critiques of same-sex "marriage," physician-assisted suicide, and scientism.[85] They also include defenses of morals legislation and the full political participation of citizens informed by their religious beliefs.[86]

III. CONCLUSION

It is clear that some courts and some legal theorists misrepresent the rational status of religious beliefs as well as their attendant moral and metaphysical beliefs. The judicial opinions we covered, most of which were issued between the 1940s and the 1970s, should not surprise us. For the jurists who authored them would not have been acquainted with the literature on the rationality of religious belief that has been a staple of Anglo-American philosophy for nearly five decades.

What should surprise us are the legal theorists. A legal academy that is fully informed and intellectually serious about religion and religious beliefs should be one in which the same sort of care and deference afforded to scholarship involving speech, privacy, racial discrimination, and criminal justice would be extended without controversy to the theological traditions and beliefs that most Americans hold dear. But, as we have seen, one finds within the literature caricatures, straw men, and dismissals, claims about the religious views of the nation's citizenry that, if they were about race, gender, or sexual orientation, would be quickly and loudly dismissed by many of these same legal theorists as instances of bigotry borne of ignorance.

I am not suggesting, of course, that theism, or Christian theism in particular, does not have serious detractors who have offered fair-minded critiques of the arguments found in the literature mentioned above. But the presence of sincere and thoughtful critics of religion armed with counterarguments no more counts against the rationality of theism and its attendant moral and metaphysical notions than does the presence of sincere and thoughtful political libertarians and conservatives armed with counterarguments count against the rationality of social democracy. I am also not suggesting, by showing that religion is not by nature irrational, that there are therefore no irrational religious beliefs or that there are not legitimate philosophical and constitutional questions that one may raise against religiously informed legislation. What I am suggesting is that there is simply no justification for a court or a legal theorist to issue a negative judgment on the rationality of all religious beliefs and their attendant notions and then to employ that judgment as an immutable standard by which to exclude a priori all such beliefs from serious consideration in policy disputes. Although one could argue that the Establishment Clause of the First Amendment was intended to "separate church and state," even if those precise words do not appear in the Constitution, it hardly follows from this that it was intended as an epistemological litmus test by which a court or a legal theorist may capriciously sequester faith from reason.

NOTES

1. John Rawls, *Political Liberalism*, rev. ed. (New York: Columbia University Press, 1996).

2. According to Rawls *reasonable comprehensive doctrines* have three main features:

One is that a reasonable doctrine is an exercise of theoretical reason: it covers the major religious, philosophical, and moral aspects of human life in a more or less consistent and coherent manner. It organizes and characterizes recognized values so that they are compatible with one another and express an intelligible view of the world. Each doctrine will do this in ways that distinguish it from other doctrines, for example, by giving certain values a particular primacy and weight. In singling out which values to count as especially significant and how to balance them when they conflict, a reasonable comprehensive doctrine is also an exercise of practical reason. Both theoretical and practical reason (including as appropriate the rational) are used together in its formulation. Finally, a third feature is that while a reasonable comprehensive view is not necessarily fixed and unchanging, it normally belongs to, or draws upon, a tradition of thought and doctrine. Although stable over time, and not subject to sudden and unexplained changes, it tends to evolve slowly in the light of what, from its point of view, it sees as good and sufficient reasons. (*Political Liberalism*, 59)

3. "Since the political conception is shared by everyone while the reasonable doctrines are not, we must distinguish between a public basis of justificaton generally acceptable to citizens on fundamental political questions and the many nonpublic bases of justification belonging to the many comprehensive doctrines and acceptable only to those who affirm them" (ibid., xix).

4. James Hitchcock, *The Supreme Court and Religion in American Life*, vol. 2, *From "Higher Law" to "Sectarian Scruples"* (Princeton, NJ: Princeton University Press, 2004), 67–76, 120–32.

5. Ibid., 128.

6. Of course, it is widely accepted by most philosophers of science that the natural sciences, such as physics, chemistry, biology, astronomy, and so on, involve more than empirical proof, requiring also a host of philosophical and conceptual assumptions in order to even get off the

ground. See, for example, Larry Laudan and Jarrett Leplin, "Empirical Equivalence and Underdetermination," *Journal of Philosophy* 88.9 (September 1991): 449–72; Thomas Kuhn, *The Structures of Scientific Revolutions*, 3rd ed. (Chicago: University of Chicago Press, 1996).

7. *United States v. Ballard*, 322 U.S. 78 (1944), 87–88.

8. *Serbian Orthodox Diocese v. Milivojevich*, 426 U.S. 696 (1976), 715–16, 716.

9. "These things shall be a statute and ordinance for you throughout your generations wherever you live. If anyone kills another, the murderer shall be put to death on the evidence of witnesses; but no one shall be put to death on the testimony of a single witness. Moreover you shall accept no ransom for the life of a murderer who is subject to the death penalty; a murderer must be put to death" (Numbers 35: 29–31—NRSV).

10. *Wolman v. Walter,* 433 U.S. 229 (1977), 265 (Stevens, J., concurring), quoting from Tr. of Oral Arg. 7, *Scopes v. State,* 154 Tenn. 105, 289 S. W. 363 (1927), on file with Clarence Darrow Papers, Library of Congress (punctuation corrected).

11. In his analysis of a Missouri statute that placed restrictions on abortion and included a preamble that asserted that human life begins at conception, Justice Stevens wrote:

> Indeed, I am persuaded that the absence of any secular purpose for the legislative declarations that life begins at conception and that conception occurs at fertilization makes the relevant portion of the preamble invalid under the Establishment Clause of the First Amendment to the Federal Constitution. This conclusion does not, and could not, rest on the fact that the statement happens to coincide with the tenets of certain religions … or on the fact that the legislators who voted to enact it may have been motivated by religious considerations. . . . Rather, it rests on the fact that the preamble, an unequivocal endorsement of a religious tenet of some but by no means all Christian faiths, serves no identifiable secular purpose. That fact alone compels a conclusion that the statute violates the Establishment Clause. . . . As a secular matter, there is an obvious difference between the state interest in protecting the freshly fertilized egg and the state interest in protecting a 9-month-gestated, fully sentient fetus on the eve of birth. There can be no interest in protecting the newly fertilized egg from physical pain or mental anguish, because the capacity for such suffering does not yet exist; respecting a developed fetus, however, that interest is valid. (*Webster v. Reproductive Health Services*, 492 U.S. 490 [1989], 566–67, 569 [Stevens, J., dissenting; notes and citations omitted])

Of course, Justice Stevens's judgment begs the question, since one cannot justify the killing of a presentient human being merely on the grounds that it lacks sentience. He is assuming—rather than arguing for—the truth of the belief that sentience is a property a human being must possess in order for the law to be justified in protecting that being from homicide.

12. *Engle v. Vitale,* 370 U.S. 421 (1962), 432.

13. *Lee v. Weisman,* 505 U.S. 577 (1992), 589.

14. Ibid., 645 (J. Scalia, dissenting).

15. Steven G. Gey, "Life after the Establishment Clause," *West Virginia Law Review* 110 (2007): 11.

16. Suzanna Sherry, "Enlightening the Religion Clauses," *Journal of Contemporary Legal Issues* 7.1 (1996): 478.

17. Ibid., 482, 479.

18. Brian Leiter, "Foundations of Religious Liberty: Toleration or Respect?" *San Diego Law Review* 47 (2010): 944–45.

19. Ibid., 945–46.

20. Ibid., 947–48.

21. Ibid., 955.

22. See Ted Poston, "Foundationalism" (updated June 10, 2010), in *Internet Encyclopedia of Philosophy: A Peer-Reviewed Academic Resource*, available at http://www.iep.utm.edu/found-ep/.

23. A self-evident belief is a belief that is true by definition or a necessary truth, for example, "All bachelors are unmarried males," "2 + 3 = 5," or "C = 2πr."

24. An incorrigible belief is a subjective belief about which one cannot be mistaken, for example, "I feel pain." It may be that one's pain is illusory, in the sense there is no neurological or physical cause of one's pain, but the feeling of pain is undeniable. Or suppose that you are Mr. Scrooge and you seem to have been awoken by what appears to be a being who claims to be the Ghost of Christmas Past. You have the incorrigible belief that you are being appeared to by the Ghost of Christmas Past, even though it may be the case that you are hallucinating, dreaming, or a neighbor is dressed up as the ghost in order to guilt you into abandoning your greed. Nevertheless, it is incorrigibly the case that you are being appeared to Ghost-of-Christmas-Pastly.

25. Beliefs that are evident to the senses are those beliefs about the world that come to us through our senses and about which we could be mistaken. When Tom sees a basketball court when he looks out into my backyard, he comes to believe that there is a basketball court in my backyard.

26. See, for example, Alvin Plantinga, *Warranted Christian Belief* (New York: Oxford University Press, 2000), 94–97.

27. Sherry, "Enlightening the Religion Clauses," 479.

28. These are self-evident truths, and so in this sense, the Narrow Foundationalist would also reject the "incontestable" prong of SR.

29. Leiter, "Foundations of Religious Liberty," 947, 955; Sherry, "Enlightening," 478. As I noted in the text, Leiter mentions "neo-Thomism" and "Intelligent Design" (947–48) but refers to no actual arguments and cites no actual publications or authors.

30. This is not to say that some of what we cover below would not also apply to other religious traditions. But given this chapter's space constraints, and the fact that virtually all interest in religion and law questions in the United States concerns the claims of Christian

citizens to shape public policy and be free of government coercion, focusing on Christian theism makes the most sense.

31. The late philosopher Greg Bahnsen once called this "the beer in the refrigerator fallacy." Just because the best way to answer the question "Is there beer in the refrigerator?" is to go and look does not mean that this is the way we find other things.

32. Although it probably need not be said, but a position's rationality, religious or otherwise, does not depend on whether all, most, or even some dissenters from the position are convinced of it based on the arguments offered by its champions. For if that were the case, one could simply dismiss the arguments offered by Gey, Sherry, and Leiter as irrational because some, perhaps many, sophisticated critics find their arguments unconvincing. Moreover, if total or near unanimity were the test for rationality, then virtually every contested point of view in the academy would be "irrational."

33. See, for example, William Lane Craig and J. P. Moreland, eds., *The Blackwell Companion to Natural Theology* (Oxford, UK: Wiley-Blackwell, 2009); Richard Swinburne, *The Existence of God* (New York: Oxford University Press, 1979); William Lane Craig, *The Kalam Cosmological Argument* (New York: MacMillan, 1979); C. Stephen Evans, *Natural Signs and Knowledge of God: A New Look at Theistic Arguments* (New York: Oxford University Press, 2010); Alvin Plantinga, *The Ontological Argument from St. Anselm to Contemporary Philosophers* (Garden City, NY: Doubleday, 1965).

34. See, for example, John Haldane, *Reasonable Faith* (New York: Routledge, 2010); Paul Mosser and Paul Copan, eds., *The Rationality of Theism* (New York: Routledge, 2003); Alvin Plantinga, *Warranted Christian Belief* (New York: Oxford University Press, 2000); Alvin Plantinga, *God and Other Minds* (Ithaca, NY: Cornell University Press, 1967); Alvin Plantinga and Nicholas Wolterstorff, eds., *Faith and Rationality: Reason and Belief in God* (Notre Dame, IN: University of Notre Dame Press, 1983); Charles Taliaferro and Jill Evans, *Image in Mind: Theism, Naturalism, and the Imagination* (New York: Continuum, 2010); Richard Swinburne, *Faith and Reason* (Oxford: Clarendon, 1983); Alvin Plantinga and Michael Tooley, *Knowledge of God* (Malden, MA: Wiley-Blackwell, 2008); Edward Feser, *The Last Superstition: A Refutation of the New Atheists* (South Bend, IN: St. Augustine Press, 2008).

35. Robert C. Koons and Gregory Bealer, eds., *The Waning of Materialism* (New York: Oxford University Press, 2010); William Lane Craig and J. P. Moreland, eds., *Naturalism: A Critical Analysis* (New York: Routledge, 2000); Stewart Goetz and Charles Taliaferro, *Naturalism* (Grand Rapids, MI: Eerdmans, 2008); Michael Rae, *World without Design: The Ontological Consequences of Naturalism* (New York: Oxford University Press, 2004).

36. Alvin Plantinga, *Warrant and Proper Function* (New York: Oxford University Press, 1993), 216–37. For critiques and defenses see, for example, Branden Fitelson and Elliot Sober, "Plantinga's Probability Arguments against Evolutionary Naturalism," in *Intelligent Design Creationism and Its Critics: Philosophical, Theological, and Scientific Perspectives*, ed. Robert T. Pennock (Cambridge, MA: MIT Press, 2001); J. Wesley Robbins, "Is Naturalism Irrational?" *Faith and Philosophy* 11.2 (1994): 255–59. For the book dedicated exclusively to assessing Plantinga's

argument, see James Beilby, ed., *Naturalism Defeated? Essays on Plantinga's Evolutionary Argument against Naturalism* (Ithaca, NY: Cornell University Press, 2002).

37. See, for example, John M. Rist, *Real Ethics: Reconsidering the Foundations of Morality* (New York: Cambridge University Press, 2002); John E. Hare, *God's Call: Moral Realism, God's Commands, and Human Autonomy* (Grand Rapids, MI: Eerdmans, 2001); J. P. Moreland, "Ethics Depend on God," in J. P. Moreland and Kai Nielsen, *Does God Exist? The Debate between Theists and Atheists* (Amherst, NY: Prometheus Books, 1993), 111–26.

38. See, for example, William Hasker, *The Emergent Self* (Ithaca, NY: Cornell University Press, 1999); Richard Swinburne, *The Evolution of the Soul*, 2nd ed. (New York: Oxford University Press, 1997); J. P. Moreland, *The Recalcitrant* Imago Dei: *Human Persons and the Failure of Naturalism* (London: SCM Press, 2009); J. P. Moreland, *Consciousness and the Existence of God: A Theistic Argument* (New York: Routledge, 2009); Ric Machuga, *In Defense of the Soul: What It Means to Be Human* (Grand Rapids, MI: Brazos Press, 2002); Mark C. Baker and Stewart Goetz, eds., *Soul Hypothesis: Investigations into the Existence of the Soul* (New York: Continuum, 2011).

39. See, for example, Davis S. Oderberg, *Real Essentialism* (New York: Routledge, 2007); John Haldane, ed., *Mind, Metaphysics, and Value in the Thomistic and Analytical Traditions* (Notre Dame, IN: University of Notre Dame Press, 2002).

40. See, for example, William Alston, "Perceiving God," *Journal of Philosophy* 83.11 (1986): 655–65; William Alston, *Perceiving God: The Epistemology Religious Experience* (Ithaca, NY: Cornell University Press, 1991).

41. See, for example, William L. Rowe, ed., *God and the Problem of Evil* (Malden, MA: Blackwell, 2001); for responses, see Brian Davies, *The Reality of God and the Problem of Evil* (New York: Continuum, 2006); Richard Swinburne, *Providence and the Problem of Evil* (New York: Oxford University Press, 1998); Alvin Plantinga, *God, Freedom, and Evil* (New York: Harper and Row, 1974).

42. See, for example, N. T. Wright, *The Resurrection of the Son of God* (Minneapolis, MN: Fortress Press, 2003); Michael R. Licona, *The Resurrection of Jesus: A New Historiographical Approach* (Downers Grove, IL: InterVarsity Press, 2011); Richard Swinburne, *The Resurrection of God Incarnate* (Oxford: Oxford University Press, 2003); Stephen T. Davis, Daniel Kendall, and Gerald O'Collins, eds., *The Resurrection: An Interdisciplinary Symposium on the Resurrection of Jesus* (New York: Oxford University Press, 1997); C. Stephen Evans, *The Historical Christ and the Jesus of Faith: The Incarnational Narrative as History* (New York: Oxford University Press, 1996); William Lane Craig, *Assessing the New Testament Evidence for the Historicity of the Resurrection of Jesus* (Toronto: Edwin Mellen, 1989).

43. See, for example, Paul Copan, ed., *Will the Real Jesus Please Stand Up? A Debate between William Lane Craig and Dominic Crosson* (Grand Rapids, MI: Baker, 1998); Paul Copan and R. K. Tacelli, SJ, eds., *Jesus' Resurrection: Fact or Figment? A Debate between William Lane Craig and Gerd Ludemann* (Downers Grove, IL: InterVarsity Press, 2000); Gary R. Habermas and Antony G. N. Flew, *Did Jesus Rise from the Dead? The Resurrection Debate*, ed. Terry Miethe (New York: Harper and Row, 1987).

44. "There is indeed no principled way to distinguish those who maintain that the Holocaust never occurred from those who maintain that . . . Jesus Christ was [God's] Son." Sherry, "Enlightening," 491.

45. Leiter, "Foundations," 954.

46. Would anyone take seriously a philosopher who dismissed the rationality of philosophical materialism because its proponents are uniformly philosophical materialists?

47. There are, in fact, some nontheists who reject belief in God but nevertheless maintain that belief in God is rational. They are sometimes called "friendly atheists," a term coined by atheist philosopher William Rowe. See Rowe, "Friendly Atheism, Skeptical Theism, and the Problem of Evil," chapter 12 of *William L. Rowe on Philosophy of Religion: Selected Writings by William Rowe*, ed. Nick Trakakis (Burlington, VT: Ashgate, 2007). There are nontheist philosophers whose works have lent support to metaphysical and epistemological beliefs congenial to, and some say central to, Christian theism. See, for example, Thomas Nagel, *Mind and Cosmos: Why the Materialist Neo-Darwinian Conception of Nature Is Almost Certainly False* (New York: Oxford University Press, 2012); Karl R. Popper, *Knowledge and the Body-Mind Problem*, ed. M. A. Notturno (London: Routledge, 1994); Bradley Monton, *Seeking God in Science: An Atheist Defends Intelligent Design* (Buffalo, NY: Broadview Press, 2009).

48. Leiter gives the impression that only theists care about the rationality of religious belief and take the arguments for it seriously. But this is simply misleading. There are in fact many accomplished nontheist philosophers who take very seriously the rationality of religious belief as well as metaphysical and epistemological issues attendant to those beliefs (e.g., existence of the soul, metaphysical realism, critiques of foundationalism), and who have made assessments of those arguments an important part of their professional work. These include Rowe, Nagel, Monton, Paul Draper, Quentin Smith, Wes Morriston, Richard Gale, Graham Oppy, and Michael Tooley. Smith, for example, states in a 2001 piece in the journal *Philo*:

> The secularization of mainstream academia began to quickly unravel upon the publication of Plantinga's influential book on realist theism, *God and Other Minds*, in 1967. It became apparent to the philosophical profession that this book displayed that realist theists were not outmatched by naturalists in terms of the most valued standards of analytic philosophy: conceptual precision, rigor of argumentation, technical erudition, and an in-depth defense of an original world-view. This book, followed seven years later by Plantinga's even more impressive book, *The Nature of Necessity*, made it manifest that a realist theist was writing at the highest qualitative level of analytic philosophy, on the same playing field as Carnap, Russell, Moore, Grünbaum, and other naturalists. Realist theists, whom hitherto had segregated their academic lives from their private lives, increasingly came to believe (and came to be increasingly accepted or respected for believing) that arguing for realist theism in scholarly publications could no longer be justifiably regarded as engaging in an "academically unrespectable" scholarly pursuit.

Naturalists passively watched as realist versions of theism, most influenced by Plantinga's writings, began to sweep through the philosophical community, until today perhaps one-quarter or one-third of philosophy professors are theists, with most being orthodox Christians. Although many theists do not work in the area of the philosophy of religion, so many of them do work in this area that there are now over five philosophy journals devoted to theism or the philosophy of religion, such as *Faith and Philosophy, Religious Studies, International Journal of the Philosophy of Religion, Sophia, Philosophia Christi,* etc. *Philosophia Christi* began in the late 1990s and already is overflowing with submissions from leading philosophers. . . . In philosophy, it became, almost overnight, "academically respectable" to argue for theism, making philosophy a favored field of entry for the most intelligent and talented theists entering academia today. A count would show that in Oxford University Press's 2000–2001 catalogue there are 96 recently published books on the philosophy of religion (94 advancing theism and 2 presenting "both sides"). By contrast, there are 28 books in this catalogue on the philosophy of language, 23 on epistemology (including religious epistemology, such as Plantinga's *Warranted Christian Belief*), 14 on metaphysics, 61 books on the philosophy of mind, and 51 books on the philosophy of science. (Quentin Smith, "The Metaphilosophy of Naturalism," *Philo* 4.2 [Fall–Winter 2001]: 195–215)

49. "It is fair to say that the arguments [for God's existence] have left the philosophical community underwhelmed. The classic contemporary work is J. L. Mackie's *The Miracle of Theism,* whose ironic title summarizes Mackie's conclusion: the persistence of belief in God is a kind of miracle because it is so unsupported by reason and evidence." Alex Byrne, "God," *Boston Review of Books* (January–February 2009), available at http://www.bostonreview.net/BR34.1/byrne.php, quoted in Leiter, "Foundations," 954–55.

50. See William Lane Craig, "Byrne on Theistic Philosophers," EPS Blog, January 5, 2009, at http://blog.epsociety.org/2009/01/byrne-on-theistic-philosophers.asp.

51. "I am going to assume—uncontroversially among most philosophers but controversially among reformed epistemologists—that 'reformed epistemology' is nothing more than an effort to insulate religious faith from ordinary standards of reasons and evidence in common sense and the sciences, and thus religious belief is a culpable form of unwarranted belief given those ordinary epistemic standards." Leiter, "Foundations," 955.

52. Ibid., 947.

53. John Kekes, *The Nature of Philosophy* (Totowa, N.J.: Rowman and Littlefield, 1980), 156–57.

54. Leiter states:

Even here, of course, we need to be careful. There are, for example, "intellectualist" traditions in religious thought—Paley's "natural theology" or neo-Thomist arguments come to mind—according to which religious beliefs (for example, belief in a Creator or, as in America recently, belief in "an Intelligent Designer") are, in fact, supported by the kinds of evidence adduced in the sciences, once that evidence is rightly interpreted. It is doubtful whether these intellectualist traditions capture the character of popular religious belief, but even if they did, there remain important senses in which they are still "*insulated from evidence.*" First, of course, it is dubious (to put the matter gently) that these positions are really serious about following the evidence where it leads, as opposed to manipulating it to fit preordained ends. Second, and relatedly, in the case of the sciences, beliefs based on evidence are also *revisable* in light of the evidence; but in the intellectualist traditions in religious thought just noted, there is no suggestion that the fundamental beliefs will be revisable in light of new evidence. Religious beliefs are *purportedly* supported by evidence, but they are still insulated from revision *in light of evidence.* (Leiter, "Foundations," 947–48; note omitted)

Sherry, in a footnote, says that what she has "in mind [are] such beliefs as creationism, see, e.g., *Edwards v. Aguillard*, 482 U.S. 578 (1987), faith healing; *Lundman v. McKown*, 530 N.W.2d 807 (Minn. Ct. App. 1995), cert. denied, 116 S. Ct. 814, 828 (1996), and the variety of commands purportedly imposed by God, *Sherbert v. Verner*, 374 U.S. 398 (1963)." Sherry, "Enlightening," 478n26.

55. Leiter, "Foundations," 945.

56. Sherry, "Enlightening," 478.

57. Gey, "Life after the Establishment Clause," 11.

58. Paul Churchland, *Matter and Consciousness* (Cambridge, MA: MIT Press, 1984), 21.

59. Paul Churchland, "Eliminative Materialism and the Propositional Attitudes," *Journal of Philosophy* 78 (1981): 67–90. According to Churchland, "eliminative materialism is the thesis that our common-sense conception of psychological phenomena constitutes a radically false theory, a theory so fundamentally defective that both the principles and the ontology of that theory will eventually be displaced, rather than smoothly reduced, by completed neuroscience. Our mutual understanding and even our introspection may then be reconstituted within the conceptual framework of completed neuroscience, a theory we may expect to be more powerful by far than the common-sense psychology it displaces, and more substantially integrated within physical science generally" (ibid., 67).

60. For the classic modern Catholic and Protestant accounts of doctrinal development, see respectively, John Henry Cardinal Newman, *An Essay on the Development of Christina Doctrine*, rev. ed., foreword by Ian Kerr (1878; Notre Dame, IN: University of Notre Dame Press, 1989); James Orr, *The Progress of Dogma* (London: Hotter and Stoughton, 1901).

61. See, for example, Pope Benedict XVI, "Faith, Reason, and the University: Memories and Reflections" (September 12, 2006), available at http://www.vatican.va/holy_father/

benedict_xvi/speeches/2006/september/documents/hf_ben-xvi_spe_20060912_university-regensburg_en.html; John Mark Reynolds, *When Athens Met Jerusalem: An Introduction to Classical and Christian Thought* (Downers Grove, IL: InterVarsity Press, 2009), 221–45.

62. See, for example, John M. Rist, *What Is Truth? From the Academy to the Vatican* (New York: Cambridge University Press, 2008); Etienne Gilson, *God and Philosophy* (New Haven, CT: Yale University Press, 1941); Etienne Gilson, *History of Christian Philosophy in the Middle Ages* (New York: Random House, 1955).

63. See, for example, Adolf Harnack, *History of Dogma*, vol. 1, trans. Neil Buchanan (Grand Rapids, MI: Christian Classics Ethereal Library, 1894), cf. C. Wayne Glick, "Nineteenth Century Theological and Cultural Influences on Adolf Harnack," *Church History* 28.2 (June 1959): 157–82.

64. See, for example, Benedict Ashley and Albert Moraczewski, "Cloning, Aquinas, and the Embryonic Person," *National Catholic Bioethics Quarterly* 1.2 (Summer 2001): 189–201. Ashley and Moraczewski note:

> Aquinas . . . did not know that the matter out of which the human body is generated is already highly organized at conception and endowed with the efficient and formal causality necessary to organize itself into a system in which, as it matures, the brain becomes the principal adult organ. Hence he was forced to resort to the hypothesis that the male semen remains in the womb, gradually organizing the menstrual blood, first to the level of vegetative life and then to the level of animal life, so as to be capable of the further self-development needed for ensoulment. But he also supposed that this entire process from its initiation was teleologically (final cause) predetermined to produce a human person, not a vegetable, an infra-human animal, or a mere embryonic collection of independent cells. That is why the Catholic Church has always taught that even if it were true that personal ensoulment takes place sometime after conception, nevertheless abortion at any stage is a very grave sin against the dignity of a human *person*. (Ibid., 200)

65. See, e.g., *Catechism of the Catholic Church: Revised in Accordance with the Official Latin Text Promulgated by Pope John Paul II*, 2nd ed. (Washington, D.C.: United States Conference of Catholic Bishops, 2000), 26–49, 1877–948, 2104–9, 2331–400; Pope John Paul II, *Evangelium Vitae: The Gospel of Life* (March 25, 1995), available at http://www.vatican.va/holy_father/john_paul_ii/encyclicals/documents/hf_jp-ii_enc_25031995_evangelium-vitae_en.html; John Paul II, *Fides et Ratio: On the Relationship between Faith and Reason* (September 14, 1998), 44–45, available at http://www.vatican.va/holy_father/john_paul_ii/encyclicals/documents/hf_jp-ii_enc_15101998_fides-et-ratio_en.html.

66. One has to be careful here, for there is a wide spectrum of views among Evangelical Protestants. See, for example, the helpful article by Presbyterian pastor Tim Keller, "Creation, Evolution, and Christian Laypeople," *BioLogos White Paper* (November 2009), available at http://biologos.org/uploads/projects/Keller_white_paper.pdf.

67. The work of the Reformed philosopher Alvin Plantinga is particularly illuminating in this regard. See, for example, Alvin Plantinga, *Where the Conflict Really Lies: Science, Religion, and Naturalism* (New York: Oxford University Press, 2012); Daniel C. Dennett and Alvin Plantinga, *Science and Religion: Are They Compatible?* (New York: Oxford University Press, 2010).

68. See, for example, Pope Pius XII, *Humani Generis* (August 12, 1950), available at http://www.vatican.va/holy_father/pius_xii/encyclicals/documents/hf_p-xii_enc_12081950_humani-generis_en.html; Pope John Paul II, "Message to the Pontifical Academy of Sciences: On Evolution" (October 22, 1996), available at http://www.ewtn.com/library/PAPALDOC/JP961022.HTM; Joseph Cardinal Ratzinger, *"In the Beginning . . .": A Catholic Understanding of the Story of Creation and the Fall*, trans. Boniface Ramsey (Grand Rapids, MI: Eerdmans, 1986).

69. See, for example, Etienne Gilson, *From Aristotle to Darwin and Back Again: A Journey in Final Causality, Species, and Evolution*, trans. John Lyon (Notre Dame, IN: University of Notre Dame Press, 1984); Brad S. Gregory, "Science versus Religion? The Insights and Oversights of the 'New Atheists,'" *Logos: A Journal of Catholic Thought* 12.4 (2009): 17–55; Sr. Damien Marie Savino, FSE, "Atheistic Science: The Only Option?" *Logos: A Journal of Catholic Thought and Culture* 12.4 (2009): 56–73; William E. Carroll, "At the Mercy of Chance? Evolution and the Catholic Tradition," *Revue des Questions Scientifiques* 177 (2006): 179–204; William E. Carroll, "Creation, Evolution, and Thomas Aquinas," *Revue des Questions Scientifiques* 171 (2000): 319–47; Michael W. Tkacz, "Thomas Aquinas versus the Intelligent Designers: What Is God's Finger Doing in My Pre-Biotic Soup?" in *Intelligent Design: Science or Religion? Critical Perspectives*, ed. Robert M. Baird and Stuart E. Rosenbaum (Amherst, NY: Prometheus Books, 2007), 275–82; Michael Tkacz, "The Retorsive Argument for Formal Cause and the Darwinian Account of Scientific Knowledge," *International Philosophical Quarterly* 43 (2003): 159–66; Edward Feser, *Aquinas: A Beginner's Guide* (Oxford, UK: Oneworld, 2009), 36–51, 110–20; Mark Ryland, "Intelligent Design Theory," in *New Catholic Encyclopedia Supplement*, ed. Robert L. Fastiggi (Farmington Hills, MI: Gale Publishing, 2009), 1:470–78; James A. Sadowsky, SJ, "Did Darwin Destroy the Design Argument?" *International Philosophical Quarterly* 28 (1988): 95–104; Avery Cardinal Dulles, SJ, "God and Evolution," *First Things* 176 (October 2007): 19–24; Machuga, *In Defense of the Soul*.

70. For theistic alternatives to intelligent design, see, for example, Simon Conway Morris, *Life's Solution: Inevitable Humans in a Lonely Universe* (Cambridge, UK: Cambridge University Press, 2003); Francis Collins, *The Language of God: A Scientist Presents Evidence for Belief* (New York: The Free Press, 2006). For the critics of intelligent design, see, for example, Bruce L. Gordon and William A. Dembski, eds., *The Nature of Nature: Examining the Role of Naturalism in Science* (Wilmington, DE: ISI Books, 2011); Del Ratzsch, *Nature, Science, and Design: The Status of Design in Natural Science*, Philosophy and Biology Series (Albany, NY: State University of New York Press, 2001); Plantinga, *Where the Conflict Really Lies*.

71. Avery Cardinal Dulles, SJ, "*Dignitatis Humanae* and the Development of Catholic Doctrine," in *Catholicism and Religious Freedom: Contemporary Reflections on Vatican II's Declaration on Religious Liberty*, ed. Kenneth L. Grasso and Robert P. Hunt (Lanham, MD: Sheed and Ward, 2006), 43.

72. *The Declaration on Religious Freedom: Dignatitis Humanae* (December 7, 1965), available at http://www.vatican.va/archive/hist_councils/ii_vatican_council/documents/vat-ii_decl_19651207_dignitatis-humanae_en.html. For "other Christians," see, for example, James E. Wood Jr., E. Bruce Thompson, and Robert T. Miller, *Church and State in Scripture, History, and Constitutional Law* (Waco, TX: Baylor University Press, 1958).

73. Leiter, "Foundations," 947.

74. There are several formulations of Kant's Categorical Imperative, the most well-known of which is: "Act only according to that maxim whereby you can, at the same time, will that it should become a universal law." Immanuel Kant, *Grounding for the Metaphysics of Morals* [1785], with *On a Supposed Right to Lie Because of Philanthropic Concerns*, trans. James W. Ellington, 3rd ed. (Indianapolis, IN: Hackett, 1993), 30.

75. The secular philosopher Karl Popper, for example, rejected mind-body physicalism. See Popper, *Knowledge and the Body-Mind Problem.*

76. Pope John Paul II, *Evangelium Vitae*; J. P. Moreland and Scott B. Rae, *Body and Soul: Human Nature and the Crisis in Ethics* (Dowers Grove, IL: InterVarsity Press, 2000).

77. Doris Gordon (President, Libertarians for Life) and Nat Hentoff (writer, *The Village Voice*) are pro-life atheists. See Doris Gordon, "Abortion Rights and Wrongs: Applying Libertarian Beliefs Correctly," available at http://www.fnsa.org/v1n2/gordon1.html (text) and at http://www.fnsa.org/v1n2/gordon2.html (endnotes); Nat Hentoff, "The Indivisible Fight for Life" (October 19, 1986), available at http://groups.csail.mit.edu/mac/users/rauch/nvp/consistent/indivisible.html.

78. See, for example, L. W. Sumner, *Abortion and Moral Theory* (Princeton, NJ: Princeton University Press, 1981).

79. See, for example, David Boonin, *A Defense of Abortion* (New York: Cambridge University Press, 2002). For a similar approach, see Kenneth Himma, "A Dualist Analysis of Abortion: Personhood and the Concept of Self Qua Experiential Subject," *Journal of Medical Ethics* 31.1 (2005): 48–55.

80. See, for example, Peter Singer and Helen Kuhse, "On Letting Handicapped Infants Die," in *The Right Thing to Do: Basic Readings in Moral Philosophy*, ed. James Rachels (New York: Random House, 1989); Alberto Giubilini and Francesca Minerva, "After-Birth Abortion: Why Should the Baby Live?" *Journal of Medical Ethics*, 39.5 (May 2013): 261–63. For a response, see Francis J. Beckwith, "Potentials and Burdens: A Reply to Giubilini and Minerva," *Journal of Medical Ethics* 39 (May 2013): 341–44.

81. There are a few pro-lifers who argue that very early on in pregnancy (roughly during the first fourteen days after conception) the unborn is not yet an individual unified organism, because it consists of pluripotent cells that are undifferentiated, and thus is not a moral subject. See, for example, Don Marquis, "The Moral-Principle Objection to Embryonic Stem-Cell Research," *Metaphilosophy* 38.2–3 (April 2007): 190–206.

82. See, for example, Stephen Napier, ed., *Persons, Moral Worth, and Embryos: A Critical Analysis of Pro-Choice Arguments* (Dordrecht, Neth.: Springer, 2011); Robert P. George and

Christopher Tollefsen, *Embryo: A Defense of Human Life*, 2nd ed. (Princeton, NJ: Witherspoon Institute, 2011); Patrick Lee, *Abortion and Unborn Human Life*, 2nd ed. (Washington, D.C.: Catholic University of America Press, 2010); Christopher Kaczor, *The Ethics of Abortion: Women's Rights, Human Life, and the Question of Justice* (New York: Routledge, 2011); Francis J. Beckwith, *Defending Life: A Moral and Legal Case against Abortion Choice* (New York: Cambridge University Press, 2007); Moreland and Rae, *Body and Soul*.

83. "We take 'person' to mean an individual who is capable of attributing to her own existence some (at least) basic value such that being deprived of this existence represents a loss to her. This means that many nonhuman animals and mentally retarded human individuals are persons, but that all the individuals who are not in the condition of attributing any value to their own existence are not persons. Merely being human is not in itself a reason for ascribing someone a right to life." Giubilini and Minerva, "After-Birth Abortion," 2.

84. Boonin, for example, notes: "For on the account of the wrongness of killing that results from this modification of the original future-like-ours argument, the existence of other individuals makes a legitimate moral demand on us in virtue of their having at least some actual desires about how their lives go. . . . A human fetus has no such desires prior to the point at which it has conscious experiences, and it has no conscious experiences prior to the point at which it has organized electrical activity in its cerebral cortex. It therefore has no such desires prior to the point at which it has organized electrical activity in its cerebral cortex." Boonin, *A Defense of Abortion*, 125, 126.

85. On marriage, see, for example, Sherif Girgis, Robert P. George, and Ryan T. Anderson, "What Is Marriage?" *Harvard Journal of Law and Public Policy* 34 (2010): 245–87; David Bradshaw, "A Reply to Corvino," in *Same Sex: Debating the Ethics, Science, and Culture of Homosexuality*, ed. John Corvino (Lanham, MD: Rowman and Littlefield, 1997), 17–30; Mary Geach, "Lying with the Body," *The Monist* 91.3–4 (July–October 2008): 523–57; Patrick Lee, "Marriage, Procreation, and Same-Sex Unions," *The Monist* 91.3–4 (July–October 2008): 422–38; John M. Finnis, "Law, Morality, and 'Sexual Orientation,'" *Notre Dame Law Review* 69.5 (1994): 1049–76. For physician-assisted suicide, see, for example, John Keown, *Euthanasia, Ethics and Public Policy: An Argument against Legalisation* (New York: Cambridge University Press, 2002). For scientism, see, for example, Plantinga, *Where the Conflict Really Lies*; Leon R. Kass, *Toward a Moral Natural Science: Biology and Human Affairs* (New York: Basic Books, 1988); Gregory, "Science versus Religion?"; Carroll, "Creation, Evolution, and Thomas Aquinas"; Edward Feser, "Blinded by Scientism," *Public Discourse* (9 March 2010), available at http://www.thepublicdiscourse.com/2010/03/1174.

86. For morals legislation, see, for example, Robert P. George, *Making Men Moral: Civil Liberties and Public Morality* (Oxford: Clarendon Press, 1993); Hadley Arkes, *Philosopher in the City: The Moral Dimensions of Urban Politics* (Princeton, NJ: Princeton University Press, 1981); Francis A. Canavan, SJ, *The Pluralist Game: Pluralism, Liberalism, and the Moral Conscience* (Lanham, MD: Rowman and Littlefield, 1995). For full political participation, see, for example, Christopher Eberle, *Religious Conviction in Liberal Politics* (New York: Cambridge University Press,

2002); Bryan McGraw, *Faith in Politics: Religion and Liberal Democracy* (New York: Cambridge University Press, 2010); Robert P. George, *A Clash of Orthodoxies: Law, Religion, and Morality in Crisis* (Wilmington, DE: ISI Books, 2001); Nicholas Wolterstorff, "Why We Should Reject What Liberalism Tells Us about Speaking and Acting in Public for Religious Reasons," in *Religion and Contemporary Liberalism*, ed. Paul Weithman (Notre Dame, IN: Notre Dame University Press, 1997), 162–81.

10

RICHARD RORTY'S SECULAR GODS AND UNPHILOSOPHIC PHILOSOPHERS

Luigi Bradizza

In his later years, Richard Rorty softened his stance toward religion. He came to accept that religious believers could be important allies in pursuit of his political project of community, love, individual flourishing, and the diminution of cruelty. However, Rorty's subordination of religious belief to his politics comes at the cost of genuine religiosity. Religious defenders of Rorty such as G. Elijah Dann are wrong to believe that Rorty's philosophy is friendly to religion. Scholars such as Alvin Plantinga have more correctly argued that Rorty's philosophy does not sufficiently allow for more traditional Christianity.[1] For Rorty, what remains of religion is religiously inspired sentiment in the service of secular liberal ideals.[2] But how secular is this project? Daniela Sorea has suggested that Rorty puts man in the place of God. By contrast, J. Wesley Robbins claims that Rorty does not "think[...] that humans are little Gods" because for Rorty, humans are not "originators of meaning and truth."[3] Sorea has the stronger claim, but it requires an elaboration she does not offer. God is understood by believers to be the creator of man. Rorty's secular idealism is, ironically, religious insofar as it replaces God with man as the re-creator of man in ideal form. In a further irony, this godlike man must be severely limited if he is to be endlessly creative. The traditional God is understood to have created man as rational and capable of grasping the objective moral truth of the world. By contrast, for Rorty's godlike man, political philosophy and endless creativity are mutually exclusive.

RORTY ON PHILOSOPHY, RELIGION, AND POLITICS

Rorty is an anti-representationalist; he believes that no one can have direct, objective knowledge of objects in the world. This limitation on our understanding is a consequence of our use of language to describe the world. Language cannot reflect, represent, or mirror the world as it actually exists.[4] Rorty's anti-representationalism leads him to deny any "metaphysical" truths, including God's existence. He is therefore an atheist.[5] Rorty argues that modern philosophy delegitimized religion and advanced atheism.[6] As pleased as he is with this outcome, Rorty also rejects modern philosophy. He is of the view that both religion and modern philosophy have been attractive for the same fundamental reason: they promise redemption, that is, they offer a unified, true, objective, and final view of the whole and our place in it.[7] One promises this redemption through faith, the other by means of rational access to objective truth. Rorty would replace both religion and representational philosophy with his own redemption-free anti-representational philosophy.

Rorty originally expressed his rejection of religious faith in quite strong terms. He argued for a thoroughly secular public life, with religion kept strictly private.[8] He was scornful toward Stephen L. Carter's wish that faith be permitted some public expression.[9] Believing himself to be picking up where Thomas Jefferson left off, Rorty argued for a complete separation of church and state.[10] As he put it, "A suitably privatized form of religious belief might dictate neither one's scientific beliefs nor anybody's moral choices save one's own."[11] Rorty blamed religion for a host of historical injustices and condemned it for its continuing involvement in American political life. He objected to the political marginalization of atheists in America by religious believers.[12] He strongly objected to politically oriented religious pressure groups and their influence on the Republican Party.[13] And he especially condemned religious believers for their objections to what he saw as the purely private and harmless sexual practices of homosexuals.[14]

By confining religion to the strictly private realm, Rorty would advance his political project: the attainment of a liberal society. On his understanding, a liberal is one who thinks "that cruelty is the worst thing we do." As an anti-representationalist, Rorty cannot give a rational and objectively valid justification for his liberalism.[15] He openly acknowledges that his political stance—and indeed all of human life—is contingent. One's moral and political views are dependent on historical, social, and linguistic factors that do not allow for an objective defense. He therefore describes himself as a liberal ironist, that is, as one who is aware of the contingency of his liberal commitments. Rorty can only *assert* the preferability of his ironic liberalism. Embedded in this liberal political order is a social culture that is maximally tolerant of—and indeed encourages—autonomous and diverse private ways of thinking, speaking, and living. As Michael Bacon puts it, "The sense of autonomy Rorty favors is a matter of embracing contingency—in particular, of seeing one's self and those things that are central to one's identity as the result of such contingencies, and re-creating them through continual redescription." The task of the state is to secure to each an environment that protects him or her from cruelty, including the cruelty of humiliation, so that each can have maximum freedom within a sphere of personal autonomy to undertake his or her own private projects of personal transformation and perfection.[16]

The public sphere is neutral between individual projects of self-creation and re-creation. Whatever people's private idiosyncrasies, Rorty expects and demands a common civic culture: "In a liberal society, our public dealings with our fellow citizens are not *supposed* to be Romantic or inventive; they are supposed to have the routine intelligibility of the marketplace or the courtroom." He goes on, "Publicly discussable compromises require discourse in a common vocabulary, and such a vocabulary is required to describe the *moral* identities a liberal society asks its citizens to have."[17] The public sphere is meant to serve the private sphere, indirectly by protecting it but also directly by redistributing wealth for the sake of a greater equality of material outcome. Rorty believes that his ironic liberalism can and should be the reigning political system in America and, eventually, the entire world.[18]

Rorty is strongly committed to his political project.[19] Indeed, politics is so central a concern for him that he believes philosophy's main function is to serve it.[20] Philosophy cannot give us objective truth, but it can help us organize our views. Philosophic "inquiry is a matter of finding coherence among beliefs, not of corresponding to an object."[21] The beliefs that Rorty has in mind are primarily political ones. The coherent intellectual story offered by philosophy can help us fit together our intellectual history to better place and explain the role of liberal ideas in our lives. Philosophy can therefore help us integrate Rorty's coming liberal regime into our intellectual history. Philosophy clarifies ideas and intellectual movements. It explains intellectual growth (or regression). But it cannot justify our moral choices or refute what we see as the bad moral choices of others.[22] Rorty therefore explicitly rejects traditional political philosophy as a guide to human action.[23] Rorty repeatedly calls for a modest role for and reduced expectations from philosophy. He claims that philosophy does not help us improve the world in tangible ways to anything like the degree of other fields of study, in particular, social science and literature. "We do not need philosophy for social criticism," Rorty told one interviewer. "We have economics, sociology, the novel, psychoanalysis, and many other ways to criticize society."[24] Nor is philosophy of much use in bolstering or advancing the humanities.[25] As D. Vaden House puts it, Rorty "positively insists that philosophy has better things to do [than providing objective knowledge], namely, providing an 'edifying' (historicising, humanizing) voice in the human conversation."[26] And for all his support for the project of the Enlightenment, Rorty certainly does not think that philosophic enlightenment will spread. He doesn't expect that ordinary people will take an interest in philosophy, nor does he insist that they do.[27]

Rorty never altered his view of the proper place of philosophy, but later in life he did allow for an increased role for religion. In a 2003 article, he retracted some of the views he had expressed nine years earlier in his somewhat harsh review of Stephen L. Carter's book.[28] Rorty's modified position amounted to allowing for—and perhaps even inviting—religiously inspired support for public liberal projects such as the welfare state and greater egalitarianism.[29] Rorty modified his views partly because he came to see that the relationship between religion and society should be determined by "cultural politics," or the public struggle over what sort of vocabulary to use, what sort of society to become, and what sorts of activities and inquiries to permit. For Rorty, "cultural politics should replace ontology," that is, questions of objective truth are not important.[30] Instead, as a philosophical pragmatist,[31] Rorty thinks we should look to how topics of discussion, language, and activities pragmatically promote or hinder the sort of society we want. It might be appropriate for a society to allow for or encourage some aspect of religion if it determines that such tolerance would be better for it than any other alternative. In Rorty's reformed view, a society can ask, "Does one or more of these religious traditions provide language we wish to use when putting together our self-image, determining what is most important to us?"[32]

Rorty also became more open toward religion because he more carefully delineated his objection to religion, stressing that he was more anticlerical than antireligious. In his view, "ecclesiastical institutions . . . are dangerous to the health of democratic societies."[33] Rorty accused religious organizations such as the Roman Catholic Church of having a history of "bigoted exclusivism" toward Jews and homosexuals, with their motive being "money and power." As Dann puts it, "For Rorty, the problem is organized religion."[34] Because ecclesiastical organizations threaten the cruelty-free liberal political order Rorty would establish, he hopes that they "will eventually wither away." He believes that religion should "be pruned back to the parish level."[35] During public remarks in 2002, though, Rorty indicated that even unorganized religion poses a threat: "Of course, shortly after one of these private American churches is founded, it develops its own little Vatican and becomes one more horrible authoritarian institution."[36] Rorty remained somewhat vague about the measures he would take to limit ecclesiastical organizations. He argued that although we should *legally* tolerate religiously inspired public statements opposing homosexuality, such statements should nonetheless be seen as "hate speech" and be subject to very strong social sanctions. People uttering such speech should be "shunned and despised" and subjected to "social ostracism."[37] At times he suggested that *legal measures* be taken against religious organizations. In a 2002 essay, he wrote, "It is possible to agree that society should grant private individuals the right to formulate private systems of belief while remaining *militantly* anti-clerical."[38] He added that "[i]ssues [of religious tolerance in public settings] require different resolutions in different countries and different centuries." Jason Boffetti notes the vagueness in Rorty's opposition to organized religion: "when orthodox theism conflicts with [Rorty's] American civil religion of democracy, traditional religious belief must yield or risk public disapproval and a range of possible, though as yet unnamed, threats."[39]

MARGINALIZING AND DEFORMING RELIGION

Rorty's revised understanding of religion and its appropriate place in our lives must cause us to wonder whether men can still be properly religious in his liberal regime. Dann argues that there is sufficient space for Christianity within Rorty's thought and defends this claim by proposing that we understand Christianity as grounded in an "edifying theology" consistent with Rorty's anti-representational philosophy. Dann therefore makes of religious belief what Rorty has made of philosophy. He presents his revised Christianity as authentic and claims it is consistent with Rorty's philosophic views and ironic liberalism.[40] By contrast with Dann, Plantinga argues that Rorty's philosophy is incompatible with Christianity to the extent that Christianity is understood representationally. And in his view, Christianity must be understood representationally. As he puts it, "It is certainly crucial to Christian belief to suppose that there *is* a way things are, and that it includes the great things of the gospel; it is crucial to Christian belief to suppose that such propositions as *God created the world* and *Christ's suffering and death are an atonement for human sin* are true."[41]

Even if we assume that Dann is correct in believing that Christianity *can* be based on "edifying theology," there are two difficulties with going on to argue that Christianity is compatible with Rorty's views. In the first place, most Christians have been and are "representational" and believe that God really exists, independently of us. Asking them to become (what we might call) anti-representational Christians is, at the very least, the equivalent of asking them to change denominations. Knowing this, many (if not most) will refuse to change. Representational Christians appear to be here to stay.[42] And so, even if Rorty would accept Dann's version of Christianity, we must conclude that Rorty is intolerant of Christianity because he is intolerant of its traditional variants.

The second difficulty with arguing that Rorty's liberal regime is compatible with Christianity is that Rorty deforms Christianity by instrumentalizing it. Rorty is correct to note an overlap between certain aspects of Christianity and his own welfare state views.[43] One might say that there is at least a touch of social gospel in all variants of Christianity, but subordinating public expressions of traditional Christianity to secular public purposes deforms it by making it a mere instrument of worldly justice. Many American Christians wish to go beyond support for (aspects of) the welfare state and advocate public moral behavior that they believe is essential to America's spiritual well-being. Their elaborated moral views often include—rightly or wrongly—opposition to homosexuality, yet Rorty would use the power of democratic consensus and social pressure to silence those who publicly invoke religiously based political views he strongly opposes.

Treating antihomosexual public speech as hate speech might be more understandable if that speech were routinely delivered in hateful tones. Yet even Rorty acknowledges that Christian "ministers sometimes try to distinguish themselves from the gay-bashers by saying that even though sodomy is an abomination, Christians must be kind and merciful even to the most disgusting and shameless sinners."[44] He goes on to argue that he would nonetheless silence them because even such qualified speech encourages gay-bashers. Rorty goes too far. Even if he is right to believe that gay-bashers find support for their illegal actions in such qualified speech, the speech would not so much be hateful as (at most) irresponsible. The most obvious response to such gay-bashers would be to enforce more effectively laws against violence and harassment. We could thereby both preserve open political debate and prevent gay-bashing. But this is an option that Rorty does not explore.[45] More generally, many conservative Christian moral teachings conflict with Rorty's liberal views, and any of those teachings could be connected to a social malady by a Rortyan liberal. For example, perhaps transgressive artists such as Andres Serrano would receive fewer death threats if conservative Christians stopped complaining publicly, even in moderate tones, about blasphemous art. And one can easily come up with many other examples. Rorty either hasn't thought through the implications of his instrumentalization of Christianity, or he has thought them through and is nonetheless satisfied to call for a truncated, overly privatized, and insufficient Christianity.

REPLACING GOD WITH MAN

Rorty believes that his atheism and anticlericalism free him from God. But Rorty's liberal utopia in effect replaces God with man. Robbins disagrees with this view of Rorty, but he doesn't take into account the immense scale of Rorty's ambition to transform human life and bring about a liberal utopia.[46] It is an ambition that exceeds human bounds at the same time that, ironically, it is restrained by them. It is these restraints that Robbins detects, but we must not overlook the ambition. Although it is secular, Rorty's utopia is so attractive to him that he quite openly sacralizes it. But let us notice that his sacred liberal utopia is the creation of *man*. Rorty has in effect divinized the authors of his sacred future. That divinization shows itself in the autonomy and self-creation of Rortyan man, a person governed by his desires, with unlimited creative powers, and the goal of personal perfection. And that divinization especially shows itself in the godlike qualities of his "strong poets."

Rorty's sacralization of the future begins with a yearning for a utopia, a heaven on earth: "We moderns are superior to the ancients—both pagan and Christian—in our ability to imagine a utopia here on earth."[47] Bringing about that utopia requires an inspirational text: "It would be best, of course, if we could find a new document to provide our children with inspiration and hope—one which was as free of the defects of the New Testament as of those of the [Communist] Manifesto."[48] In another work, Rorty describes J. S. Mill's *On Liberty* and *Utilitarianism* as "sacred texts" of "leftist politics."[49] He calls for a "religion of literature, in which works of the secular imagination replace Scripture as the principal source of inspiration and hope for each new generation."[50] Rorty's liberal utopia is one in which cruelty is eliminated, people love one another, and there is an (eventual) global community of politically like-minded individuals who secure for each other an egalitarian society that enables each to undertake his or her own private projects to the maximum extent possible, for the greatest human happiness possible. Rorty adopts religious language—if not overt religious beliefs—in describing this utopia. He has a "sense that holiness resides only in an ideal future," and he continues, "My sense of the holy, insofar as I have one, is bound up with the hope that someday, any millennium now, my remote descendants will live in a global civilization in which love is pretty much the only law." He allows that he has "unjustifiable hope" that this utopia will come about, a hope that sounds very much like faith.[51] He would spread his sense of the holy to his fellow citizens. Rorty seems quite favorably disposed toward (on his interpretation) Whitman's and Dewey's "hope for a casteless and classless America in the place traditionally occupied by knowledge of the will of God. They wanted that utopian America to replace God as the unconditional object of desire." He sees no "viable leftist alternative to [their] civic religion" aimed at making "social justice . . . our country's principle goal."[52]

The citizens of Rorty's sacred future are radically autonomous. He argues for human autonomy in part as a replacement for what he regards as religious believers' unhealthy dependence on their faith. For Rorty, religious belief offers meaning and comfort to some, but it is clear that he sees this as a weakness.[53] He traces at least some of the appeal of religion among ordinary believers to their belief that they require redemption. They believe themselves to be radically inadequate, imperfect, and partial, and they seek in religious belief some measure of healing for these flaws by an authority independent of and above themselves. Rorty argues that people are not naturally sinful, and so they do not need their sins forgiven.[54] Neither do they need a source of authority outside of themselves for their moral views. Indeed, Rorty strongly objects to the simple citing of scripture in defense of a moral position.[55] His autonomous man is self-consciously free of nature, religion, the dictates of an allegedly objective and universal reason, societal conventions (apart from those he chooses to adopt), and in general, any external or "objective" authority.

Rather than submitting to a standard of behavior determined by some authority outside of themselves (be it revelation, nature, or universal reason), men should shape and reshape their lives in line with their own desires. Rorty approves of William James's view that all human demands should be satisfied on no other grounds than that they are demands, limited only by the proviso that they not conflict with the demands of others. Indeed, Rorty tells us that, "on a pragmatist account, the only point of having beliefs in the first place is to gratify desires."[56] Man is ruled by what is most particular to him: not God, human nature, or universal reason, but his own desires.

A man's autonomy and desires drive his creativity, particularly as that creativity is directed at himself and his own life. Rortyan man is infinitely creative; there is no theoretical upper limit to his creativity.[57] His creativity is expanded by the use of science. Rorty acknowledges the efficacy of modern natural science in increasing our ability to predict and control nature, even as he denies the claims of typical scientists that they gain an objective understanding of actual objects in the world.[58] Consistent with scientific claims, Rorty places no upper limit on our ability to predict and control nature. And so there are in principle no natural restrictions on our ability to create and re-create ourselves and our lives. This absence of limits goes well beyond the modern project of using natural science for the relief of man's estate, limited as that project is by a "metaphysical" understanding of the world and by one's reason. For Rorty, science is joined to and permits unlimited creative and re-creative powers for the self, with no limits to our ability to imagine new selves.

The goal of Rortyan man is personal perfection.[59] There is no end point to human development—Hegelian or otherwise—that defines or limits this perfection. Therefore, neither history nor human creativity and re-creativity have a terminus, and so there is infinite change possible, without the pathos of an ending (except, of course, one's death). In sum, Rortyan man gives his own life its shape, its meaning, and its perfection. Autonomous man becomes the creator and re-creator of himself in perfect form. He creates himself in his own image.[60]

For Rorty, the highest degree of autonomy and creativity is found in the greatest artists, the strong poets. They are godlike human figures, shaping and reshaping themselves and others in accordance with their own supremely autonomous imagination and immense talents. Such individuals are trailblazers who discover new ways of living, craft new vocabularies for describing and re-describing human possibilities, and co-opt other people through attractive and compelling presentations. They represent the high points of human cultural achievement and they are the most powerful agents of social change: "In my view, an ideally liberal polity would be one whose culture hero is [Harold] Bloom's 'strong poet' rather than the warrior, the priest, the sage, or the truth-seeking, 'logical,' 'objective' scientist."[61]

Rorty sees "literary" poets (as opposed to, for example, "religious" or "philosophic" poets) as particularly strong, and his typical examples include such authors as Harriet Beecher Stowe, Proust, Nabokov, Orwell, and Dickens.[62] Depending on their art, these strong poets can move us to shape and reshape our understanding of our private life and its possibilities, or they can shape and reshape our understanding of political affairs and what can and should be done in our civic relations with each other.[63] It is important to note here that the strong poet works not by means of rational persuasion, but by appealing to and enlarging the sentiments of his audience.[64] Indeed, Rorty describes the work of a strong poet who sensitizes his reader to the suffering of others as "sentimental education."[65] Rorty places art above philosophy and religion as the most effective means of bringing about large-scale personal and social transformations. He told an interviewer that "literature is more important [than philosophy] for moral progress, because it contributes to the widening of the moral imagination." Referring to Dickens, Stowe, and Orwell, Rorty asserts that "a whole lot of people can suddenly undergo a gestalt switch as a result of reading a novel."[66]

LIMITED SECULAR GODS

Despite his godlike qualities, Rortyan man is in important respects quite limited. He is limited by anti-representational philosophy, for he can never attain objective knowledge of things in the world.[67] And although Rorty acknowledges the efficacy of modern natural science, he sees it as offering us only pragmatic means of coping with and describing nature, regardless of the predictive power and control over nature it gives us. We might see this anti-representational limitation as meaningless if we could affirm that objects in the world are nothing more than linguistic constructions, but in fact Rorty believes that *something* independent of our thoughts really exists in the world and interacts with us.[68]

Our limitation is, again, based on language, on its inability to represent or mirror the world. Rortyan man therefore knows that he cannot have objective knowledge of something that actually exists; some aspect of reality is closed to his mind. We might still see this limitation as meaningless if we could be persuaded, with Rorty, that the desire for such objective knowledge is a product of weakness, of being unable or unwilling to face up to the responsibility we have for shaping our lives and our views. As Owen puts it, "The ironist looks upon the need to know the whole as an unhealthy one, as a sickness."[69] But this deflection doesn't answer individuals who seek knowledge of reality as a way of courageously confronting and overcoming their limits. Even if Rorty's anti-representationalism is correct (indeed, precisely if it is), Rorty cannot *objectively* argue against the desire of someone for transcendence, for the surmounting of anti-representational limits. He can, at most, claim that this desire cannot be satisfied and so will not promote our happiness. Yet even if it is unsatisfiable, the desire for transcendence could be properly reflected in a recognition of our radical and permanent incompleteness. And perhaps this sort of self-understanding is necessary for our happiness, particularly if we see this incompleteness as true and have a need for truth. Rorty attempts to mute the desire for transcendence by claiming that neither "the quest for truth" nor "the quest for God is hard-wired" in us. Instead, "both are matters of cultural formation."[70] But even if he is right about this, we can conclude only that individuals seeking transcendence *can* change this aspect of themselves; we cannot conclude that they *should* change.

In fact, Rorty goes part way to accepting a desire for transcendence. Asked by Gianni Vattimo whether "there [is] any feeling of dependence that one could not consider pathological," Rorty replied by favorably recounting Dewey's understanding of how we can "join[. . .] the human with the non-human universe." Dewey allowed for a "kind of vague romantic pantheism [that] is the only expression of a sense of dependence we need—recognizing that we are part of a larger whole." This larger whole, Rorty tells us, can consist of "the books you read or your cultural tradition or the physical universe" or some combination of these. Rorty agrees that what Vattimo calls this "vague pantheistic attitude" is appropriate to a "half-believer."[71] Rorty does not necessarily include himself in the company of half-believers, but by describing such a sense of dependency as non-pathological, Rorty makes an important—if not fully elaborated—concession to the human recognition of our partialness and incompleteness.[72]

Taken to its representational limit, a feeling of dependence leads to a desire for completeness, for wholeness, and from there to a desire for objectivity, that is, for a true understanding of one's place in the larger reality. For Rorty, however, the desire for objectivity is at odds with the desire for solidarity he thinks we should all share:

> Insofar as a person is seeking solidarity, she does not ask about the relation between the practices of the chosen community and something outside that community. Insofar as she seeks objectivity, she distances herself from the actual persons around her not by thinking of herself as

a member of some other real or imaginary group, but rather by attaching herself to something which can be described without reference to any particular human beings.

Rorty here traces the desire for objectivity to "the tradition in Western culture which centers around the notion of the search for Truth," and which holds that "the idea of Truth [is] something to be pursued for its own sake, not because it will be good for oneself, or for one's real or imaginary community."[73] But in fact Rorty is posing a false choice. Socrates (whom Rorty correctly identifies in this article as an important figure in this tradition) sought Truth as part of a community of philosophically minded friends. And what of communities of religious believers collectively seeking knowledge of God and His will? But if objectivity and solidarity are compatible, and if objectivity is desired as part of the search for wholeness, and if the search for wholeness is legitimate, then we must see Rorty's philosophy as closing off an important path to human flourishing.

Perhaps the most severe limit on Rortyan man is that experienced by ordinary people. They lack the talents of the exceptional men, the strong poets, and they even fall short of the less exceptional intellectuals, so they cannot free themselves from the contingency of other people's language.[74] As Rorty puts it, autonomy "is something which certain particular human beings hope to attain by self-creation, and which a few actually do." Indeed, Rorty does not see how ordinary people can even be brought to be ironic.[75] The root of the limitation in ordinary people lies in ineradicable human inequality. Rorty quietly acknowledges and accepts the view that most men can neither rise nor be brought to the level of the exceptional few. To his credit, Rorty is not clouded by envy. He welcomes the existence of great men. As he put it in an interview, "We who are not heroes are made modest by the presence of the heroic." But he offered no account of or cause for their existence. He told another interviewer that "you are completely dependent on the occasional emergence of geniuses like Kant, Hegel, Heidegger, and Wittgenstein. I insist that we're all at the mercy of people of genius."[76] Most of us will never be their intellectual equals: "Each new generation ought to acknowledge the greatness of such figures [as, for example, Hegel, Wordsworth, Blake, and Schiller], and aspire to follow their example, even while knowing that the vast majority of such attempts will be futile, and perhaps even ludicrous."[77] Indeed, it is in part because so few can emulate greatness that he is so insistent in advocating economic redistribution. Whether due to conventional or natural causes, human inequality is, for Rorty, a permanent feature of the human condition, and we can at most compensate for this by positive efforts to equalize (some) outcomes. In his view, redistribution of income can give all people an opportunity to actualize their desires and personal projects.

But this attempt to equalize outcomes can be only partly successful. We are led to wonder what sort of citizens most men will be if they cannot rise to the level of Rorty's intellectual liberal ironists and strong poets. Rorty acknowledges that an "ideal citizen" of his liberal utopia has talents exceeding that of ordinary people. These ordinary people will be at most "commonsensically nominalist and historicist" but, again, not ironists.[78] They bear a striking resemblance to the sorts of Christians he criticizes, ones who, in arguing for or against public policy, provide no argument beyond a scriptural citation. Such Christians, he argues, "should not justify their support of or opposition to legislation *simply* by saying 'Scripture says' or 'Rome has spoken; the matter is closed' or 'My church teaches.'" For Rorty, a simple appeal to a religious authority is out of bounds. But so too is a simple appeal to a *secular* authority: "I would not consider myself to be seriously discussing politics with my fellow-citizens if I *simply* quoted passages from [J. S.] Mill at them, as opposed to using those passages to help me articulate my views."[79] Rorty wants thoughtful citizens. But the "commonsensically nominalist and historicist" ordinary citizens in his liberal utopia are no more articulate than the Christians he criticizes. Rorty's strong poets and intellectuals cannot universalize thoughtful citizenship. And so they can hardly be expected to go further and utterly transform ordinary men.[80] This is a striking limitation on Rorty's secular gods, and it calls into question the utopian possibilities of his liberal order.

Rorty's secular gods, his strong poets, now come into view as something less than divine: they are secular priests leading their flock. In a discussion of the topic of the "privatization of perfection," Rorty attributes to J. S. Mill and others the view, with which he agrees,

> that poetry should take over the role that religion has played in the formation of individual human lives. They also agree that nobody should take over the function of the clergy. For poets are to a secularized polytheism [which holds that "human values" are "incommensurable" and therefore cannot be ranked][81] what the priests of a universal church are to monotheism. Once you become polytheistic, you will turn away not only from priests but from such priest-substitutes as metaphysicians and physicists—from anyone who purports to tell you how things *really* are.[82]

They may eschew representationalism and metaphysics, but Rorty's strong poets are no less the leaders of the various polytheistic faiths of his secular utopia than actual priests are of their traditional faith.[83] Because ordinary people in Rorty's liberal utopia are consumers and not producers of the poetry that transforms them, theirs is a condition of dependence and subordination, but without the transcendent freedom offered ordinary Christians by their traditional faith.

Perhaps even the strong poets are not free. In House's view, everyone in Rorty's world—including the strong poets—might be fully subject to natural necessity. As he puts it, Rorty's philosophy leaves it "unclear whether nature is a product of human creativity or human creativity the outcome of natural causal forces."[84] Rorty "argues that someday a perfected physics will offer a complete description of humans, including a description of their speech dispositions." At the same time, Rorty views men as potentially "free creations of our own descriptive powers."[85] House notes the ambiguity in Rorty's thought here, but does not resolve it. M. A. Casey goes further than House in his critique of Rorty: "The reality of human life for Rorty is that we are all the products of contingency, of meaningless necessity." Self-creation is a "pretence" that amounts to "therapy" in the face of this necessity: "There is never self-creation as such, even for the artistic few: only the semblance of it." In Casey's view, the pretence and the therapy extend to the strong poets and are only more obvious in the case of Rorty's ordinary men.[86]

Casey's stronger critique appears to hit closer to the mark than House's more tentative speculation. Rorty offers no mechanism for free will or a free choice that escapes necessity. There is certainly nothing like the Kantian rational autonomy of the will in Rorty's thought. Indeed, Rorty seems favorably disposed to Whitman's and Dewey's view that, on his reading of their thought, the traditional "religious impulse" is related to "the infantile need for security, the childish hope of escaping from time and chance." And time and chance appear to have man fully in their grip, because Rorty allows that he "see[s] the self as centerless, as a historical contingency all the way through." By not exempting the strong poets from these descriptions, Rorty provides support for Casey's view.[87]

If Rortyan man is free, his freedom is indistinguishable from arbitrariness, an arbitrariness deeply connected to Rorty's philosophy. Ironically, the limits to knowledge traced by anti-representationalism are essential to the endless creativity that is a feature of Rortyan man. Were he to have transcendent knowledge of God and His Word, or the natural world, including his own human nature, he would be required to submit himself morally to claims derivable from that knowledge. He could then no longer exercise endless creativity and self-redefinition.[88] Rorty has traded one set of limits for another but has gained, he believes, the freedom to do what he wishes with his life. The fruits of this freedom, however, are arbitrary self-assertions. House criticizes "the arbitrariness that stems from Rorty's claim that the historical process has no point." The continuing "human conversation" Rorty seeks "lives, not by the pursuit of the truth about the world, nor by the truth about human nature, but through bare self-assertion."[89] Rorty tries to escape the charge that he promotes arbitrariness by redefining the term as "the conviction that one's own social practice is the only social practice one will ever need and that one does not need to fuse horizons with anybody else because one's own social practice is already sufficient."[90]

But having conceded that individuals can be arbitrary, it is a small step to allowing that collectivities can have a fused view that is no less arbitrary than the individual views it replaces.[91]

And so, Rorty's sacralized secular utopia lacks the divine creatures necessary to bring it about. Rorty's godlike strong poets are given the role, but they lack the necessary powers. They are limited by human inequality, and by their own lack of access to objective truth. They are further limited by the aimless wanderings of their redescriptions.

CONCLUSIONS

Rorty's philosophy is mainly critical, that is, he uses philosophy to destroy the Western philosophic tradition insofar as it seeks objective truth through reason—and religion insofar as it seeks to know the real God. Wayne Hudson and Wim van Reijen note "the tough-minded eliminative side" of Rorty's philosophy and also point out that Rorty fails to "provide adequate methods" for a more positive philosophic project.[92] Rorty himself says: "I think of pragmatism as primarily therapeutic philosophy—therapy conducted on certain mind-sets created by previous philosophers." It "frees you up from various old habits and convictions."[93] But what fills the void created by anti-representationalism? Rorty does not offer us wisdom; rather, he frees us from philosophy's love of wisdom in preparation for his radical political project of endless creativity. Owen is therefore correct to conclude that Rorty "is not a philosopher but a moralist."[94]

Having freed us from objective truth, Rorty nonetheless understands that we must choose and act. Unable to use universal reason or revelation as a guide, we are thrown back upon ourselves. More precisely, we are thrown back upon our passions—for this is what remains to guide the unguided. We are at any rate thrown back upon *someone's* passions; Rorty cannot assure us that our passions are our own and that we are not in effect moved by—"at the mercy of"—the passions of the strong poets. The case for faith and political philosophy as guides rests, as it always has, on whether we are satisfied to be at the mercy of *anyone's* passions.

NOTES

1. G. Elijah Dann, *After Rorty: The Possibilities for Ethics and Religious Belief* (London: Continuum, 2006), 3; Alvin Plantinga, *Warranted Christian Belief* (Oxford: Oxford University Press, 2000), 423–25.

2. Some critics of Rorty's views on religion, including Plantinga, are receptive to many of

Rorty's liberal ideals, but justify those ideals on non-Rortyan grounds. See Plantinga, *Warranted Christian Belief*, 423–24.

3. Sorea writes that Rorty's "religion of the future . . . is at most heresy, which places the human instead [i.e., in place] of God, similar to the manner in which communist regimes did." Daniela Sorea, "Observations with Respect to the Future of Religion Prefigured by R. Rorty and G. Vattimo," *Bulletin of the Transilvania University of Brasov*, series 7, *Social Sciences and Law* 2.51 (2009): 240. J. Wesley Robbins, "'You Will Be like God': Richard Rorty and Mark C. Taylor on the Theological Significance of Human Language Use," *Journal of Religion* 72.3 (July 1992): 392.

4. Richard Rorty, *Philosophy and the Mirror of Nature* (Princeton, NJ: Princeton University Press, 1979), 10–12.

5. Richard Rorty, "The Historiography of Philosophy: Four Genres," in *Truth and Progress* (Cambridge: Cambridge University Press, 1998), 249; Richard Rorty, "Cultural Politics and the Question of the Existence of God," in Nancy K. Frankenberry, ed., *Radical Interpretation in Religion* (Cambridge: Cambridge University Press, 2002), 71, 74. Rorty later wished that he had described himself as anticlerical rather than an atheist. Richard Rorty, "Anti-clericalism and Atheism," in Mark A. Wrathall, ed., *Religion after Metaphysics* (Cambridge: Cambridge University Press, 2003), 39–40. But in fact, at no point in his life did Rorty believe in the existence of God. See also Rorty, "Anti-clericalism and Atheism," 38.

6. Rorty, "Anti-clericalism and Atheism," 43; Richard Rorty, "The Decline of Redemptive Truth and the Rise of a Literary Culture [2000]," John M. Olin Center, University of Chicago, at http://olincenter.uchicago.edu/pdf/rorty.pdf (accessed July 31, 2013), 3–5; Richard Rorty, *Contingency, Irony, and Solidarity* (Cambridge: Cambridge University Press, 1989), 68.

7. Rorty, "Decline of Redemptive Truth," 2–3.

8. Richard Rorty, "Religion as Conversation-Stopper," in *Philosophy and Social Hope* (1994; Harmondsworth: Penguin, 1999), 169; Rorty, *Contingency, Irony, and Solidarity*, xvi.

9. Rorty, "Religion as Conversation-Stopper," 171.

10. Richard Rorty, "The Priority of Democracy to Philosophy," in *Objectivity, Relativism, and Truth*, 175; Rorty, "Religion as Conversation-Stopper," 169.

11. Rorty, "Religious Faith, Intellectual Responsibility and Romance," in *Philosophy and Social Hope*, 150.

12. Rorty, "Religion as Conversation-Stopper," 169.

13. Richard Rorty, "Failed Prophecies, Glorious Hopes," in *Philosophy and Social Hope*, 204–5.

14. Richard Rorty, "Ethics without Principles," in *Philosophy and Social Hope*, 86; Richard Rorty, *Take Care of Freedom and Truth Will Take Care of Itself: Interviews with Richard Rorty*, ed. Eduardo Mendieta (Stanford, CA: Stanford University Press, 2006), 58, 75, 81.

15. Rorty, *Contingency, Irony, and Solidarity*, xv (quote), 54–55.

16. See Richard Rorty, "Responses to Critics," in Yong Huang, ed., *Rorty, Pragmatism, and Confucianism: With Responses by Richard Rorty* (Albany: State University of New York Press, 2009), 299; Michael Bacon, "Richard Rorty: Liberalism, Irony, and Social Hope," in Catherine

H. Zuckert, ed., *Political Philosophy in the Twentieth Century: Authors and Arguments* (Cambridge: Cambridge University Press, 2011), 207 (quote); Rorty, *Contingency, Irony, and Solidarity*, xiv, 102.

17. Richard Rorty, "Moral Identity and Private Autonomy: The Case of Foucault," in *Essays on Heidegger and Others* (Cambridge: Cambridge University Press, 1991), 196 (emphases his).

18. Rorty, *Contingency, Irony, and Solidarity*, 85. For his ironic liberalism, see Rorty, "Cosmopolitanism without Emancipation," in *Objectivity, Relativism, and Truth*, 218–20; also Richard Rorty, "An Ethics for Today," in *An Ethics for Today: Finding Common Ground between Philosophy and Religion* (New York: Columbia University Press, 2011), 17.

19. Casey Nelson Blake notes Rorty's increased interest in politics after his 1989 *Contingency, Irony and Solidarity*. Casey Nelson Blake, "Private Life and Public Commitment: From Water Rauschenbusch to Richard Rorty," in *A Pragmatist's Progress? Richard Rorty and American Intellectual History*, ed. John Pettegrew (Lanham, MD: Rowman and Littlefield, 2000), 87.

20. Rorty, *Contingency, Irony, and Solidarity*, 196–97; Richard Rorty, "Habermas, Derrida, and the Functions of Philosophy," in *Truth and Progress*, 309–10.

21. Richard Rorty et al., "Dialogue: What Is Religion's Future after Metaphysics?" in Richard Rorty and Gianni Vattimo, *The Future of Religion*, ed. Santiago Zabala (New York: Columbia University Press, 2005), 58.

22. Rorty, *Contingency, Irony, and Solidarity*, 51–52, 54–55; see also Rorty, *Take Care of Freedom*, 47, 79; Richard Rorty, "Globalization, the Politics of Identity and Social Hope," in *Philosophy and Social Hope*, 232; Richard Rorty, "Unger, Castoriadis, and the Romance of a National Future," in *Essays on Heidegger and Others*, 190–91.

23. Richard Rorty, "Philosophy as Science, as Metaphor, and as Politics," in *Essays on Heidegger and Others*, 25; Rorty, "Globalization, the Politics of Identity and Social Hope," 232; also Rorty, *Contingency, Irony, and Solidarity*, xiv.

24. Rorty, *Take Care of Freedom*, 45. See also Richard Rorty, "Afterword: Intellectual Historians and Pragmatic Philosophy," in Pettegrew, *Pragmatist's Progress*, 210; Rorty, "Philosophy as Science," 24–26.

25. Richard Rorty, "Science as Solidarity," in *Objectivity, Relativism, and Truth*, 44–45; Richard Rorty, "Texts and Lumps," ibid., 78.

26. D. Vaden House, *Without God or His Doubles: Realism, Relativism and Rorty* (Leiden: E. J. Brill, 1994), 132.

27. Rorty, "Anti-clericalism and Atheism," 38.

28. Stephen L. Carter, *The Culture of Disbelief* (New York: Anchor, 1994).

29. Richard Rorty, "Religion in the Public Square: A Reconsideration," *Journal of Religious Ethics* 31.1 (Spring 2003): 142–43, 147–48. For Rorty's view of the connection between Christian charity and liberalism, see Rorty et al., "Dialogue," 65, where he argues that "in the late eighteenth century . . . Christian charity changed into *liberté, egalité, fraternité*." See also Rorty, *Take Care of Freedom*, 47; Rorty, "Failed Prophecies, Glorious Hopes," 205.

30. Rorty, "Cultural Politics," 55.

31. Steven Kautz, *Liberalism and Community* (Ithaca, NY: Cornell University Press, 1995), 88.

32. Rorty, "Cultural Politics," 70, also 75–76, 71 (quote).

33. Rorty, "Anti-clericalism and Atheism," 40.

34. Rorty, "Religion in the Public Square," 145, also 141–42, 146; see Rorty, "Ethics for Today," 7–8; Rorty et al., "Dialogue," 79; G. Elijah Dann, "Philosophy, Religion, and Religious Belief after Rorty," in Rorty, *Ethics for Today*, 40.

35. Rorty, "Religion in the Public Square,"142, 148, also 141–42.

36. Rorty et al., "Dialogue," 70.

37. Rorty, "Religion in the Public Square," 143, 148.

38. Rorty, "Cultural Politics," 76 (emphasis added). There is a tenuousness to Rorty's notion of individual rights, because they have their origin not in God or nature but purely in convention.

39. Ibid.; also Rorty, "Religion in the Public Square," 141; Jason Boffetti, "How Richard Rorty Found Religion," *First Things* 143 (May 2004): 30.

40. See Dann, *After Rorty*, 169–78, 192–93. Dann also notes that Rorty's thought is compatible with Gianni Vattimo's thoroughly secularized Christianity. See Dann, "Philosophy, Religion," 47–49, 51–52; cf. Rorty, "Ethics for Today," 24–25; and see Rorty, "Anti-clericalism and Atheism," 40–41. Dann's thought here is somewhat similar to that of Hartmut von Sass, in "Religion in a Private Igloo? A Critical Dialogue with Richard Rorty," *International Journal for Philosophy of Religion* 70 (2011): 203–4, 215.

41. Plantinga, *Warranted Christian Belief*, 425 (his emphasis).

42. Rorty seems to disagree: "But what counts as religious may [in the future] be as different from what we call religious as Proust is from Dante or Warhol from Fra Angelico." Richard Rorty, "Reply to Jeffrey Stout," in *The Philosophy of Richard Rorty*, ed. Randall E. Auxier and Lewis Edwin Hahn (Chicago: Open Court, 2010), 547.

43. Rorty focuses on Psalm 72 and 1 Corinthians 13. Rorty, "Religion in the Public Square," 143, 147.

44. Ibid., 145.

45. As an alternative to Rorty's anticlericism, Andrew Fiala proposes retaining religion while purging it of antihomosexual talk. Andrew Fiala, "Militant Atheism, Pragmatism, and the God-Shaped Hole," *International Journal for Philosophy of Religion* 65 (2009): 150.

46. See Robbins, "You Will Be Like God," 392, 397–98, 402.

47. Rorty, "Failed Prophecies, Glorious Hopes," 208. For a sense of his yearning, see Rorty, "Unger, Castoriadis,"191–92; Richard Rorty, "Looking Backwards from the Year 2096," in *Philosophy and Social Hope*, 243–51; Rorty, "Ethics for Today," 14; also Boffetti, "How Richard Rorty Found Religion," 25.

48. Rorty, "Failed Prophecies, Glorious Hopes," 208.

49. Rorty, "Religion in the Public Square," 142.

50. Richard Rorty, *Achieving Our Country: Leftist Thought in Twentieth-Century America*

(Cambridge, MA: Harvard University Press, 1998), 136.

51. Rorty, "Anti-clericalism and Atheism," 44, 45; see also Rorty, "Religious Faith, Intellectual Responsibility, and Romance," 160–61.

52. Rorty, *Achieving Our Country*, 18, 101; for more of his religious language, see ibid., 132–33.

53. Rorty, "Religion in the Public Square," 142.

54. Rorty, "Ethics for Today," 13.

55. Rorty, "Religion in the Public Square," 147.

56. Rorty, "Religious Faith, Intellectual Responsibility, and Romance," 153; see also Rorty, "Ethics for Today," 15.

57. Rorty, *Contingency, Irony, and Solidarity*, xvi; see also Rorty, *Take Care of Freedom*, 69–70.

58. He states that "there is no reason to praise scientists for being more 'objective' or 'logical' or 'methodical' or 'devoted to truth' than other people." Rorty, "Science as Solidarity," 39.

59. Rorty, *Contingency, Irony, and Solidarity*, xiv, 102; Richard Rorty, "Pragmatism as Romantic Polytheism," in *The Revival of Pragmatism: New Essays on Social Thought, Law, and Culture*, ed. Morris Dickstein (Durham: Duke University Press, 1998), 24.

60. House hints at something like a rebellion by Rorty against God with the aim of displacing Him: "The real issue for Rorty is, as Humpty Dumpty said in defense of his idiosyncratic use of words, who is going to be the master." House, *Without God or His Doubles*, 125; also 124.

61. Rorty, *Contingency, Irony, and Solidarity*, 53 (quote), see also xvi, 20, 37, 143; also Rorty, "Responses to Critics," 295. But Rorty also places Christ, Galileo, and Hegel in the category of strong poets. See Rorty, "Ethics without Principles," 87; Rorty, *Contingency, Irony, and Solidarity*, 12–13. The strong poet is something of an egotist. Joan C. Williams argues that for Rorty's strong poet, "true self-fulfillment lies solely in self-interest." Joan C. Williams, "Rorty, Radicalism, Romanticism: The Politics of the Gaze," in Pettegrew, *Pragmatist's Progress*, 76. Indeed, Rorty denies that "there is something over and above what Cardinal Ratzinger called 'the ego and its desires.'" Rorty, "Ethics for Today," 15. Graham Longford argues that the Rortyan strong poet poses a danger to others, because Rorty cannot keep the public and private spheres adequately separated. See Graham Longford, "'Sensitive Killers, Cruel Aesthetes, and Pitiless Poets': Foucault, Rorty, and the Ethics of Self-Fashioning," *Polity* 33.4 (Summer 2001): 569–92, esp. 582–86. Rorty himself acknowledges and approves of the "Romantic egoism" of the strong poets and believes they can be made safe for society. Rorty, "Responses to Critics," 299.

62. For Stowe, see Rorty, *Contingency, Irony, and Solidarity*, 141. For Proust, ibid., 98–108; Rorty, *Take Care of Freedom*, 67. For Nabokov, see Rorty, *Contingency, Irony, and Solidarity*, 144–68. For Orwell and Dickens, see Richard Rorty, "Heidegger, Kundera, and Dickens," in *Essays on Heidegger and Others*, 79–81.

63. Rorty, *Take Care of Freedom*, 67; Rorty, *Contingency, Irony, and Solidarity*, 141.

64. Rorty, "Heidegger, Kundera, and Dickens," 81. See also Gary Gutting, *What Philosophers Know: Case Studies in Recent Analytic Philosophy* (Cambridge: Cambridge University Press,

2009), 199.

65. Richard Rorty, "Human Rights, Rationality, and Sentimentality," in *Truth and Progress*, 180, also 181.

66. Rorty, *Take Care of Freedom*, 67, 123; also 48–49.

67. Ironically, as J. Judd Owen points out, this is one great truth that "say[s] something quite substantial about the world, as it is in itself." J. Judd Owen, *Religion and the Demise of Liberal Rationalism: The Foundational Crisis of the Separation of Church and State* (Chicago: University of Chicago Press, 2001), 65.

68. Richard Rorty, "Charles Taylor on Truth," in *Truth and Progress*, 86; Richard Rorty, "Against Unity," *Wilson Quarterly* 22.1 (Winter 1998): 31; Rorty, "Texts and Lumps," 80–81; also Richard Rorty, "Inquiry as Recontextualization: An Anti-dualist Account of Interpretation," in *Objectivity, Relativism, and Truth*, 97.

69. Owen, *Religion and the Demise of Liberal Rationalism*, 43.

70. Rorty, "Anti-clericalism and Atheism," 44.

71. Rorty et al., "Dialogue," 78.

72. See Nicholas H. Smith, "Rorty on Religion and Hope," *Inquiry* 48.1 (February 2005): 86–87.

73. Richard Rorty, "Solidarity or Objectivity?" in *Objectivity, Relativism, and Truth*, 21.

74. Williams, "Rorty, Radicalism, Romanticism," 72.

75. Rorty, *Contingency, Irony, and Solidarity*, 65 (quote), 87, also 89–92. In a later interview, he seems to back away from this view. Rorty, *Take Care of Freedom*, 46–47. However, in a still later interview, he returns to his original view that most people cannot be ironic. Rorty, *Take Care of Freedom*, 81.

76. Rorty, *Take Care of Freedom*, 73, 145; see also Rorty, *Contingency, Irony, and Solidarity*, 143.

77. Rorty, *Take Care of Freedom*, 73.

78. Rorty, *Contingency, Irony, and Solidarity*, 61, 87.

79. Rorty, "Religion in the Public Square," 147 (his emphasis).

80. See Rorty, "Human Rights, Rationality, and Sentimentality," 181–82; Rorty, *Achieving Our Country*, 53–54.

81. Rorty, "Pragmatism as Romantic Polytheism," 23.

82. Ibid., 24 (his emphasis).

83. See Boffetti, "How Richard Rorty Found Religion," 28.

84. House, *Without God or His Doubles*, 117.

85. Ibid., 121.

86. M. A. Casey, *Meaninglessness: The Solutions of Nietzsche, Freud, and Rorty* (Lanham, MD: Lexington Books, 2002), 88–89.

87. Rorty, *Achieving Our Country*, 18; Rorty, "Priority of Democracy to Philosophy," 188.

88. See Owen, *Religion and the Demise of Liberal Rationalism*, 65.

89. House, *Without God or His Doubles*, 140.

90. Rorty et al., "Dialogue," 59; cf. Rorty, "Ethics for Today," 26.

91. Rorty's definition of "arbitrary" presents problems for his strong poet, who in his singular creativity and uniqueness, stands apart from others. Rorty tells us that "the Romantic poet is exemplary because he does not ask, 'How does my work fit in with everything around me?' but instead asks that everything around him accommodate itself to his work." Rorty, "Responses to Critics," 299.

92. Richard Rorty, Wayne Hudson, and Wim van Reijen, "From Philosophy to Postphilosophy: Interview Conducted by Wayne Hudson and Wim van Reijen," in Rorty, *Take Care of Freedom*, 22; see also 79.

93. Rorty, *Take Care of Freedom*, 125; see also ibid., 79; Richard Rorty, "Habermas and Lyotard on Postmodernity," in *Essays on Heidegger and Others*, 176; Rorty, "John Searle on Realism and Relativism," in *Truth and Progress*, 76.

94. Owen, *Religion and the Demise of Liberal Rationalism*, 66.

11

CONVERTING SECULARISM

R. J. Snell

In his classic analysis of intellectuals under the Soviet regime, Czeslaw Milosz borrows from a 1932 Polish novel, *Insatiability*, and its portrayal of European decadence: "nothing but a study of decay: mad, dissonant music; erotic perversion; widespread use of narcotics; dispossessed thinking." Already stricken by anomie, the denizens of the fictional regime also learn of a massive invading army that threatens their very existence. Just then, fortunately, "a great number of hawkers appear in the cities peddling Murti-Bing pills."[1]

As it turns out, Murti-Bing was a Mongolian philosopher who had incarnated his philosophy into pills. Anyone using them "became serene and happy. The problems he had struggled with until then suddenly appeared to be superficial and unimportant. He smiled indulgently at those who continued to worry about them, [especially those] pertaining to unsolvable ontological difficulties. A man who swallowed Murti-Bing pills became impervious to any metaphysical concerns." Free from care about the meaning of existence, users were free also from fear, responding with quiet indifference to the approach of the foreign invasion, turning instead to socially useful art and work—for a time. But since the users "could not rid themselves completely of their former personalities, they became schizophrenics." Humanity cannot always be ignored or suppressed, certainly not without disruption of psyche.[2]

In what follows, I note the growing sense that something is wrong with public discourse in the contemporary West. Despite our attempts to live out the philosophy of Murti-Bing and keep comprehensive questions about the human good out of our discourse, human reality cannot be truncated forever, always finding ways to emerge. Using the work of Steven D. Smith, Charles Taylor, and Bernard Lonergan, I argue that denying comprehensive discourse ignores an ontologically constitutive aspect of human reality, truncates human meaning to the level of animal knowing, and requires therapy in the form of intellectual conversion. Secularism needs converting so we can be human again.

THE TRUNCATED CONVERSATION

The chorus of alarm at the state of contemporary discourse, politics, and civil society is deafening, although I will not needlessly cite multiple examples. Still, it is remarkable how thinkers opposed on so many other issues can agree that something is wrong. Chief Rabbi Jonathan Sacks, for instance, argues that Western culture has fragmented to such an extent that sources of common identity around which diverse groups can build a "home together" have all but disappeared, and with significant effect:

> Liberal democracy is in danger. . . . Nation states of the West are becoming places where free speech is increasingly at risk, non-political institutions are becoming politicized, university campuses are turning into ideological arenas, and a combination of political correctness and ethnic-religious separatism are eroding the graciousness of civil society. . . . Culture is fragmenting into non-communicating systems of belief in which civil discourse ends and reasoned argument becomes impossible. The political process is in danger of being abandoned in favour of the media-attention-grabbing gesture, with the threat of violence never far from the surface.[3]

While her attitudes toward religion differ quite dramatically, Susan Jacoby sounds a similar theme, warning of an age of "American Unreason," suffering from "general decline in American civil, cultural, and scientific literacy," and the resulting polarization caused when "the field of debate is often left to those who care most intensely." She claims that "dumbness" is defined downward, and "it becomes much easier to convince people of the validity of extreme positions." This decline is manifest in speech, political life, media, cultural life, and on it goes, "exacerbated by a new species of semiconscious antirationalism, feeding on and fed by an ignorant popular culture of video images and unremitting noise that leaves no room for contemplation or logic."[4]

The polarizing and silo-making effects of extremism are noted as well by Mary Ann Glendon's description of the current discourse on rights, which, "in all its absoluteness, promotes unrealistic expectations, heightens social conflict, and inhibits dialogue that might lead towards consensus, accommodation, or at least the discovery of common ground." Moreover, "these traits promote mere assertion over reason giving."[5] In this claim she finds support from Alasdair MacIntyre for whom "the most striking feature of contemporary moral utterance is that so much of it is used to express disagreements; and the most striking feature of the debates . . . is their interminable character. . . . There seems to be no rational way of securing moral agreement in our culture." Lacking rational grounding, moral disagreements tend to root themselves in arbitrary belief and consequent shrill protest at the other sides' arbitrariness.[6]

We could go on, but the history and proliferation of such alarm is ably reviewed in many places, including Steven D. Smith's recent *The Disenchantment of Secular Discourse.* Like those above, Smith observes the shallowness of contemporary discourse in culture, politics, and law, although his diagnosis is interesting. Refraining from the usual criticisms of public education, the media, new technology, and other "culprits," Smith sees in them "descriptions more of symptoms than of underlying causes," while the "problem runs deeper."[7]

Juxtaposing the optimistic hopes for Reason that were evident in the Enlightenment (found also in its cheery disciples such as Henry Steele Commager) with the deflated expectations of our own age, Smith traces the disruption of Reason by reasonableness.[8] Such deflation is perhaps most obvious in the work of John Rawls, for whom it would be absurd to think that reason would dispel pluralism "by leading people to converge on a unified truth—certainly not about ultimate or cosmic matters."[9] Abandoning claims to comprehensiveness or even real justification for our political beliefs seems an odd demand, but pluralism entails recognition that "no one's truth is going to prevail," and consequently "Reason is displaced by 'reasonableness'—which in effect amounts to a willingness *not* to ask too much of, or to assign too much responsibility to, reason."[10]

Now, while Rawls claims that his version of public reason—reasonableness—allows workable public answers to the issues at hand, the fact remains that public reason requires a truncation of our questions, insisting that we do not ask publically about those things that matter most. Consequently, claims Smith:

> we can notice the way in which shallowness in discourse is actually *prescribed by* some of the most influential political thought of our time. . . . It is hardly an exaggeration to say that the very point of "public reason" is to keep public discourse shallow—to keep it from drowning in the perilous depths of questions about "the nature of the universe," or "the end and the object of life," or other tenets of our comprehensive doctrines.[11]

Nor is Murti-Bing the domain of Rawls alone; one could think also of Richard Rorty, who rather happily prescribes abandoning any hope "that being right about philosophical matters is important for right action" or that there was "a way of holding reality and justice in a single vision."[12] Hope replaces knowledge, and democracy trumps philosophy, so Rorty suggests we simply refrain from asking the relevant questions.

Smith describes our situation as Weber's iron cage "in which life is lived and discourse is conducted according to the stern constraints of secular rationalism."[13] Charles Taylor's analysis of the secular is helpful here. In asking what it means to live in a secular age, Taylor distinguishes Secularity 1, the disestablishment of national churches or separation of church and state, from Secularity 2, a condition where few people attend religious services or believe in God, and from Secularity 3, a change "in *what it is to believe*."[14] Unlike societies in which religious belief is the norm, Secularity 3 regards belief as one option among many, thus altering the experience of belief. When belief is viewed as optional, and when believers acknowledge that others make sense of the world differently, and apparently with no loss of fullness, then belief's status changes, perennially looking over its shoulder at other options, wondering about them.[15] Consequently, commitment to a tradition is thought intrinsically private, with little expectation that others will "converge" on its unified truth. Pluralism governs even faith, and reasonableness demands holding faith quite loosely, at least publically. When Smith refers to the iron cage of the secular, I suggest we keep Secularity 3 in mind, for Secularity 3 most adequately articulates the truncation of questions, the squelching of reason in the supposition that big questions are noncognitive, nonrational.

Such truncation is quite odd, Smith thinks, even schizophrenic, for Murti-Bing-type relief from ultimate questions can only be temporary. Life in the cage is fundamentally dishonest, for "we have done violence to many of our deepest convictions," and trying to engage in public reason from a truncated foundation "turns out to be a pretty shabby and unsatisfactory affair." Consequently, we *smuggle*, for while "modern secular vocabulary purports to render inadmissible notions such as those that animated premodern moral discourse . . . our deepest convictions rely on such notions, and . . . we have little choice except to smuggle such notions into the conversation—to introduce them incognito under some sort of secular disguise." While it may be possible to do science within the iron cage, public reason does "violence to many of our deepest convictions." Consequently, to make our arguments at all plausible, we become smugglers, always making an "argument that depends on an illicit and undisclosed premise . . . even if . . . not consciously aware."[16] Murti-Bing works only for a time, then the person lapses into schizophrenia.

DISEQUILIBRIUM AND MORAL SPACE

Charles Taylor explains why comprehensiveness cannot be completely eradicated and always emerges, even if only as smuggling.[17] Like other animals, we experience desires and appetites for a variety of needs and goods, but unlike the other animals we also have second-order desires about our own appetites; we can desire to overcome a particular desire, for instance, out of a sense that some appetites are more and others less worthwhile. In evaluating the worth of our desires, claims Taylor, we are capable of "strong-evaluations," which go beyond mere prudential calculus to judge the worth of desires against our self-interpretation, how we value and understand our own subjectivity.[18] Since humans are strong-evaluators, we always interpret ourselves along with our desires, although self-interpretation, in Taylor's somewhat Heideggerian reading, always involves a projection forward of who we wish to be and not just a static description of who we find ourselves to be now. We experience our desire from the viewpoint of an engaged agent, as subjects always involved in shaping their own identities.

The capacity to evaluate requires a framework, a horizon of meaning in which our various values—plural and largely irreducible to each other—are placed in relationship to each other in a vision of a complete, ordered, and good life. In *Sources of the Self* Taylor identifies three categories of strong values, those values serving as focal points of our moral framework, namely, values related to (1) the notion that human life is worth respect; (2) notions of a rich and meaningful life, a life worth having; and (3) notions of our own dignity with respect to others.[19] While Taylor believes that frameworks are always historical and contingent, the *fact* that humans require a framework is necessary—for absent a framework, our self-interpretations and subjectivity would be rendered meaningless. Consequently, value, or moral space, while potentially perspectival and fluctuating in terms of content, is constitutive of human reality—we cannot be what we are without evaluative frameworks:

> The claim is that living within such strongly qualified horizons is constitutive of human agency, that stepping outside these limits would be tantamount to stepping outside what we would recognize as integral, that is, undamaged human personhood. . . . To know who I am is a species of knowing where I stand. My identity is defined by the commitments and identifications which provide the frame or horizon within which I can try to determine from case to case what is good, or valuable, or what ought to be done, or what I endorse or oppose. In other words, it is the horizon within which I am capable of taking a stand.[20]

Note the claim of "undamaged human personhood." Rather than pretending that humans could somehow manage without moral normativity, Taylor suggests that any such lack would be an abnormality, "an appalling identity crisis," even sinking to the level of the "pathological."[21]

Further, claims Taylor, since our evaluations are multiple and nonreducible and since our self-interpretations vary even within our own histories, our frameworks tend toward a terminus, a focal point of our moral horizons, centered on *hypergoods*, goods "incomparably more important than others . . . of overriding importance."[22] It is these goods that determine the direction of our lives, around which we orient our purpose and meaning, and against which we judge not only our strong-evaluations but also our sense of how successfully we have determined our previous strong-evaluations. In short, without hypergoods we would lack a self or the capacity to judge the quality and worth of our lives.

Hypergoods are first in our sense of self, they form the starting points of our deliberation and interpretations, and as the source of meaning and action cannot be derived or deduced from some sort of methodological starting point—they are not the sort of thing the sciences can or ought to control. In fact, Taylor is highly critical of naturalism's claim that "the meaning-dimension of human existence is ultimately a realm of subjective illusion . . . only properly understood when considered from the point of view developed by modern natural science."[23] Meaning cannot be reduced to a mode distinct from moral agency; such philosophical anthropology is inadequate to our own engaged and involved agency and selfhood, claims Taylor.

Nor does it follow that because values are nonscientific they should be discounted or set aside from public discourse. According to Smith, the move to so-called reasonableness occurred because of a sense that pluralism could not be solved or undone by Reason's unity; and so questions about deepest worth, hypergoods, were to be purposely left out of our conversations. Taylor would disagree. While it is the case that our own moral agency and selfhood are constituted by our moral space, it does not follow that moral space is individualistic. Indeed, for Taylor, hypergoods are considered self-transcending, not merely constructed by us but experienced as prior to us. While moral agency requires choice and involvement, still involvement and choice are significant only because "*independent of my will* there is something noble, courageous, and hence significant in giving shape to my own life."[24]

Moral frameworks are thus not merely subjective, nor are they accidental to our identity. Consequently, being asked to set them aside in favor of public reasonableness is akin to being asked to set aside our own lives, our own purposes—it is being asked to sacrifice our moral agency on the altar of the public. Taylor believes this ought not and cannot be done as it would entail a profound self-contradiction to choose to violate one's own capacity for agency. Further, while value is constitutive of our identity, this is not merely private, for any anthropology suggesting that one already has an identity—either as an individual or as a group—prior to and independent of engagement with the Other would appear to misunderstand the dialogical nature of moral frameworks. Rather than simply having some sort of monological moral identity or framework that one can subsequently set aside or partially truncate so as to enter the space of pluralistic reasonableness, we find our moral identity is thoroughly dialogical, always involved with others in forming its own-self.[25]

We "become moral agents, capable of understanding ourselves," claims Taylor, not in solitary inner discourse, whatever early modern thinkers may have presumed, but "through our acquisition of rich human languages of expression . . . covering not only the words we speak, but also other modes or expression whereby we define ourselves." Expressive languages are not self-generated, "people do not acquire the languages needed for self-definition on their own" but, rather, through "interaction with others who matter." Further, the fundamentally dialogical relation concerns not merely the origin of language but is constant and ongoing. We do not simply acquire a language and then proceed in isolation, especially for the most important of things: "We define our identity always in dialogue with, sometimes in struggle against, the things our significant others want to see in us." Monological conceptions, it turns out, are inadequate anthropology.[26]

From Taylor, then, we have an account for the symptoms described by Smith, who claimed that modern discourse has become a somewhat shabby affair in that it attempts to truncate our questions, truncate our reason, and limit public conversation to something rather less than matters of ultimate import. This fails. Consequently we are forced to smuggle in higher values so that argument can occur at all, although the smuggling is itself a form of truncation and distortion. The reason for the contemporary shabbiness cannot be skirted, however, for it is an ontological matter governed by philosophical anthropology; it is simply *the way we are*, although Taylor need not rely upon reification of human nature, essentialism, or static deduction—his is a phenomenological account.

Consequently, the "reasonableness" of our current situation is in fact thoroughly unreasonable, rooted in an impossible and unreasonable requirement of setting aside what matters most. Such a setting aside is a truncation of our moral frameworks, and thus a negation of our moral agency and selfhood. Murti-Bing cannot work indefinitely.

TRUNCATED SUBJECTIVITY

In the remaining space, I further explore the notion of truncation and its consequences. I argue that Bernard Lonergan's account of truncated intelligence helps us understand the malaise of contemporary moral argument and maintain a philosophical anthropology in keeping with Taylor's commitment to value as ontologically constitutive of the human. Also, I suggest that Lonergan's explanation clarifies the necessity of intellectual conversion for a recovery of comprehensive debate and an end of schizophrenic smuggling.

It is, Lonergan suggests, easy to neglect human subjectivity in our reflections on human nature and examine ourselves from the viewpoint of abstract definitions that cannot but be alien to our lived, concrete reality.[27] While the tradition has often depended upon a metaphysics of the soul, studying "the subject is quite different, for it is the study of oneself inasmuch as one is conscious" and "prescinds from the soul, its essence, its potencies . . . for none of these is given in consciousness."[28] The study of subjectivity need not exclude a study of the soul, but neither are these identical studies, and it is quite easy to overlook the subject or think the subject explained when one is attending to a metaphysical exposition.

While the neglected subject "does not know himself," the "truncated subject not only does not know himself but also is unaware of his ignorance and so, in one way or another, concludes that what he does not know does not exist." Such truncation occurs in a variety of ways, generally through a form of reductionism whereby a part of human subjectivity is confused for the totality, and usually because the epistemic access to that partial truth is illicitly declared the only epistemic access that counts. Thus it is that "behaviorists would pay no attention to the inner workings of the subject; logical positivists would confine meaning to sensible data and the structures of mathematical logic; pragmatists would divert our attention to actions and results."[29]

Not all truncations are so obvious, however. In fact, the truncations with the greatest implications occur through a very subtle mistake, namely, a mistaken grasp of objectivity in knowing.[30] Objectivity is complex, and coming to terms with genuine human knowing even more so. One of the tasks of Lonergan's massive *Insight: A Study in Human Understanding* was to articulate the basic duality of human knowing, to distinguish animal knowing and its picture-thinking from genuinely human knowing and its commitment to intelligence and reasonableness.[31] As animals, a goodly amount of our conscious intentionality concerns our relations to bodies out there in the world—making money, finding a mate, raising children, building a house, fixing the car, finding a train station in an unfamiliar city, and so on. However complex these activities and realities happen to be, they are fundamentally the same sort of realities occupying the attention of other animals, and however complex and sophisticated our apprehension, these realities are imagined as bodies, as entities out there in the world. Consequently, our mode of being relative to bodies is extroversion, a concern for the external, the bodies one can touch, see, or at least imagine touching and seeing, the way a child might imagine God in heaven being a big person "up there somewhere," but still a body and still modeled after what is touchable or seeable. In extroversion, thus, reality is modeled after the sorts of things that can be seen, and objectivity is modeled after "taking a good look."

But not all knowing is animal extroversion, for we live not only in a world of bodies but also in a world mediated by meaning and intelligence where the true and real is not what can be touched or seen (or imaginably touched or seen) but, rather, understood and reasonably affirmed. Language and thought expand the world of reality, for "words denote not only what is present but also what is absent or past or future, not only what is factual but also the possible, the ideal, the normative." The larger world of meaning "does not lie within anyone's immediate experience," nor is it even "the totality of all worlds of immediate experience," for meaning "does not merely repeat but goes beyond experiencing," and it is in this larger world of meaning that humans "live out our lives."[32]

Truncated subjectivity occurs, then, when all knowing is reduced to the sort of objectivity proper to extroversion. This mistake can take subtle form. Lonergan claims that because the truncated subject does not know itself, often confusing one element of human knowing for the whole, the truncated subject is unlikely to grasp the complexity and polymorphic range of genuine objectivity. And while adult humans are obviously capable of grasping intelligibility and affirming reasonability, "it is one thing for them to function and it is quite another to become explicitly aware that they function." For the truncated, "what is meant by an 'object' and 'objective,' is something to be settled not by any scrutiny of one's operations and their properties, but by picture-thinking," for which an object "has to be something one looks at" and knowing some version of "seeing all that there is to be seen."[33]

Now, once picture-thinking, or a naïve extroversion, takes over, "immanence is an inevitable consequence," for the only real admitted is the sort of real that could in principle be seen or observed, and reality is reduced to the world of bodies rather than what can be intelligently conceived and reasonably affirmed in the fully human world.[34] When the subjects are truncated, so too is their world. Immanence, the denial of transcendence, is not merely a rejection of the possibility of the supernatural or the role of the supernatural in life, as in Secularity 1 and 2; instead, the very conditions of belief change, in the immanence of picture thinking. In fully human knowing mediated by meaning, our questions are not merely about what can be intuited or seen but about intelligible unity and patterns of meaning, and so also is understanding, which is a grasp of intelligible cause not at all like looking at bodies in front of us. Once given over to immanence, however, "understanding too must be merely immanent and merely subjective."[35] The conclusion of subjectivity is particularly interesting here, where reasonableness has been defined as limiting questions and debate to less consequential matters, since matters of ultimate concern are thought to be merely subjective and not governed by reason, unlike the supposedly publically accessible matters of everyday policy.

I suggest, then, a vicious circle. Once we've neglected the human subject and its full range of knowing, questions are reduced and truncated to that which is accessible to picture thinking, but since picture thinking will not accept the rational status of non-extroverted reality it considers non-truncated questions as entirely subjective and immune from reasonable arguments and discussions, all of which neglects the full range of the human subject and its range of questions, thus beginning the cycle again. The situation of Secularity 3—also the situation where pluralism is apparently so robust that reason cannot operate concerning ultimate questions—is at least partially explained by noting the dominance of extroversion and the illicit use of standards of objectivity proper to our animal knowing as standards of our fully human knowing.

TRUNCATED INTELLIGENCE AND DECLINE

I suspect, then, that in our current discourse we rely on smuggling because of a prior illicit exportation of objectivity as used in extroversion into our fully human knowing. Once transported, in our extroverted objectivity we find the comprehensive questions about the human good entirely subjective, even arbitrary, and rather sensibly decide to limit our gaze to matters of more practical concern. Of course, the refusal of comprehensiveness is sensible if and only if extroversion is the only form of knowing, which it is not. Lonergan calls this illicit use of extroversion as the standard of fully human knowing *the cognitional myth*, for having (1) thought that knowing is like seeing, and (2) objectivity is like taking a good look, and (3) the real is that sort of reality that can be looked upon, the world of meaning clearly fails those tests.[36]

As abstract and arcane as this cognitional-epistemological dispute may seem, the consequences for praxis and human living are quite tangible in matters of human progress and decline. As Lonergan conceives it, human intelligence is the condition of progress, for, all things being equal, unrestricted intelligence makes things better, and progress is possible so long as the intelligence is not distorted:

> This process of new ideas can spread through the whole good of order. You start changing the situation at one point, but that change in the situation will involve repercussions all through the good of order. New ideas will start popping up everywhere. There will result augmented well-being, and it affects each of the aspects of the human good: the flow of particular goods becomes more frequent, more instance, more varied; . . . new types of goods are provided; the society enjoys democracy and more education; . . . there is status for all, because everything

is running smoothly; . . . there are happy personal relations, a development in taste, in aesthetic value and its appreciation, and in ethics, in the autonomy of the subject; finally, there is more time for people to attend to their own perfection in religion.[37]

Of course, human intelligence is often distorted, impeded by sin, ignorance, or confusion, and Lonergan offers quite sophisticated accounts of the various impediments.

While civilization could develop in a steady advance of intelligent progress, this is not guaranteed, and decline is quite possible, maybe even probable, as humans flee from intelligence:

> The flight from understanding blocks the insights that concrete situations demand. There follow unintelligent policies and inept courses of action. The situation deteriorates to demand still further insights, and as they are blocked, policies become more unintelligent and action more inept. What is worse, the deteriorating situation seems to provide the uncritical, biased mind with factual evidence in which the bias is claimed to be verified. So in ever increasing measure intelligence comes to be regarded as irrelevant to practical living. Human activity settles down to a decadent routine and initiative becomes the privilege of violence.[38]

Impeding intelligence results in decline, of either the shorter or the longer cycle. Lonergan explains that shorter cycles of unintelligent thought, value, policy, and situation are generally caused by individual or group bias where the possible contributions of certain individuals or groups are rejected because of an irrational refusal or because intelligence is forced, crammed into the cleverness of finding new and better pleasures and advantages for me and mine rather than allowing intelligence to seek the truth where it can be found.

More worrisome is the longer cycle of decline, which Lonergan believes is caused by general bias, an irrational and truncated practicality that limits intelligence to those matters considered immediately practical or having a discernible practical benefit. General bias fails to take a long view of things, rejecting the full range of intelligence with the retort "What good is this anyway?" Consequently, such biased intelligence truncates the full range of questions. We insist that certain questions not be asked—we reject comprehensiveness—and thus lose out on those "impractical" ideas and questions that could eventually inform good policies and actions, and we thus maintain corrupt conditions while forbidding the very source of deliverance.

As Lonergan charts longer patterns of decline, the immediate problems and conflicts of the social situation can likely worsen as the intelligence, policy, and action fragment and become something less than fully intelligent—stupidity ensues. More relevant, comprehensive intelligence is disregarded: "Culture retreats into an ivory tower. Religion becomes an inward affair of the heart. Philosophy glitters like a gem with endless facets and no practical purpose."[39] Note how similar this account is to the prescription of Rawls or Rorty for whom culture and religion and philosophy become akin to luxury goods, pleasant perhaps but not public or useful, things to be kept to oneself, merely subjective, and to be thrown overboard in the face of public pluralism. Of course, this is a distortion of intelligence and its usual capacity to ask everything and anything about everything, including questions of ultimate value. Distorted intelligence can be reduced to mere animal knowing and instrumentalization. Such a society no longer can even identify the norms of human living, for its knowing is not human.

INTELLECTUAL CONVERSION

If this is at all correct, then the shabby state of contemporary public discourse, the lack of comprehensive query and its problematic implications for moral identity, the relativistic tendency of pluralism as construed by contemporary discourse, and the conditions of belief in Secularity 3 share a cause, namely, the cognitional myth. Consequently, they share a solution, which Lonergan terms *intellectual conversion*. Intellectual conversion is *not* religious conversion, although it does allow space for religion; nor is intellectual conversion forced, for it simply asks human subjects to pay attention to—and allow the free exercise and value of—the full range of their subjectivity, the full range of their questions. It is quite vital to grasp that no special pleading occurs here, there is no reference to mysticism or grace or the supernatural. All that is asked is for humans to note that the normal exigency of their questioning admits of no reason to arbitrarily demand that questions stop here, or here, or here. Instead, questioning is potentially unlimited, asking about the total intelligibility of all that is, including the possibility of a completely unconditioned principle of intelligibility, say God. But this is the normal and natural exigency of questions, and so intellectual conversion merely introduces humans to themselves, asking them to know themselves and let themselves be fully human.

Lonergan's disciples are fond of noting the intellectual conversion of Augustine in the *Confessions*, a conversion occurring well before the religious conversion. Throughout the text Augustine has struggled to overcome the vestiges of Mani in his thought, for even after he's rejected the doctrine, Augustine struggles to overcome his *image* of God, whom he imagines as a body because he has not "followed the intelligence of the mind . . . but the mind of the flesh . . . living outside [himself], seeing only with the eye of the flesh."[40] Further, his attempts to understand the "intelligence of the mind" falter, for he imagines the mind from the pattern of extroversion, his "mind moved within the confines of corporeal forms," which is "miserable folly." While he, like everyone, uses intelligence, he cannot yet "see [his] mind."[41]

In Augustine's interpretation of this impasse, the problem is not the arguments for or against God's existence, the problem is that he *imagines* God, thinking that all reality must be reducible to the reality proper to extroversion: "Nor did I think anything existed which is not material. *That was the principal and almost sole cause of my inevitable error.*"[42] He slowly makes progress toward God, not by thinking about God but by getting the nature of human intelligence correct, discovering (that is, converting to fully human knowing) "it was not in a place" that intelligence resides.[43] At last, by grace, he realizes that it is possible for God to exist when he ascends from "bodies to the soul . . . and from there to its inward force . . . to the power of reasoning . . . it withdrew itself from the contradictory swarms of imaginative fantasies, so as to discover the light by which it was flooded."[44] This is intellectual conversion:

> a radical clarification and, consequently, the elimination of an exceedingly stubborn and misleading myth concerning reality, objectivity, and human knowledge. The myth is that knowing is like looking, that objectivity is seeing what is there to be seen and not seeing what is not there, and that the real is what is out there now to be looked at. Now this myth overlooks the distinction between the world of immediacy, say, the world of the infant and, on the other hand, the world mediated by meaning.[45]

Primarily, intellectual conversion is realizing the reality of fully human knowing; it is possible by ending the neglect and truncation of human subjectivity that considers all reality must be body-like. It also frees intelligence to avoid general bias, decline, and the shabby affair of needing to smuggle value into an arbitrarily truncated and thereby pretty shabby discourse.

CONVERTING SECULARISM: PARTING THOUGHTS

In claiming the need for secularism to convert, I am decidedly not claiming the conversion of Secularity 1 or 2. It's possible that there is no God, that decreased religious observance is desirable, or that religion is separated from the affairs of state for good reason. All of this is open for further debate. But this is precisely my point—*all* of this is open for debate, and for real, rigorous, and rational *debate*. Any claim that questions should be forgone or any ultimate matters set aside for the sake of reasonableness is an entirely unreasonable thing to do, for it is the sort of claim dependent on neglecting, then truncating, the normal and natural exigencies of human intelligence and reason. We ask questions about ultimate matters because it is deeply in keeping with our subjectivity—human nature, if you prefer—to do so, and restrictions on our normal range of questions cannot but be an arbitrary limit.

I am not claiming that space needs to be made for matters of ultimate concern because there is some special domain or faculty of faith. In fact, my claim is quite modest, simply that comprehensive questions are within the realm of debate because they are within the realm of our normal intelligent questioning. We ask such questions precisely because we can, and, in fact, "the question of God . . . lies within man's horizon. Man's transcendental subjectivity is mutilated or abolished, unless he is stretching forth towards the intelligible, the unconditioned, the good of value. The reach, not of his attainment, but of his intending is unrestricted."[46] Our consciousness is violated, "abolished" in its exigency, when we are forced to be truncated, and there is no reason to do this to ourselves. In fact, it would seem that the problem with the cultured despisers of religion in the public discourse is not that they are too rational but that they are hardly rational enough. Religion does not demand the conversion of Secularity 3 in a hostile takeover of reason or freedom or self-governance, and religion does not arrogate the domain of reason. Instead, religious questions do what they do best, they allow the human to be human, they allow the world to be the world, they allow reason to be reasonable—again, and at last.

NOTES

1. Czeslaw Milosz, *The Captive Mind*, trans. Jane Zielonko (New York: Vintage Books, 1953), 4.

2. Ibid., 4–5.

3. Jonathan Sacks, *The Home We Build Together: Re-creating Society* (New York: Continuum, 2007), 11.

4. Susan Jacoby, *The Age of American Unreason* (New York: Pantheon Books, 2008), 297, 298, xii.

5. Mary Ann Glendon, *Rights Talk: The Impoverishment of Political Discourse* (New York: The Free Press, 1991), 14.

6. Alasdair MacIntyre, *After Virtue: A Study in Moral Theory* (Notre Dame, IN: University of Notre Dame Press, 1984), 6 (quote), 68–69.

7. Steven D. Smith, *The Disenchantment of Secular Discourse* (Cambridge, MA: Harvard University Press, 2010), 7, 11.

8. Following Smith's own usage, the capitalization here distinguishes Reason as an Enlightenment Myth from reason in the sense of the use of human intelligence. This distinction is respected throughout this essay.

9. Smith, *The Disenchantment of Secular Discourse*, 14.

10. Ibid., 15–16.

11. Ibid., 17.

12. Richard Rorty, *Philosophy and Social Hope* (New York: Penguin Books, 1999), 19.

13. Smith, *Disenchantment of Secular Discourse*, 23.

14. Charles Taylor, *A Secular Age* (Cambridge: Belknap Press, 2007), 3.

15. Ibid., 3–7.

16. Smith, *Disenchantment of Secular Discourse*, 27, 26–27, 25, 37.

17. A more detailed summary of Taylor is found in my forthcoming book, co-authored with Steven D. Cone, *Authentic Cosmopolitanism: Love, Sin, and Grace in the Christian University* (Eugene, OR: Pickwick, forthcoming).

18. Nicholas H. Smith, *Charles Taylor: Meaning, Morals and Modernity* (Malden, MA: Polity, 2002), 87–90.

19. Charles Taylor, *Sources of the Self: The Making of the Modern Identity* (Cambridge, MA: Harvard University Press, 1989), 14–15.

20. Ibid., 27.

21. Ibid., 31.

22. Ibid., 62.

23. Smith, *Charles Taylor*, 6–7.

24. Charles Taylor, *The Ethics of Authenticity* (Cambridge, MA: Harvard University Press, 1991), 39.

25. Charles Taylor, *Multiculturalism: Examining the Politics of Recognition*, ed. Amy Gutmann (Princeton, NJ: Princeton University Press, 1994), 32. One could also think of the social character of human identity in Heidegger, for whom relation to "the-They" is primordial and non-optional. See Martin Heidegger, *Being and Time*, trans. John Macquarrie and Edward Robinson (New York: Harper and Row, 1962), 149–68.

26. Taylor, *Multiculturalism*, 32.

27. Bernard Lonergan, "The Subject," in *The Lonergan Reader*, ed. Mark D. Morelli and Elizabeth A. Morelli (Toronto: University of Toronto Press, 1997), 420–35, esp. 421.

28. Ibid., 424.

29. Ibid.

30. Ibid., 425.

31. Bernard Lonergan, *Insight: A Study of Human Understanding*, vol. 3 of *Collected Works of Bernard Lonergan*, ed. Frederick E. Crowe and Robert M. Doran (Toronto: University of Toronto Press, 1992).

32. Bernard Lonergan, *Method in Theology* (New York: Seabury Press, 1972), 77.

33. Lonergan, "The Subject," 426–27.

34. Ibid., 427.

35. Ibid., 428.

36. Lonergan, *Method*, 238. See also R. J. Snell, *Through a Glass Darkly: Bernard Lonergan and Richard Rorty on Knowing without a God's-eye View* (Milwaukee, WI: Marquette University Press, 2006), 69–71.

37. Bernard Lonergan, *Topics in Education: The Cincinnati Lectures of 1959 on the Philosophy of Education*, vol. 10 of *Collected Works of Bernard Lonergan*, ed. Robert M. Doran and Frederick E. Crowe (Toronto: University of Toronto Press, 1993), 51.

38. Lonergan, *Insight*, 8.

39. Ibid., 254.

40. Augustine, *Confessions*, trans. Henry Chadwick (New York: Oxford University Press, 1991), 3.6.

41. Ibid., 4.15.

42. Ibid., 5.10 (emphasis added).

43. Ibid., 7.7.

44. Ibid., 7.17.

45. Lonergan, *Method*, 238.

46. Ibid., 103.

CONTRIBUTOR BIOGRAPHIES

Francis J. Beckwith is professor of philosophy and church-state studies, and resident scholar in the Institute for Studies of Religion at Baylor University. He is the author of over a dozen books including *Politics for Christians: Statecraft as Soulcraft* (InterVarsity Press, 2010) and *Defending Life: A Moral and Legal Case against Abortion Choice* (Cambridge University Press, 2007).

Luigi Bradizza is assistant professor of political science at Salve Regina University. He is author of *Richard T. Ely's Critique of Capitalism* (Palgrave Macmillan). He also is author of "Elite Education and the Viability of a Lockean Society," which appeared in *The Review of Politics* (Fall 2008) and "Madison and Republican Cosmopolitanism," which appeared in *Cosmopolitanism in the Age of Globalization: Citizens with States*, edited by Lee Trapanier and Khalil M. Habib (University of Kentucky Press).

J. Budziszewski, an ethical and political theorist, is professor of government and philosophy at the University of Texas, Austin. A specialist on the classical natural law tradition, he is completing a commentary on Thomas Aquinas's *Treatise on Law*, to be published by Cambridge University Press. His earlier works include *The Resurrection of Nature* (Cornell), *The Nearest Coast of Darkness* (Cornell), *True Tolerance* (Transaction), *Written on the Heart: The Case for Natural Law* (IVP), *The Revenge of Conscience* (Spence), *What We Can't Not Know: A Guide* (Ignatius Press), and *The Line Through the Heart* (ISI).

Paul R. DeHart is assistant professor of political science at Texas State University. He is author of *Uncovering the Constitution's Moral Design* (University of Missouri Press, 2007) as well as a number of articles and chapters, including "The

Dangerous Life: Natural Justice and the Rightful Subversion of the State," *Polity* (July 2006), "Covenantal Realism: The Self-Referential Incoherency of Conventional Social Contract Theory and the Necessity of Consent," *Perspectives on Political Science* (July 2012), "Reason and Will in Natural Law," in *Natural Law and Evangelical Political Thought* (Lexington Books, 2012), "Fractured Foundations: The Self-Contradiction between Locke's Ontology and His Moral Philosophy," *Locke Studies* (2012), and "Leviathan Leashed: On the Incoherence of Absolute Sovereignty," *Critical Review* (Winter 2013).

Ralph C. Hancock holds degrees from BYU and Harvard and has taught political philosophy at Brigham Young University since 1987; he is also president of the John Adams Center for the Study of Faith, Philosophy and Public Affairs. His most recent book is *The Responsibility of Reason: Theory and Practice in a Liberal-Democratic Age* (Rowman and Littlefield), and a new edition of his *Calvin and the Foundations of Modern Politics* has recently been published by Saint Augustine's Press.

Carson Holloway is associate professor of political science at the University of Nebraska at Omaha. He is the author of *The Way of Life: John Paul II and the Challenge of Liberal Modernity* (Baylor University Press, 2008), *The Right Darwin? Evolution, Religion, and the Future of Democracy* (Spence Publishing, 2006), *All Shook Up: Music, Passion, and Politics* (Spence Publishing, 2001), and the editor of *Magnanimity and Statesmanship* (Lexington Books, 2008).

Robert C. Koons is professor of philosophy at the University of Texas at Austin. He is author of *Paradoxes of Belief and Strategic Rationality* (Cambridge University Press) and *Realism Regained* (Oxford University Press). Most recently he co-edited (with George Bealer) *The Waning of Materialism* (Oxford University Press).

Peter Augustine Lawler is Dana Professor of Government at Berry College and executive editor of the scholarly quarterly *Perspectives on Political Science*. He is author or editor of fifteen books and more than two hundred articles and chapters; he served on President Bush's Council on Bioethics.

R. J. Snell is associate professor and director of the philosophy program at Eastern University where he also is research director of the Agora Institute for Civic Virtue and the Common Good. Among his writing is *Through a Glass Darkly: Bernard Lonergan and Richard Rorty on Knowing without a God's-eye View*, and the forthcoming books *Authentic Cosmopolitanism: Love, Sin, and Grace in the Christian University* (with Steve Cone), and *The Perspective of Love: Natural Law in a New Mode*.

James R. Stoner, Jr., is professor of political science at Louisiana State University and a former chair of the department. He is author of *Common-Law Liberty: Rethinking American Constitutionalism* (Kansas) and *Common Law and Liberal Theory: Coke, Hobbes, and the Origins of American Constitutionalism* (Kansas). From 2002 to 2006 he served on the National Council on the Humanities.

Micah Watson is assistant professor of political science and Director of the Center for Politics & Religion at Union University in Jackson, Tennessee. He works in the intersection between political thought and religion and did his graduate work at Baylor University and Princeton University. Most recently, he has co-edited *Natural Law and Evangelical Political Thought* (Lexington Press, 2012).

INDEX